G22541

To Susanne

with thanks for all the help

[illegible signature]

30.9.2003

Social Foundations of Markets, Money and Credit

Where does the power of money come from? Why is trust so important in financial operations? How does the swapping of gifts differ from the exchange of commodities? Where does self-interest stop and communal solidarity start in capitalist economies?

These issues and many more are discussed in a rigorous, yet readable, manner in *Social Foundations of Markets, Money and Credit.* It is shown in particular that capitalist economies are permeated with non-economic relations that flow from the exploitative relations of production. Lapavitsas focuses especially on money, the aspect that markets have in common, and critically analyses its economic and non-economic characteristics.

This carefully argued book will prove interesting and valuable to students and researchers not only in economics, but also in sociology and anthropology. Well-informed critics of capitalism will also find it a useful read.

Costas Lapavitsas is Senior Lecturer in Economics at the School of Oriental and African Studies, University of London, UK. He is co-editor of *Development Policy in the Twenty-First Century*, also available from Routledge.

Routledge frontiers of political economy

1 **Equilibrium Versus Understanding**
Towards the rehumanization of economics within social theory
Mark Addleson

2 **Evolution, Order and Complexity**
Edited by Elias L. Khalil and Kenneth E. Boulding

3 **Interactions in Political Economy**
Malvern after ten years
Edited by Steven Pressman

4 **The End of Economics**
Michael Perelman

5 **Probability in Economics**
Omar F. Hamouda and Robin Rowley

6 **Capital Controversy, Post Keynesian Economics and the History of Economics**
Essays in honour of Geoff Harcourt, volume one
Edited by Philip Arestis, Gabriel Palma and Malcolm Sawyer

7 **Markets, Unemployment and Economic Policy**
Essays in honour of Geoff Harcourt, volume two
Edited by Philip Arestis, Gabriel Palma and Malcolm Sawyer

8 **Social Economy**
The logic of capitalist development
Clark Everling

9 **New Keynesian Economics/Post Keynesian Alternatives**
Edited by Roy J. Rotheim

10 **The Representative Agent in Macroeconomics**
James E. Hartley

11 **Borderlands of Economics**
Essays in honour of Daniel R. Fusfeld
Edited by Nahid Aslanbeigui and Young Back Choi

12 **Value, Distribution and Capital**
Essays in honour of Pierangelo Garegnani
Edited by Gary Mongiovi and Fabio Petri

13 **The Economics of Science**
Methodology and Epistemology as if Economics Really Mattered
James R. Wible

14 **Competitiveness, Localised Learning and Regional Development**
Specialisation and prosperity in small open economies
Peter Maskell, Heikki Eskelinen, Ingjaldur Hannibalsson, Anders Malmberg and Eirik Vatne

15 **Labour Market Theory**
A constructive reassessment
Ben J. Fine

16 **Women and European Employment**
Jill Rubery, Mark Smith, Colette Fagan, Damian Grimshaw

17 **Explorations in Economic Methodology**
From Lakatos to empirical philosophy of science
Roger Backhouse

18 **Subjectivity in Political Economy**
Essays on wanting and choosing
David P. Levine

19 **The Political Economy of Middle East Peace**
The impact of competing trade agendas
Edited by J. W. Wright, Jnr

20 **The Active Consumer**
Novelty and surprise in consumer choice
Edited by Marina Bianchi

21 **Subjectivism and Economic Analysis**
Essays in memory of Ludwig Lachmann
Edited by Roger Koppl and Gary Mongiovi

22 Themes in Post-Keynesian Economics
Essays in honour of Geoff Harcourt, volume three
Edited by Peter Kriesler and Claudio Sardoni

23 The Dynamics of Technological Knowledge
Cristiano Antonelli

24 The Political Economy of Diet, Health and Food Policy
Ben J. Fine

25 The End of Finance
Capital market inflation, financial derivatives and pension fund capitalism
Jan Toporowski

26 Political Economy and the New Capitalism
Edited by Jan Toporowski

27 Growth Theory
A philosophical perspective
Patricia Northover

28 The Political Economy of the Small Firm
Edited by Charlie Dannreuther

29 Hahn and Economic Methodology
Edited by Thomas Boylan and Paschal F. O'Gorman

30 Gender, Growth and Trade
The miracle economies of the postwar years
David Kucera

31 Normative Political Economy
Subjective freedom, the market and the state
David Levine

32 Economist with a Public Purpose
Essays in honour of John Kenneth Galbraith
Edited by Michael Keaney

33 The Demise of Involuntary Unemployment
Michel De Vroey

34 The Fundamental Institutions of Capitalism
Ernesto Screpanti

35 Transcending Transaction
The search for self-generating markets
Alan Shipman

36 Power in Business and the State
An historical analysis of its concentration
Frank Bealey

37 Editing Economics
Essays in honour of Mark Perlman
Hank Lim, Ungsuh K. Park and Geoff Harcourt

38 Money, Macroeconomics and Keynes
Essays in honour of Victoria Chick, volume one
Philip Arestis, Meghnad Desai and Sheila Dow

39 Methodology, Microeconomics and Keynes
Essays in honour of Victoria Chick, volume two
Philip Arestis, Meghnad Desai and Sheila Dow

40 Market Drive and Governance
Reexamining the rules for economic and commercial contest
Ralf Boscheck

41 The Value of Marx
Political economy for contemporary capitalism
Alfredo Saad-Filho

42 Issues in Positive Political Economy
S. Mansoob Murshed

43 The Enigma of Globalisation
A journey to a new stage of capitalism
Robert Went

44 The Market
Equilibrium, stability, mythology
S. N. Afriat

45 The Political Economy of Rule Evasion and Policy Reform
Jim Leitzel

46 Unpaid Work and the Economy
Edited by Antonella Picchio

47 Distributional Justice
Theory and measurement
Hilde Bojer

48 Cognitive Developments in Economics
Edited by Salvatore Rizzello

49 Social Foundations of Markets, Money and Credit
Costas Lapavitsas

50 Rethinking Capitalist Development
Essays on the economics of Josef Steindl
G. Heihnsohn and O. Steiger

Social Foundations of Markets, Money and Credit

Costas Lapavitsas

Routledge
Taylor & Francis Group
LONDON AND NEW YORK

First published 2003
by Routledge
11 New Fetter Lane, London EC4P 4EE

Simultaneously published in the USA and Canada
by Routledge
29 West 35th Street, New York, NY 10001

Routledge is an imprint of the Taylor & Francis Group

Typeset in Baskerville by Wearset Ltd, Boldon, Tyne and Wear
Printed and bound in Great Britain by MPG Books Ltd, Bodmin

British Library Cataloguing in Publication Data
A catalogue record for this book is available from the British Library

Library of Congress Cataloging in Publication Data
Lapavitsas, Costas, 1961–
Social foundations of markets, money, and credit / Costas Lapavitsas.
p. cm. – (Routledge frontiers of political economy; 49)
Includes bibliographical references and index.
1. Capitalism. 2. Marxian economics. 3. Money. 4. Credit. 5. Economics – Sociological aspects. I. Title. II. Series.

HB501.L265 2003
330.12'2–dc21

2003046661

ISBN 0-415-31805-X

Contents

Acknowledgements xi
Introduction 1

PART I
Commodities, markets and capital 7

1 Social relations underpinning commodity markets 9
1.1 Products and commodities 10
1.2 The economic and the non-economic spheres of capitalist society 14
1.3 Class relations in the capitalist economy 17
1.4 Capital and commodities 21
1.5 Markets without commodities, and markets in commodities not produced by capital 26

2 Commodities and gifts 31
2.1 Commodities and gifts as tokens of market and non-market relations 31
2.2 Commodity and gift exchangeability 33
2.3 The role of use value in commodity exchange 37
2.4 Non-market relations in creation and deployment of labour power 42

PART II
Money and credit 47

3 Money's monopoly over the ability to buy 49
3.1 The peculiar role of money in capitalist exchange 49
3.2 The theoretical problem of money's emergence and the labour theory of value 53
3.3 The 'simple, isolated, or accidental form of value' 57

3.4 The 'total or expanded form of value' 58
3.5 The 'general form of value' and the role of social custom 59
3.6 The 'money form of value' 63
3.7 The specific character of monetary exchange in contrast to barter 64
3.8 Money as source of social power 66

4 The social content of credit relations **68**
4.1 Trust and the structure of the capitalist credit system 69
4.2 Non-economic foundations of commercial (trade) credit relations 72
4.3 The role of trust in the operations of banking (monetary) credit 76
4.4 The social character of money market credit 82
4.5 Central bank credit 84
4.6 Conclusion 86

PART III
Theoretical approaches to the social relations sustaining markets and money **89**

5 Social norms and institutions in the capitalist economy **91**
5.1 Rationality and social norms in economic analysis 92
5.2 Institutions and markets 98
5.3 Information-theoretic analysis and neoclassical economics 101
5.4 The 'embeddedness' of the capitalist economy in social relations 104
5.5 'Social capital' and the capitalist economy 107

6 The emergence and functioning of money **112**
6.1 Money as means of exchange 113
6.2 Money as unit of account 119
6.3 'Multiple' markets and money 124
6.4 'Limited-purpose' and 'general-purpose' money 128

7 Money as unit of account and means of exchange in a socialist society **131**
7.1 Socialism as the conscious ascendancy of the non-economic 131
7.2 Labour money 135

Notes 140
Bibliography 152
Index 168

Acknowledgements

This book has been in the making for some time and owes debts to several people. The heaviest is due to Ben Fine, whose broad interests and undiminished intellectual curiosity provided much of the inspiration to write. His suggestions, even when critically phrased, were always penetrating and at times decisive in shaping the work. Makoto Itoh offered well-balanced advice, especially on the finer points of Uno doctrine, interpreted from his own distinctive standpoint. John Weeks made useful comments on the presentation of Marxist and neoclassical economic theory. Alfredo Saad-Filho read drafts and helped make the analysis less arcane. Susanne MacGregor cast a critical eye and restrained the more egregious assertions regarding social theory. Stergios Skaperdas made sensible remarks, drawing on his knowledge of neoclassicism. Others have made comments on particular topics at various points in time. Michiaki Obata's remarks at a seminar delivered some time ago in Tokyo influenced the argument on gifts and commodities in Chapter 2 in ways he probably did not realise at the time. Danny Miller's generous comments on a draft of the same chapter made me feel less uncomfortable about discussing anthropological literature. Chris Cramer also made relevant points on the same topic. Giannis Milios commented on other parts of the text from a Marxist standpoint, as did Yiorgos Stassinopoulos. Finally, Lesley Hoggart helped improve the clarity and approachability of the text.

The end result is entirely the author's responsibility. The aim has been to produce an academic work of use to those engaged in confronting capitalist profit-making and the mechanisms of money and credit. Trust, power, moral obligation and solidarity have both social and individual determinants. The importance of this point was often disregarded as neoliberalism rose triumphant. The economic storms that broke toward the end of the 1990s have brought renewed demands for communal solidarity and for limits on the power of money and credit. But no social change in this direction can have a lasting effect unless it challenges directly the social foundations of capitalist markets.

Introduction

Economic theory and policy across the world are currently dominated by neo-liberalism. Its adherents believe that free markets have beneficial economic properties, and that there is no alternative to markets in organising economy and society. The neo-liberal outlook has held sway for more than two decades in the USA, Europe and Japan, while being gradually imposed on the developing world. Yet its results have been deeply disappointing. Since the early 1980s, growth rates have been generally poor, real incomes have stagnated and the productivity of labour has risen uncertainly and haltingly. Meanwhile, income inequality has widened, absolute poverty in the developing world is vast, and economic instability (partly due to a succession of financial bubbles) has become an entrenched part of life. Free markets have performed less well than their advocates either expected or wished.

Disillusionment with the performance of free markets has grown palpably among social scientists, grassroots organisations, labour unions, and even some economic policy-makers. Searching questions are asked about the functioning of markets, especially the role of non-economic (or even social) relations. Social relations and institutions are increasingly thought to have a determining influence on the way markets work as well as on their efficiency. Hardly any official pronouncement on economic policy today, especially those by international organisations such as the International Monetary Fund and the World Bank, fails to mention the importance of social institutions as well as trust, honesty, confidence, credibility, reliability, moral integrity, and the like. This broader focus is apparent even in economic theory. Models now explicitly acknowledge and incorporate behavioural norms and social customs in analysing economic decision-making. The 'new political economy', for instance, theorises norms and social custom – notions that would have been considered beyond the analytical ambit of economists in the past. Similarly, the 'new economics of finance' and the 'new economics of the labour market' emphasise the importance of access to information for the performance of markets. The list could be easily extended.

In a similar spirit, the new economic sociology attempts to establish non-economic explanations for the emergence and functioning of markets. 'Network theory', for instance, seeks to demonstrate the importance of the social relations within which markets and commodity exchange are 'embedded'. The newly-minted concept of 'social capital' has risen rapidly to prominence, attempting in part to capture non-economic and social influences on economic processes. Its enthusiastic adoption by the international economic organisations is a token of the rising influence of non-economic concerns in economic policy-making. In anthropology, similarly, the old debate on the gift has taken on a new lease of life. The contrast between gift and commodity acts as proxy for the opposition between the world of moral (or cultural) imperatives and the world of pecuniary gain. Contrasted to the commodity, the gift is deemed to capture the moral, customary and power aspects of economic and social life. In political science, finally, it is widely assumed that norms of association, institutional learning and the exercise of power are fundamental to the efficient operation of the capitalist economy.

In Marxist theory, the relationship between the economic and non-economic aspects of social life has always attracted much attention. Long before neoclassical theory turned its attention to social norms and institutions, all strands of Marxist political economy examined the interaction between the economic and the non-economic spheres of the capitalist mode of production. The classical corpus of Marxism, after all, rests on analysis of capital as both economic phenomenon and set of social relations. Capitalist economic relations are typically assumed to set the tone for non-economic relations, but non-economic practices and institutions impinge upon the capitalist economy in a variety of complex ways. Classical Marxism, moreover, insists on theory being historically specific, avoiding abstract generalisations about human beings and focusing on society's class structure. Nonetheless, Marxist political economy has been marginal to the recent revival of interest in the non-economic aspects of the capitalist economy. Its absence has been most notable in connection with the anti-capitalist movement of the last decade. The disparate currents of that movement, despite their ideological and organisational differences, are agreed that non-economic concerns should take precedence over capitalist profit-making. The anti-capitalist movement insists that economic policy should be shaped by the non-economic requirements of social cohesiveness, solidarity among people, moral obligation toward the poor and the weak, respect for social customs, and care for the environment. Remarkably, it has not drawn more systematically on Marxist theory while formulating its demands for alternative policies.

Mindful of this vacuum, this book examines non-economic relations in capitalist markets, using Marxist analytical techniques and paying particular attention to money and credit. It aims to show that the class foundations of the capitalist economy are fundamental to the interplay between the economic and the non-economic, especially in the realm of markets.

Clearly, there is no simple way of demonstrating the role of social class in this respect. It is possible, for instance, to lapse into a caricature of materialism and propose some version of 'economic determinism' whereby all that is deemed necessary is knowledge of capitalist economic processes because, presumably, non-economic processes are derivative of economic relations. But this type of vulgar Marxism is now marginalised, if not extinct. Rather, two related claims are made in this book. First, the capitalist economy is permeated by non-economic relations that are specifically capitalist, and directly reflect the economy's class character. Typical examples are workplace relations of power and authority between capitalists and workers, but also of solidarity among workers. Second, there is a profusion of other non-economic relations in the capitalist economy that are systematically marshalled and placed at the service of capitalist enterprises. Familial relations among parents and children, for instance, are integral to creating the ability to work and securing a regular supply of workers to industry. Money and credit, moreover, represent relations of trust and power in capitalist markets that are mobilised to facilitate the profit-making activities of industry. As a consequence, relations of trust and power acquire a social and specifically capitalist character.

Capitalism as social system is not defined by markets, money and credit. For capitalism to emerge, a distinctive set of relations of production must be socially established – a class of capitalists and a class of workers with unequal property rights over the means of production, and an attendant disparity of economic and social power. Once capitalist relations of production have been established, markets inevitably proliferate and organise the economic life of society. Thus, at the start of the book, the connection between markets and capitalism is explored in depth. It is shown that capitalist commodity markets represent the most developed form of commercial give and take, and function as theoretical reference points for other markets. Qualitative differences are shown to exist between products and commodities as well as between markets in produced commodities, markets in non-produced objects, and even 'pretend' markets. By adopting a strong interpretation of Marxist economic theory, it is then demonstrated that money has a monopoly over the ability to buy. Specifically, money is shown to be an outgrowth of commodity exchange, the product of economic and non-economic relations among commodity owners. Credit, on the other hand, stands for trust embodied in capitalist market practices and institutions. Breaking fresh theoretical ground, it is shown that interpersonal (or inter-enterprise) trust and power in the capitalist economy acquire an increasingly social character through the institutional mechanisms of credit. The credit system is a set of social mechanisms that socialises trust and power in the interests of capitalist profit-making.

The interaction between economic and non-economic relations in the capitalist economy is evidently a vast and complex topic, and this slim book has no pretensions to comprehensive treatment. Politics and the state were left out of the account, despite their importance as non-economic relations and institutions, on the grounds that they require independent and full treatment in a separate work. Even then, reviewing relevant literature from other disciplines was a fraught exercise. It proved necessary to concentrate attention on the interplay of economic with non-economic relations in the field of money and credit. That was the basis on which debates and individual contributions were selected from economics, sociology and anthropology. By the same token, work in biology was ignored, despite having much to say on altruism, selfishness, moral obligation and power – often from a Marxist standpoint. Particularly difficult was deciding how far to go in discussing sociological classics, such as Durkheim's *Division of Labour in Society*, or Weber's *Economy and Society* and *The Protestant Ethic and the Spirit of Capitalism.* It is arguable, for instance, that Tonnies' original distinction between *Gemeinschaft* and *Gesellschaft* in *Community and Association* offers deeper insights into the interaction of the economic with the non-economic than the currently fashionable notion of 'social capital'. In the end, for reasons of space and balance, they were not discussed directly, though their influence on the book's arguments can be discerned at several junctures. In short, the literature reviewed constitutes mostly economic, sociological and anthropological work of the last three decades with a direct bearing on money and credit.

The book is organised as follows. Part I lays out a view of markets, commodities, and capitalism based on Marxist political economy. Specifically, Chapter 1 discusses commodities and markets, defining capital as a set of social relations and an economic phenomenon. Analytical emphasis is laid on the distinction between the form and substance of commodity value, and its implications for analysis of markets for produced commodities, for non-produced objects and for 'pretend' markets. Chapter 2 reconsiders the debate on the gift as the antithesis of the commodity. It is shown that the distinction ignores the use value of commodities, and therefore disregards non-economic relations that originate in transacting and deploying commodities as useful things. Part II turns to money and credit. Chapter 3 presents an original analysis of the relationship between money and markets, focusing on the economic and non-economic relations among commodity owners. Money is shown to emerge as monopolist of the ability to buy, the universal equivalent. Consequently, money possesses unique economic and social power in a capitalist society. This analysis relies on an interpretation of Marx's theory of value, which stresses the distinction between form and substance of value. Chapter 4 then turns to capitalist credit, and shows that interpersonal (and inter-enterprise) trust and power become embodied in the institutions and assets that comprise the social mechanisms of the credit system. Capitalist credit is initially a private relationship between two contracting parties, but becomes increasingly social as the layers of the credit system are traversed. However, because capitalist credit is based on money-making, it also has a noxious and fraudulent character. Part III then considers some relevant economic, sociological and anthropological theory. Chapter 5 discusses the rise of non-economic concepts in contemporary mainstream economic theory, focusing on 'institutionalist' and 'information-theoretic' economics. The relevant sociological literature of 'networks' and 'social capital' is also considered in this context. Chapter 6 discusses theoretical views related to the emergence of money and its functions in commodity exchange. It is shown that identifying money with its functions, especially means of exchange or unit of account, leads to problematic results for theory. Concluding, Chapter 7 briefly considers the implications for money as unit of account and means of exchange that would follow a socialist transformation of capitalist society. A socialist society would combine a complex division of labour with social solidarity and conscious management of social resources. Much of the social power of money, deriving from its unique ability to buy, would thereby disappear.

Part I

Commodities, markets and capital

1 Social relations underpinning commodity markets

The 'market' appears to be a simple concept, naturally lending itself to analysis by social science in general and economics in particular. This assumption is so commonly made that it is not even noted in theoretical work. The core of neoclassical economics, for instance, consists of theoretical analysis of commodity exchange in the market. Similarly, recent sociological work on the 'embeddedness' of markets in social relations takes the market as this point of departure. But the assumption is misleading. There is no such thing as a 'market in general', nor is the 'market' a simple concept that could serve as starting point for theory. On the contrary, markets are complex concepts that have to be constructed from simpler categories. The fundamental category in this respect is the most elementary component of markets, the commodity.[1] To undertake analysis of markets, commodities have to be examined first, identifying their differences with products and, at a further remove, with other traded objects. For this purpose, it is necessary to specify the social relations under which products become commodities. Analysis of commodities makes it possible to identify qualitative differences among markets, particularly between markets in produced commodities, markets in objects unrelated to production (such as financial and real estate assets) and even 'pretend' markets, i.e. trading practices attached to phenomena that have nothing to do with commerce (for instance, the practice of bribing).

The first section of this chapter considers the difference between products and commodities, and shows that it is necessary to pursue socially and historically specific analysis. In particular, capitalist social conditions are privileged terrain for theoretical analysis of commodities, because the products of capital are commodities immediately and automatically. Commodities produced by capital fully encapsulate the inherent aspects of all commodities, and provide a reference point for other traded things and their markets. Capitalist social relations are discussed in the second and third sections, paying particular attention to the interplay of the economic with the non-economic. Class is a salient aspect of capitalist social relations, especially with regard to property over resources as well as authority and fiat at the point of production. In this light, it is shown in the fourth section that the value of commodities produced by capital is dictated primarily by economic factors. Capitalist relations of production and exchange give social substance to commodity value (abstract human labour) and determine exchange ratios and relative prices. By the same token, commodities not produced by capital lack the social substance of value, and their exchange ratios and relative prices are strongly susceptible to the influence of non-economic relations. Moreover, for traded objects unrelated to production, non-economic relations play a decisive role in determining exchange ratios and prices. Thus, in the fifth section, markets are shown to be differentiated according to their underlying social relations of production to such an extent that in 'pretend' markets the form of the commodity becomes attached to things and transactions that have no economic content at all.

1.1 Products and commodities

In mainstream economic theory, market agents are rational individuals with different tastes and preferences (this is discussed more extensively in Chapter 5). The exclusive aim of market agents is personal gratification through consumption of commodities that are obtained in exchange for commodities they already hold. Individuals have neither social nor private relations that openly influence their regular give and take in the market. They do not even know each other – the market is assumed to be 'anonymous'. In so far as individuals have any determination other than 'human being', it is as 'commodity owner'. When other fundamental characteristics of individual agents are explicitly acknowledged, such as kinship, gender, ethnicity and friendship, awkward problems emerge for theory. It is intuitively implausible, for instance, that father and son would exchange things, services and favours in purely egoistic fashion, or as apparent equals. Similarly, members of hostile ethnic groups are unlikely to shun violence in their give and take, naturally complying with the principle of *quid pro quo*. Thus, economic theory typically postulates a pure 'economic' outlook for its agents by assuming away relations other than those that might arise among 'rational egoists'. The mode of operation of individuals in economic models is fundamentally determined by the ownership of and desire for commodities.[2]

In all societies, however, there is a vast range of products that are possessed, consumed and exchanged in ways unrelated to commercial exchange. These include family services, things produced for personal consumption, and gifts. Despite not being bought in markets, it is apparent that they influence the decision-making of the 'economic individual', whose only purpose is, after all, to seek gratification from consumption. This difficult issue is often tackled by economic theory by means of a simple expedient: it is assumed, implicitly or explicitly, that everything is (or could be) a commodity. Yet it is far from obvious that possession and consumption of products could be logically equated with possession and consumption of commodities. Even in contemporary capitalism, in which commodities permeate most areas of social life, there are things produced that indisputably lie outside the market, such as objects of great national or religious significance – unique symbols of past wars, the crown jewels, venerated church icons. Products certainly can, and do, become commodities, but this is neither automatic nor immediate. It is therefore incumbent on theory to specify the social and historical conditions under which the transformation of products into commodities takes place, instead of assuming it away.

It could be thought, perhaps, that much of the difficulty would melt away if a definition of the commodity was adopted that applied across history and society. Commodities, for instance, could be defined simply as things that are bought and sold. The difference between commodities and products would then become irrelevant and all that would matter would be the owner's intention to trade, which could be expressed toward anything and under any social conditions. However, the deficiencies of this definition become apparent as soon as the qualitative differences between traded objects come into view. As objects of trade the products of human labour belong to a different category compared to things provided by nature, and even more compared to economic titles, claims on others, or abstract cultural practices. Analogously, the market for motorcars belongs to a different category to the market for fishing rights, or the market for financial derivatives, or even the market for access to the ear of the Minister for Public Construction. To be more specific, pricing behaviour, institutional structure and customary practices in the market for motorcars are closely related to production of motorcars, a process that requires hired labour and the use of machinery and raw materials. In contrast, no production activities are involved in markets for fishing rights or financial derivatives, and if the traded objects take a concrete form at all, it is mostly as scraps of paper. Prices, institutions and customary practices in these markets reflect the absence of production, as is shown below. The need to differentiate between products and commodities in a historically and socially specific way cannot be eliminated through mere definitions.[3]

The neglect of social and historical conditions of commodity trading by neoclassical economics has its roots in Smith, for whom human beings have an innate tendency to 'truck, barter and exchange' (1776, p. 17) that sets them apart from other animals. The social conditions under which commodity trading takes place are not as important to Smith as the trans-historical aspect of trading, which he adduces to human nature. Consequently, in a celebrated paragraph Smith (1776, p. 53) exemplifies his argument by having a deer-hunter and a beaver-hunter (from a 'nation of hunters') meet, agree on the rate of exchange of one beaver to two deer, trade, and depart satisfied with their purchases. Yet Smith's example bears no relation to observed hunter-gatherer practices, as anthropological work made clear long ago.[4] If the deer-hunter and the beaver-hunter belonged to the same band, it would not enter their heads to trade, for the game would probably belong to the group as a whole. If they belonged to different bands but still happened to meet, they would be as likely to ignore each other, or even to fight, as to trade. Smith's trans-historical approach is thus predicated on ignoring the social conditions within which trade occurs or, more accurately, on making the tacit assumption that social conditions are such that, when producers meet, they neither fight nor ignore each other but engage in trade as a matter of course. This tacit supposition injects an element of universality to Smith's analysis of commodity exchange, allowing him to attribute the existence of commerce to a 'natural' human disposition to trade. But the universality is artificial. Smith's deer- and beaver-hunters are not at all 'primitives' engaging in barter – they are capitalist traders dressed up in loincloths.

Ignoring the social and historical conditions under which products become commodities leads to major theoretical difficulties. The commodity is best analysed in socially and historically specific terms. The snag is, however, that commodity trading has historically occurred under a remarkable variety of social conditions. Commercial activities, for instance, were deeply familiar to ancient Phoenicians, Greeks and Romans. Similarly, there was domestic and foreign trade of rice and other goods in imperial China and Japan, and the Silk Road brought into contact a multitude of peoples from the western reaches of China to Byzantine Constantinople for more than a millennium. After the discovery of the Americas and the beginning of the modern era, commodity trading gradually expanded and spread across the world. The dominant capitalist social conditions of the last two centuries, finally, have sustained an explosion of commodity trading and markets with neither historical precedent nor parallel. If indeed products become commodities according to underlying social and historical conditions, there seems to be an inordinate variety of such conditions compatible with commodity trading. Where should the theorist start?

The approach adopted in this book derives from an interpretation of Marx's work that relies on Fine and Harris (1979) and Weeks (1981). Broadly speaking, analysis focuses first on markets for produced commodities, and then identifies important qualitative differences with other markets. These differences can be ascertained because the social and historical conditions under which products become commodities are explicitly considered. Specifically, it is assumed that capitalist social relations provide apposite terrain for analysis of commodities. There are two fundamental reasons for this assumption. First, capitalism has sustained an unprecedented expansion of commodity trading in the history of humanity.[5] Commodity trading in non-capitalist societies, substantial as it might have been during particular historical periods, pales into insignificance compared to that under capitalism. Second, and partly resulting from the first, capitalism encourages full development of all economic aspects of the commodity, including value, price, money, interest, and so on. Theory, therefore, is able to penetrate the mysteries of commodity value, the social form of commodities, the types of labour that contribute to commodity value, the transformation of products into commodities, but also the widespread and systematic emergence of markets in things that are not produced at all. In other words, trading in commodities produced under capitalist relations is assumed to constitute the fully developed form of all trading. Consequently, analysis of capitalist commodity trading allows for concepts to be formulated and conclusions to be drawn that afford insights into other trading. This theoretical position derives directly from Marx (1939; see 1973, pp. 105–106) for whom the fully developed form of a social phenomenon provides vital insights into its less-developed forms.[6] Admittedly Marx (p. 105) uses an unfortunate analogy to demonstrate his argument:

> Human anatomy contains a key to the anatomy of the ape. The intimations of higher development among the subordinate animal species, however, can be understood only after the higher development is already known.

This nineteenth century view of biological evolution as progress, with humanity at its peak, is now obsolete – apes are neither a 'subordinate' nor a 'less developed' form of human beings. Nevertheless, Marx's methodological point is powerful, and does not hinge on his example: theoretical analysis of a social phenomenon should focus on its most developed form, even if less developed forms appear independently, or earlier in historical time. This methodological principle underpins the work in this book.

However, the approach adopted here has also been influenced by the outlook of the Uno (1980) current of Japanese Marxism.[7] In particular, conclusions drawn about markets in commodities produced by capital are not expected directly to apply to markets for things that are not produced, or to non-capitalist commodity markets. Analogously, analysis of commodities produced under capitalist conditions does not immediately reveal what also holds for commodities produced under feudal, tribal or other non-capitalist conditions. In short, the fully developed aspects of the commodity are not directly and immediately its general aspects. This does not mean, however, that there is one theory for capitalist commodities, another for feudal commodities, yet another for tributary society commodities, and so on. There are common features of trading across markets, societies and historical periods, which could be illuminated through analysis of commodities produced under capitalist conditions – as is shown in more detail below. But in establishing what is general about markets, it is important not to contradict the historical order of precedence of market-related phenomena. This point is of paramount importance for the substance of commodity value – arguably the most important economic aspect of the commodity – defined by Marxist political economy as abstract human labour. For the approach adopted here, abstract human labour is a specifically capitalist phenomenon, the result of capitalist social relations of production, and refers to commodities produced under capitalist relations. It applies neither to objects traded generally in a capitalist economy, nor to commodities traded in non-capitalist societies. Commodity value as abstract labour is a social category whose existence requires capitalist conditions of production, and hence only the analysis of commodities produced under capitalist conditions could reveal its substance. The significance of this point will become apparent in demonstrating the emergence of money out of commodity exchange in Chapter 3.

To analyse commodities further, it is necessary to discuss capitalist social relations more fully. In the next section it is shown that social class is a decisive aspect of capitalist economic and non-economic relations. Markets are the social organisers of the capitalist economy, but their importance derives ultimately from the class structure of capitalist society.

1.2 The economic and the non-economic spheres of capitalist society

The first step in specifying the nature of capitalist social relations is to distinguish between capitalism as a social system in theory and capitalism as social reality in particular countries. The appropriate concepts are capitalism as a mode of production and capitalism as a social formation, developed by post-war French Marxism and associated closely with Althusser.[8] The capitalist mode of production is an integral whole of economic, political, ideological and cultural relations that have a specifically capitalist character. A capitalist social formation, on the other hand, is a historical entity that contains more than one mode of production, though the capitalist dominates the others. In this book the focus is exclusively on the capitalist mode of production, also referred to as capitalist society. A characteristic feature of the capitalist mode of production is that its economic aspects stand apart from its political, ideological and cultural aspects (Fine and Harris, 1979, pp. 12–15). The capitalist economy constitutes a separate social sphere, and has a degree of autonomy from the rest of society that is not found in other modes of production. There is a multitude of links between the economic sphere and the spheres of politics, law, ideology, family, tradition and custom that comprise the rest of capitalist society. Economic relations among capitalists, for instance, give rise to political relations, and legal and ideological relations can also generate economic interaction. But the most striking feature of the capitalist economy is its historically unprecedented degree of autonomy from the rest of society. This autonomy derives, at one remove, from the pervasive role of markets in the capitalist economy, but, at a further remove, originates in the class structure of capitalist society.

Readers familiar with Marxist theory will have already recognised the distinction between 'economic base' and 'social superstructure'. It is not intended here to rehearse old debates about the relationship of the two, especially arguments regarding the dominance of the 'base' over the 'superstructure'. However, the continuing importance of this Marxist distinction can be simply demonstrated by drawing a parallel with contemporary economic theory. In the extremely influential economics of 'institutions' and 'transactions costs', associated with North (1990) and Williamson (1975), the institutional structure of society determines the performance of the economy (this is discussed in more detail in Chapter 5). Specifically, the social mechanisms that finesse and enforce the law of contract, the institutional practices that establish rules of the game among economic agents, even the religious and moral beliefs in society, are supposed to affect transactions costs and thus to determine economic efficiency. For our purposes, it is notable that this current of mainstream economics in effect recognises the distinction between 'base' and 'superstructure' in the capitalist mode of production, further claiming that the non-economic 'superstructure' sets the terms within which the economic 'base' functions. Williamson (2000, p. 597), while distilling the major findings of 'transactions costs' economics during the last three decades, has even produced a diagrammatic depiction of social relations, in the form of four successive layers. He identifies the following, from the bottom up: (i) a layer of narrowly economic relations, (ii) a layer of 'governance' relations through which legal regulations are enforced, (iii) a layer of formal institutional relations, above all laws relating to property rights, and finally (iv), a layer of informal institutional relations (called 'social embeddedness') that are customary, ideological and religious. Each layer apparently has its own appropriate form of theory – for the first, straightforward neoclassical theory, for the second, transactions costs economics, for the third, economics of property rights as well as political theory, for the fourth, sociology or similar 'social theory'. Thus Williamson, one of the most influential figures in contemporary economic theory, maintains that capitalist social relations are vertically layered – the economy being at the bottom. He presents this view as an original idea, with no mention of Marx's distinction of 'base' and 'superstructure', and little of Marx's philosophical sophistication.

In classical Marxism, economic relations are assumed to have primacy over other social relations. This is a much maligned idea, and the simplest way of indicating how it is interpreted in this book is to refer again to Williamson's vertical layering of social relations. Williamson (2000, pp. 596–598) claims that ultimate determination within his proposed structure lies with the cultural and ideological relations at the top, though 'feedback' between all layers is also acknowledged. Beliefs, ideas and prejudices, which take hundreds or even thousands of years to change, percolate through to the layers below and finally determine what happens in the economy. However, this apparently plausible argument has nothing to say on how ideas and beliefs are themselves determined and altered. In contrast, Marx's vertical layering of the capitalist mode of production draws on dialectical materialism, for which the consciousness of human beings derives from the social relations in which they engage. This is a powerful assertion based on Marx's early philosophical researches and expressed lucidly in his own work, above all in the *Theses on Feuerbach* (see Marx, 1975), as well as in *The German Ideology*, jointly written with Engels (Marx and Engels, 1845–1846). Ideas, notions, concepts and beliefs reflect the material and social reality within which human beings live. The most important aspect of that reality is the economic, i.e. the production and reproduction of material life. By this token, to a distinctly capitalist economy correspond distinctly capitalist politics, ideology, law, and even religion. This view shaped the mature work of Marx (1859) on political economy (see 1970, pp. 20–21), and it is worth quoting at length:

> In the social production of their existence, men inevitably enter into definite relations, which are independent of their will, namely relations of production appropriate to a given stage in the development of their material forces of production. The totality of these relations of production constitutes the economic structure of society, the real foundation, on which arises a legal and political superstructure and to which correspond definite forms of social consciousness. The mode of production of material life conditions the general process of social, political and intellectual life.

But dialectical materialism is not crude materialism that tries to explain the head by looking at the stomach. The realm of consciousness is also shaped by human volition. Human action is driven by consciousness, and therefore operates as an independent factor in society; it is an objective social force through which people change economy and society. Moreover, through social action people also actively make themselves. From this follows a conclusion that is particularly alien to neoclassical economics, namely that human consciousness is neither an individual nor a given magnitude, but is constantly shaped by the collective action of its bearers. This fundamental premise informs the analysis of non-economic relations in this book, and places them within the context of capitalist economic relations. Non-economic relations of fiat, authority and solidarity, for instance, are intrinsic to capitalist production and have a direct capitalist character. Relations of power, trust, and moral obligation, on the other hand, often acquire a capitalist character by being placed at the service of capitalist economic activity. To develop these arguments it is necessary to look more closely at the sphere of the capitalist economy.

1.3 Class relations in the capitalist economy

It is standard practice in economic theory to analyse the capitalist economy as comprising production, distribution of income, and exchange of output. The distinguishing feature of Marxist political economy in this respect is its assumption that production is the dominant aspect of the economy. Thus Marxist analysis of the capitalist economy commences with the social relations of production, a starting point that has profound implications for commodities and markets.[9] More specifically, it is postulated that a set of characteristic class relations can be found at the core of capitalist production. On the one hand there are capitalist producers, who are independent, autonomous, in competition with each other, and possessing both the means of production and the final output as their private property. On the other hand there are workers, who are employed to operate the means of production but own neither them nor the finished product. Thus at the heart of capitalist society are distinctive property rights and specific social relations that prevail in production. Property rights and production relations mark out two fundamental and antagonistic classes: the capitalist class and the working class.

From this standpoint, capitalist production is neither merely a technical process that results in useful products, nor simply a rational way of combining resources to produce output efficiently. It is also the most fundamental terrain for class relations to unfold between capitalists and workers, containing intrinsic and prominent non-economic components. Capitalist workplaces are permeated with hierarchy, authority and fiat, running vertically from the capitalist to the worker. Contemporary economics recognises the existence of fiat within the firm, and often contrasts it with the state of equality among market agents (discussed in Chapter 5). But, for neoclassicism, hierarchical authority at the workplace is at most a 'rational' way of improving efficiency, perhaps by reducing the transactions costs of production. The class content of workplace relations of authority is meticulously ignored by economists. Consequently, phenomena of conflict, antagonism and struggle at the workplace are treated as irrational and alien to the essence of capitalist production. In contrast, for classical Marxism, hierarchy and fiat at the workplace are necessary in order to make possible the exploitation of workers by capitalists. The aim of capitalist production is to obtain profit from the sale of finished output, which is the exclusive property of the capitalist. The deeper source of profit, however, is the systematic exploitation of workers at the workplace – i.e. the performance of labour over and above the length of time for which an equivalent has been paid to workers as money wages. The point here is not to become entangled in contentious arguments about the provenance of capitalist profits, but to stress the importance of non-economic relations in the Marxist treatment of profit. Exploitation of workers would be impossible in the absence of vertical relations of fiat and authority at the point of production. The capitalist's power at the workplace determines conditions and methods of work, with which the worker must comply. Conflict and struggle between capitalists and workers emerge inevitably in the course of production. Consequently, capitalist production is also characterised by horizontal non-economic relations, which are typically ignored by mainstream economic theory.[10] Capitalist workplaces are permeated by collegial relations of solidarity, mutual support and moral obligation among workers. Collective relations among workers ultimately acquire institutional forms through the creation of trade unions, a general phenomenon of capitalist production that makes it possible for labour to confront the pressures and strains of capitalist production. Trade unions are formal mechanisms created by workers in order effectively to intervene in conflicts over working conditions and working time, thus limiting exploitation by capitalists.

The class relations of capitalist production also influence the distribution of the final product into wages and profits. Since workers have no property in the means of production and do not own the finished output, wages are the only means they have of acquiring goods and services for themselves and their families. The real wage reflects, on the one hand, the consumption norms prevalent among workers, and on the other, the level of the productivity of labour. Profits, in contrast, accrue to capitalists because they own the finished output as well as being able to enforce practices at work that result in exploitation of workers. The actual levels of income that accrue to both workers and capitalists are partly determined through distributional struggle between the two classes, according to organisational, institutional, ideological and political factors. At any moment in time there is a distributional balance of power between the capitalist class and the working class, which varies significantly across sectors and enterprises.

The class relations of production and distribution, in turn, accord an exceptionally important role to markets in the capitalist economy. For one thing, capitalist production generates a broad network of markets where none existed previously. If independent, autonomous and specialised producers are to obtain inputs, they must enter into exchange relations with the capitalists who produced them. By the same token, producers must also channel their output into the market in search of buyers. Thus as soon as capitalist property rights and production relations are established in any sector of the economy, a large array of markets comes into existence among capitalists. 'Intermediate' markets in plant, equipment, and means of production in general are characteristically capitalist markets. The most important market in a capitalist economy, however, is that for labour power. Capitalist producers must be able to obtain labour power of requisite skills, for specific periods of time, and with a degree of flexibility in hiring and firing. Consequently, there must exist a social class that regularly hires itself out in the labour market. For the capitalist mode of production to prevail, a labour market has to be created in which the capacity to labour is traded as a commodity across society. Moreover, given the existence of a labour market, still more markets have to emerge that allow workers to obtain necessary means of consumption. Thus markets for final consumption proliferate and expand as capitalist accumulation proceeds and the working class grows. They are further boosted by the luxury consumption of capitalists out of profits.

It follows that markets act as social organisers in the capitalist mode of production. They allow resources (including labour power) to be shared out among capitalist producers, and facilitate distribution of aggregate output as wages and profits. Moreover, markets fulfil this function without conscious intervention by the state or other authorities. Changes in prices operate as signals to producers, consumers and workers, leading to changes in individual decision-making, and effecting alterations in the distribution of resources and output. Despite operating automatically, and even anarchically, markets have an organising effect on the aggregate allocation of resources and output. The unusual autonomy of the economy within the capitalist mode of production is a consequence of the automatic organising role of markets. They provide a degree of integration and unity of motion to the capitalist economy that does not require conscious measures by non-economic bodies. Therefore, the economy appears to be cut off from the rest of society – from politics, religion, morality, and ideology. However, despite making it possible for the capitalist economy to hold together, markets reveal little of the deeper reality of capitalist production. On the contrary, the role of markets in capitalist society, uniquely important as it is, derives ultimately from the social relations of production.

A difficult issue in connection with the organising role of markets in the capitalist economy is 'commodity fetishism', an original contribution by Marx (1867, Ch. 1) to social science. In a nutshell, Marx claimed that the social relations among commodity producers often appear as relations between things, especially as quantitative relations between commodities. Commodity owners that meet for purposes of trade already have social relations with each other – for instance, relations of property, of differential access to resources, of work, even of hierarchy and power. Within the market they inevitably create still more social relations, such as relations of seller to buyer, of creditor to debtor, or of client to supplier. However, their social relations are subsumed under the rates of equivalence established between their commodities. In capitalist commodity markets, for instance, the social relations of capitalist production vanish out of sight. Fundamental social relations of the capitalist mode of production, such as producer independence, autonomy in deciding how to deploy resources, absolute property rights over inputs and output, exclusive right of capitalists to profits, and the hiring of wage labourers who lack property rights over productive resources, are collapsed into the price at which goods are offered for sale. In short, the social relations among capitalists and between capitalists and workers appear in the market as relations between things (commodity exchange ratios). These relations are constantly rebalanced in the sphere of production and across society, but the only evidence that the market provides of such rebalancing is that commodities are sold at different prices.

'Commodity fetishism' implies that the capitalist economy appears as an automatically operating universe of things, despite ultimately comprising relations and phenomena created by human action. The 'objective' aspect of the capitalist economy results from the organising role of the market, and dominates economic perceptions. A clear, if extreme, example of the 'objective' or 'stand aloof' character of the capitalist economy is offered by economic crises. Whatever other aspects they might have, capitalist economic crises always involve disruption of domestic or world markets. Crises entail the inability of capitalists to sell, hence falls in prices of commodities or other assets. Falling commodity prices usually lead to declines in profitability for capitalist enterprises, emergence of commodity stockpiles, and excess capacity to produce output. Such phenomena typically appear as 'objective' developments, created by the autonomous movement of the economy. By the same token, the steps taken to restore profitability (including laying off workers, reducing wages, and imposing a myriad of constraints on private lives) appear as unfortunate but 'objectively' necessary measures. Politics, family, personal development, and even morality are forced to bow to the seemingly ineluctable and 'objective' imperatives of a crisis-stricken capitalist economy.

'Commodity fetishism' could lead to theoretical confusion and neglect of the social relations underpinning and surrounding markets. However, it is worth stressing that 'commodity fetishism' is not simply a false inversion of the underlying social reality of capitalism, making capitalist relations appear as relations among things. It is mistaken to presume, as a consequence of commodity fetishism, that the 'real' relations of a capitalist economy are social relations among people, while those observed among commodities in capitalist markets are simply a façade. Rather, capitalist economic relations are fundamentally social relations but also genuinely relations among things (Fine, 2002, pp. 67–77). Capitalist production and distribution rest on the underlying realities of resource allocation, productivity of labour, and time required for production. These are material aspects of social life that are summed up in the prices of commodities brought to market. Capitalists make profits through their production relations with workers, but they must also buy, make and sell things in order to obtain these profits. The need to obtain inputs and dispose of products in a huge network of markets implies that the capitalist economy inevitably acquires an 'objective' and 'thing-like' aspect. It is important to bear this in mind, if Marxist economics is not to degenerate into flights of fancy about the 'true' essence of the capitalist economy as relations among human beings.[11]

In the following sections it is shown that capitalist class relations are fundamental to determining the value of commodities. The interplay of the economic and the non-economic is made clear in relation to the substance of commodity value, and the relative prices of commodities. Markets are subsequently differentiated according to the social relations that are directly relevant to their operations. Non-economic relations are shown to play a pivotal role in markets for commodities not produced by capital, traded objects unrelated to production, or even traded objects unrelated to the economy.

1.4 Capital and commodities

Capital, then, comprises a set of class relations between capitalists and workers, which are both economic and non-economic. In the sphere of production, capital consists of relations of exploitation between capitalists and workers based on power and fiat. In the sphere of distribution, capital consists of relations of antagonism and struggle between capitalists and workers, but also norms of consumption for workers, within limits posed by the productivity of labour. In the sphere of exchange, finally, capital consists of a range of commercial relations: there are relations between capitalists and workers in the labour market, among capitalists in markets for means of production, and between capitalists and their customers in the markets for means of consumption.

However, capital is also an economic phenomenon in a strict sense. It stands for the constant, self-repeating motion that connects production to exchange and obeys its own impulse, rather than the motivations of individual economic agents. This aspect of capital is typically captured by the 'circuit of (industrial) capital', a series of transformations that follow each other in strict succession.[12] The circuit commences with capital as a sum of money that is spent in the markets for means of production and labour, and aims at obtaining inputs for the production process (investment). After completing the purchase of inputs, capital leaves the sphere of exchange and takes the form of productive capacity. The process of production takes place under the power and control of capitalists, resulting in exploitation of workers and generation of profits (surplus value). Profits belong to capitalists, who have exclusive property rights over the finished output. After production, capital assumes the form of commodity output (which already contains profit) and seeks sale in the sphere of exchange. When finished output is successfully sold, capital returns to the money form, completing the circuit and allowing capitalists to obtain money profits and recoup the initial investment. Capital can then continue its circular motion, either on the same scale, if profits are consumed privately by their capitalist owners, or expanded, if some money profits are reinvested. In brief, the technical side of the circuit comprises the following three flows (or transformations): (i) from money to production inputs; (ii) from production inputs to finished output; and (iii) from finished output to money capital. Since the movement of capital is continuous, the circuit also comprises three stocks coexisting in time (which can be readily observed on the balance sheets of capitalist enterprises): (i) money; (ii) plant, equipment, raw materials, and workers; (iii) finished goods. Moreover, capital requires time to traverse the circuit. There is circulation time taken up by, first, seeking sellers of inputs, and second, seeking buyers for the finished output; there is also production time taken up by transforming production inputs into finished goods. Finally, the motive force of the circuit has nothing to do with producing goods and services for the benefit of people or society. Rather, capital engages in its circular motion with the aim of maintaining and expanding itself through the successful extraction of profit.

It follows that output produced by capital is aimed exclusively at the market, rather than the gratification of the producer. The products of capital do not have to be transformed into commodities – they are commodities directly and immediately. Analogously, in any economy in which production is dominated by capital, the bulk of products comprise commodities as a matter of course. This is ultimately the reason why commodities produced by capital represent the fully developed form of commodities. To be more precise, commodities produced by capital demonstrate clearly and completely the two inherent aspects of all commodities: they are at once things of use and things of value. In line with this claim, the social relations characteristic of commodities as things of value are discussed in this chapter, drawing on the first three chapters of the first volume of Marx's *Capital*. The social relations specific to commodities as things of use are considered in the next chapter.

Marx's (1867, Ch. 1) discussion of commodities as things of value starts by recognising that commodities have 'exchange value', that is, they always exhibit a quantitative equivalence with each other. His subsequent analysis of exchange value, however, profound as it is, leaves considerable room for ambiguity. Without venturing directly into the Marxist debates on value, the position taken in this book is that exchange value is not a static property of commodities. Rather, exchange value develops according to the social relations of production, distribution and exchange. The social relations summed up in the exchange value of commodities produced by capital are profoundly different from the social relations summed up in the exchange value of commodities produced otherwise. They are even more different from the social relations relevant to the exchange value of traded objects that are not produced at all. All commodities have exchange value, but only commodities produced by capital possess it as a fully developed property. The reasons have to do with the social relations of capitalist production, as is shown below.[13]

The process of development of exchange value can be briefly sketched, drawing broadly on Marx's discussion. In commodity exchange that occurs haphazardly or accidentally, the exchange value of commodities has a rudimentary and unstable form. Inconsistent or arbitrary equivalences could hold from one transaction to the next, without any inherent tendency for discrepancies to be eliminated. For commodities A and B, for instance, the following exchange values could obtain, without real (as opposed to logical) contradiction:

x of A = y of B
x of A = g of B

If several commodities were involved in haphazard or accidental exchanges, the ratios at which they were actually exchanged might also be intransitive. The following exchange values, for example, could in practice materialise for commodities A, B, and C, without any tendency for their evident absurdity to be eliminated:

x of A = y of B
y of B = z of C
x of A = h of C

As commodity exchange becomes regular and broad, however, there is development of exchange value, which now takes the form of transitive and regular quantitative ratios among commodities. In expanded and general commodity exchange, the exchange values of commodities become more consistent and mutually compatible. A money commodity also emerges, and exchange value assumes the more developed form of money price. When money is systematically used in the process of exchange, there is little arbitrariness of quantitative ratios between commodities, and prices tend to be transitive.

The question that naturally arises here is, what are the social relations that bring regularity and transitivity to exchange values as commodity exchange becomes general, also transforming exchange values into money prices? The claim made in this chapter, as indicated above, is that they are very different in markets for commodities produced by capital as compared to other markets. For commodities produced by capital, these social relations can be ascertained immediately from Marx's own analysis of exchange value. Though it is not stated explicitly, Marx assumes in Part One of the first volume of *Capital* that the mode of production is already capitalist.[14] Marx then postulates that, as things of value, all commodities are qualitatively identical. Specifically, all commodities possess a common substance of value (abstract human labour) created in the course of their production, and contained by them in definite amounts. It follows immediately that the quantitative ratios among commodities can be neither arbitrary nor intransitive. At any given time, each commodity has a definite exchange value that prevails across markets and is compatible with that of others. Suppose, for example, that commodities A, B, and C already contained the following amounts of value substance:

1 of A = k of value substance
1 of B = l of value substance
1 of C = m of value substance

It would then be trivially true that the exchange values of these commodities would be definite and transitive:

$$1 \text{ of } A = (k/l) \text{ of } B = (k/m) \text{ of } C$$

Exchange value, therefore, must have a developed form, given that commodities contain a common value substance. To substantiate his argument about value substance, Marx (1867, pp. 131–137) proposes the well-known distinction between concrete and abstract labour. Concrete labour is specific to person, time, place and skill, and produces the use value of a commodity – for instance, shoe-making, car-making, clothes-making, etc. In contrast, abstract labour is general, featureless, homogeneous, and provides the substance of the value of a commodity.[15] For the Marxist approach adopted in this book, abstract labour is understood to comprise a social (as opposed to natural) substance, an economic magnitude that results from actual economic processes. Abstract labour is not merely a mental construct, a theoretical notion extracted from the concrete labours that create useful products. A theorist could, for instance, calculate rates of equivalence among qualitatively different concrete labours on the basis of some abstract principle, such as energy expenditure by the labourer. Thus diverse concrete labours could be rendered equivalent with each other by being reduced to some abstract standard, such as calorie consumption. But this would be a purely mental exercise that would mean nothing at all for the practice of exchange. In contrast, abstract labour as social substance implies that concrete labours are translated into a common substance in practice. In other words, social and economic processes exist that continually compare and contrast concrete labours, making them commensurate with each other. The economic functioning of society itself establishes equivalences among diverse concrete labours. Abstract labour becomes the social substance of commodity value only when social relations make it a social reality, as opposed to a mere mental abstraction.

The deeper significance of assuming capitalist social relations in order to analyse the commodity is now evident. The most fundamental social relations required for emergence of abstract labour are those of wage labour – i.e. the very relations that lie at the heart of the capitalist mode of production. Specifically, concrete labours are made commensurate with each other in practice as workers move indifferently between employments (occupationally and geographically), lacking hereditary rights over jobs. The content of their work effort is also homogenised across industries as workers are generally subjected to capitalist authority and discipline at the workplace.[16] Furthermore, abstract labour also becomes a social reality due to commercial relations attached to inputs and finished output. As capitalist producers engage in constant buying and selling (shifting resources across branches of industry) they impose equivalences on the output of disparate productive activities, and make concrete labours commensurate with each other. Nevertheless, in the absence of a deep and well-functioning labour market, capitalist producers would be unable to obtain sufficient labour inputs according to requirements. Consequently, they would be unable to shift resources flexibly across industries, the actual establishment of equivalences among finished products would become problematic, and working conditions would differ profoundly across the economy. In other words, generalised commercial transactions are a necessary but not sufficient condition for abstract labour to become a social substance. What is required for the latter is also wage labour as society-wide practice in both market and workplace, i.e. fully fledged capitalism. In sum, abstract labour is a historically specific social substance that is established as social norm under capitalist conditions of production and through the process of market competition. In the absence of the social relations of the capitalist mode of production, abstract labour has no existence as social substance.

The exchange value of commodities produced by capital is anchored in the abstract human labour they contain. Put differently, the quantitative ratios of commodities in capitalist markets (relative prices) are based on value substance. This is despite abstract human labour appearing directly neither in quantitative ratios, nor in commodity prices expressed in units of money.[17] The close relationship between substance and form of value derives exclusively from the relations of the capitalist economy. Two of its characteristic elements are particularly important. The first is the unprecedented spread of commodity markets. Commodities produced by capital bear definite and transitive prices partly because of repeated and extensive transactions within the enormous network of capitalist markets. Regular buying and selling, applying to the bulk of society's output, provides a measure of regularity to prices. Habitual and systematic transacting with a view to money profit inevitably eliminates major discrepancies and absurdities in commodity prices. The second element, however, is more important; namely, extraction of profit at the point of production. Suppose, for example, that the relative price of a particular commodity remained above the level justified by its value substance relative to others.

It follows that the profitability of its producers would be above average. Consequently, fresh capital would enter the industry, bringing with it additional resources and labour-power. An increase in the supply of the commodity would result and, other things equal, the commodity's relative price would begin to fall. Capital would continue to move into the industry until the relative price reached a level compatible with the commodity's value substance. At that point, capital profitability for the industry would be consistent with the average. The opposite process would take place if a commodity's relative price remained below the level justified by its value substance. Thus, the definitive regulator of prices of commodities produced by capital is the drive to extract profits through the exploitation of labour. The search for profit ensures ultimate compliance of the form of value (exchange value or relative price) with the substance of value (abstract labour). Definite and transitive commodity prices in capitalist markets rely partly on extensive buying and selling, but derive ultimately from the capitalist relations of production.

By the same token, for commodities that are not produced by capital, or for traded objects that are not products at all, there is no connection between substance and form of value. Exchange values and prices in such markets are determined without direct connection with the social relations of production. This constitutes a significant qualitative difference between markets in commodities produced under capitalist conditions, and all other markets. The following section explores this difference in more depth.

1.5 Markets without commodities, and markets in commodities not produced by capital

In the capitalist mode of production there is a broad array of labours that do not count as the substance of value. Similarly there are products and activities that cannot, or do not, count as commodities.[18] Thus, labours performed in the spheres of distribution and exchange do not produce commodities even though they may appear to do so. Such labours, moreover, do not create value (Fine and Harris, 1979, Ch. 3). Workers employed in much of state provision of health and education, for instance, do not contribute to creation of abstract labour. The bulk of the services provided by these workers – schooling, skill acquisition, socialisation of children, illness prevention and treatment – do not count as commodities. The same holds for workers employed in commerce (retail and wholesale) and workers employed in the miscellaneous activities of the financial sector (such as banking and stock market operations). The services they provide belong to the sphere of exchange, dealing with finished commodities and money.[19]

Moreover, there are also activities and things that assume the form of commodities, despite being inherently unrelated to commodities. In some instances, this could arise purely due to the form of money payment made. A typical example is land, which as a traded object involves no labour in production. However, property rights over land allow the owner to appropriate surplus value as rent. Thus land (real estate) markets are formed in which property rights over land are traded, their prices determined through discounting future payments of rent. Another example is stocks and shares, both of which similarly involve no labour in production. However, they can take the form of commodities because they afford to their owner a claim on profits to be generated in the future. Therefore they are bought and sold in stock markets at prices determined through discounting of future payments of interest and dividends. Insurance policies also take the commodity form – their buyers are entitled to a contingent claim on money necessary to cover accidental and unforeseen events, and their seller obtains profits by concentrating and investing the premia paid for policies. In this category of traded objects that simply assume the commodity form also belong entirely non-economic relations to which money payments are attached. These relations could include, for instance, the charging of fines ('the price of wrongdoing'), bribery ('the price of a favour'), and outright fraud and corruption ('the price of honesty'). Such activities assume the form of value and resemble commodity trading, despite being entirely unrelated to commodities through production or otherwise. They give rise to 'pretend' markets.[20]

Therefore, it is possible for the form of value in the capitalist mode of production to become completely detached from the substance of value. Promises to pay, claims on future income, things obtained from nature, and even social relations and moral sentiments can assume the form of value, without having any direct connection with value as abstract labour. An extensive array of markets (even 'pretend' markets) that are totally unrelated to commodities and their production comes into being. Prices in these markets reflect heavily the influence of non-economic factors, and retain strong elements of arbitrariness. That is not to deny the possibility of price regularity, even arising due to economic mechanisms. In the markets for land, or stocks and shares, for instance, prices are based on discounting the profits likely to be generated by capitals engaged in production. Consequently, these prices cannot move for long in a direction that is contrary to the movement of the rate of profit, determined by exploitation of workers in production. However, the absence of mechanisms anchoring land and stock prices onto the substance of value (in contrast to produced commodities) implies that they also exhibit strong volatility and arbitrariness. Non-economic factors, such as psychological swings of optimism, political change, or even purely institutional manipulation of trading, play a strong determining role for prices of land and financial assets. For other markets of this type, especially 'pretend' markets, prices could be determined exclusively by non-economic factors. Price regularity might be the result of simple repetition of transactions, or of legal and statutory relations. The level of bribes (the 'price of a favour'), for instance, is pure social custom that is specific to place, time, culture, and the frequent repetition of bribing. The level of fines (the 'price of wrongdoing'), on the other hand, is typically set by law; it might or might not reflect custom, but is nevertheless validated through repetition.

Separation of value form from value substance under capitalist conditions makes it possible to draw powerful conclusions about commodities and markets in non-capitalist societies. Value substance in non-capitalist societies is largely absent for a variety of reasons. Non-capitalist societies typically lack the refinement of labour division found in the capitalist mode of production. Moreover, it is highly unusual for non-capitalist producers to be independent, autonomous and in competition with each other. Non-capitalist societies also lack broad and stable labour markets, though instances of wage labour can often occur at their margins. Only capitalist society contains a large social class that is separated from the means of production and moves freely between jobs. By the same token, non-capitalist economies do not constitute separate sets of institutions and practices operating in a self-contained and automatic way. Instead, the operation of non-capitalist economies is heavily dependent on relations of kinship, rank, custom, and political or social authority. In sum, commodity value in non-capitalist societies cannot be a materially based social norm expressed through competition. The social mechanisms for equating diverse concrete labours and transforming them into abstract labour are undeveloped or non-existent.

The absence of the substance of value in non-capitalist societies has profound implications for commodities and markets. It follows immediately that exchange value in non-capitalist societies is a formal property of commodities, unrelated to the deeper reality of production. When commodity owners meet randomly and occasionally, the exchange values of their commodities are arbitrary and intransitive, as was explained in the previous section. If commodity exchange became frequent, regular and widespread, exchange values could shed some of their arbitrariness. Money would also emerge, making exchange values more definite and transitive. However, such phenomena would be entirely unrelated to abstract labour. Instead, they would result from customary patterns of material life and elemental economic responses to the availability of resources, both partially reflected through commodity exchange. If commodity prices became definite and transitive, that would be because of customary market relations of demand and supply, associated with repeated transactions. Relevant economic factors would include volumes of agricultural output, levels of metal ore production, availability of means of transport, and habits of eating, drinking and clothing. But prices would still bear no systematic connection to production, and markets would not operate as social organisers of economic activity. Non-capitalist societies lack the economic mechanisms characteristic of capitalist society that link relative prices to the reproduction of material life through the profitability of capital. Since prices are unrelated to value substance as a deeply based social norm, they reflect non-economic factors, including tradition, custom, moral concerns and the dictates of power. For this reason, prices in non-capitalist societies retain a strong element of arbitrariness and capriciousness.

Transition to capitalism can be seen, accordingly, as the process through which exchange value ceases to be a formal property of commodities and becomes rooted in the very structure of production. But such an evolution of exchange value would not result simply from proliferation and expansion of commodity operations. The spread of commodity transactions does not itself produce capitalism – the market is not capitalism. It is perfectly possible for markets to proliferate and commodity exchange to become widespread without capitalist social relations coming into being. Commodity prices would then be heavily influenced by social custom, tradition and non-economic manipulation. In contrast, if capitalist social conditions came into being, commodity prices would comply with underlying economic realities (abstract labour), and there would also occur an unprecedented spreading of markets. For that, however, the class structure of society must be altered, including creation of a working class and a capitalist class (by detaching groups of producers from the means of production and transferring money wealth across society). These social changes are far more profound and difficult to bring about than merely encouraging the emergence and growth of market trading.

In sum, the formal similarities among markets conceal great qualitative differences. Theoretical analysis could account for these differences, provided that it focused first on markets for commodities produced under capitalist conditions. The reason is that commodities produced by capital demonstrate fully the relationship between form and substance of value. In the capitalist mode of production products are systematically turned into commodities as a result of the class structure of capitalist society. Consequently, the underlying social relations of production are summed up in abstract labour as the substance of value, and economic mechanisms exist which ensure compliance of commodity prices with the value substance of commodities. However, the commodity form is also adopted by a wide variety of capitalist activities that are unrelated to value as abstract labour, or even unrelated to the economy altogether. Markets for land, shares, stocks, and insurance, or 'pretend' markets for favours, punishments, extortion and so on, are not to be confused with commodity markets. The material realities of production have a remote and indirect effect on their prices, if they have an effect at all. Instead, such prices are strongly influenced, or even wholly determined, by non-economic factors. Furthermore, in non-capitalist societies value substance is typically absent. Markets for commodities produced under non-capitalist conditions are modulated by non-economic factors of custom, accident, moral imperatives, hierarchy and power. Their prices are not systematically connected to production of material life. Prices could acquire regularity, if market exchanges become repeated and extensive, but that would result partly from traditional practices of buying and selling, and partly from customary patterns of social provision.

2 Commodities and gifts

2.1 Commodities and gifts as tokens of market and non-market relations

Gift exchange has long attracted theoretical interest in social science because of its implications for reciprocity, morality and rules in social intercourse. Polanyi *et al.* (1957), for instance, turned reciprocity and gift-giving into fundamental notions for analysis of non-market-based societies. Gouldner (1960) claimed that reciprocity represents a universal 'moral norm' for all societies. There have been entire theories of 'social exchange' resting on reciprocity (Homans, 1958; Blau, 1964) and, if Levi-Strauss (1949, 1958, 1962) is properly included in this field, even theories of the origin of human society based on reciprocal, gift-like, exchange of women. Mauss' (1925) famous essay on the gift, moreover, is one of the most heavily debated texts in the social sciences (see commentary by Levi-Strauss, 1950, and Sahlins, 1974, Ch. 4).[1]

Nevertheless, since the early 1980s analytical interest in reciprocity has reached quite a different level of intensity.[2] The currently prominent theory of 'social capital', for instance, relies partly on the concept of reciprocity (though not of the gift), and the early work of one of its originators, Coleman (1972, 1975), was within the current of 'social exchange'.[3] The pre-eminent role in renewing theoretical interest in the gift, however, has been played by anthropological research. The distinction between commodity and gift has become gradually established as analogue for the distinction between market and non-market relations. To be more specific, commodities are typically distinguished from gifts on the basis of their respective exchangeability. Untrammelled and full exchangeability is assumed completely to characterise the commodity, while moral, social, customary and other factors strongly condition exchangeability of the gift. Thus the 'commodity' has come to stand for rationality (especially of the instrumental variety), individualism, a strict calculus of material gain and loss, impersonal relations, and the holding together of society through the invisible glue of the market. In contrast, the 'gift' stands for moral obligation, collective concerns, personal relations that survive and continue after exchange, imprecise and often non-material rewards, and the holding together of society through visible and open relations based on volition, rank and the like.[4]

An analytical polarity is often postulated in the literature between commodity economies and gift economies. According to this approach, gift exchange and gift economy are appropriate concepts for capturing non-market transactions among agrarian producers, landowners, factory managers, workers, professionals, and so on. Gift-like reciprocity can influence the distribution of output, and consequently give shape and direction to production. Therefore, non-market and even non-economic social relations, such as hierarchy and prestige, could impinge directly upon the economic core of society. In this vein, gift-like relations and the gift economy can be thought of as a barrier (or bulwark, if preferred) against the development of capitalist relations. The web of reciprocal obligations created by gifts is not conducive to expansion of market exchange, since the latter presupposes impersonal relations driven by cold calculation of self-interest. Custom, hierarchy, prestige and mutual obligation appear to play no intrinsic role in the world of commodities, and their overwhelming presence in the world of gifts can be seen as an obstacle to development of a market economy. On the other hand, these non-market relations could also create favourable conditions for corruption and 'cronyism', both of which necessarily take the form of 'gifts'.[5] The implications for the analysis of advanced capitalism are also profound, since the demarcation line between market and non-market relations is blurred in the realm of the family and the welfare state, especially in education and health provision. Does capitalist development imply destruction of non-market relations, the relentless shrinking of the realm of custom, trust and moral obligation, which is supposedly captured by the gift? Is the world of the gift irrelevant to capitalist calculation of returns? Should the welfare state be analysed on the basis of gift relations?[6]

This chapter reconsiders the distinction between commodities and gifts and shows that it is misleading to identify commodities with market and gifts with non-market relations. Capitalist commodities and trading generate a broad range of non-market (and non-economic) relations of trust, custom, power, and hierarchy. They arise spontaneously alongside the relations of money-making, strict comparison of returns, and narrow calculation of means and ends. But the character of these non-market relations is also shaped by capital as an economic activity and as a framework of motives, aims and practices. This claim is demonstrated by analysing commodities as things of use, i.e. by focusing on their 'use value'. A major weakness of the commodity-gift literature is its exclusive concentration on commodity exchangeability, at the expense of usefulness or, more accurately, use value. When the role of use value is considered in commodity trading as well as in the subsequent deployment of commodities in production and consumption, it becomes clear that commodities continually generate non-market relations. In this light, capitalist and non-capitalist economies are not distinguished from each other because of a presumed shrinking of the realm of non-market relations in the former. Rather, the capitalist mode of production leads to emergence of a multitude of non-market relations that are stamped by capital.[7]

2.2 Commodity and gift exchangeability

The work of Gregory (1980, 1982, 1997) has been influential in the recent debate on commodities versus gifts. Gregory (1982, p. 12) proposes the following elegant distinction:

> Marx was able to develop a very important proposition: that commodity exchange is an exchange of alienable things between transactors who are in a state of reciprocal independence . . . The corollary of this is that non-commodity (gift) exchange is an exchange of inalienable things between transactors who are in a state of reciprocal dependence. This proposition is only implicit in Marx's analysis but it is . . . a precise definition of gift exchange.

Gregory uses this distinction as foundation for a theory of 'gift-based societies, characterised by kinship-based groups (clans), as opposed to 'commodity-based' societies, characterised by social classes. Theoretical interest in the subsequent debate has concentrated on demonstrating more fully the impact of non-market factors (moral, customary, kinship, religious, and so on) on gift exchange, while also discussing the social relations expressed in the latter. Thus Gregory's distinction has been (critically) employed in analysing the different roles of men and women in the process of production and exchange (Strathern, 1988). It has also been used to distinguish between things that are exchanged and things that are not exchangeable at all (Weiner, 1992). To be sure, the neatness of Gregory's distinction has also been subjected to sustained critique. Parry (1986; see also Parry and Bloch, 1989), for instance, has shown that certain gifts with religious associations are alienable in traditional Indian society. Scepticism has been expressed on whether the 'gift' is an adequate notion for characterisation of an entire economy (Thomas, 1991). Still others have rejected the notion of a sharp dichotomy between commodity and gift, preferring to see the two as poles in a 'spectrum of give and take' that extends from transactions 'dictated by a sense of obligation and commitment' (the gift pole) to transactions 'merely or principally dictated by a desire to obtain certain objects by means of exchange' (the commodity pole)

(Valeri, 1994, p. 18). According to this view, ascertaining the precise point on the spectrum at which particular transactions lie is much less important than specifying the nature of the relationship between transacting parties.

For our purposes, it is significant that Gregory's distinction between commodities and gifts (and the social and personal relations between the parties in related transactions) evidently rests on the characteristic features of the exchangeability of commodities in contrast to that of gifts. In subsequent literature there has been no quarrel with this aspect of Gregory's distinction. Rather, its implicit acceptance has contributed to the emergence of the notion of a 'spectrum' or 'continuum' of exchange transactions, with gift at one end and commodity at the other, which is accepted by both those who are critical of Gregory's distinction (such as Valeri, 1994) and those who are sympathetic to it (Carrier, 1994a, p. 361; see also 1991, 1992a). It is worth noting that Gregory (1997, Ch. 2) rejected the view of exchangeability as a 'continuum' and expressed strong support for treating commodity and gift as polar opposites. It is shown in this chapter that the binary opposition between commodity and gift cannot adequately serve Gregory's purposes because it is exclusively based on the property of exchangeability. The commodity, however, already contains a binary opposition between use value and exchange value. When use value is properly considered, the polar opposition between commodities and gifts disappears.

Significantly, close analytical focus on the exchangeability of commodity and gift is not limited to recent literature but goes back to the originators of this debate – that is, to Malinowski and Mauss. In his classic work on the gift, Mauss (1925) is most heavily exercised by locating the roots of the obligation to reciprocate gifts in primitive society, while also seeking explanations for the obligation to give and the obligation to receive gifts. In a much-analysed passage, he claims that the origin of the obligation to reciprocate lies with the 'spirit' of the gifted object – the Maori *hau* – that remains tied to the person of the original giver.[8] The mystical character of Mauss' argument has been noted, particularly by British anthropologists (for instance, Radcliffe-Brown, 1951, pp. 47–51), and indeed he appears at times almost to believe that a *hau* really resides in the gift. Mysticism aside, it is indisputable that the power of Mauss' essay derives from his erudite discussion of the rules of 'legality and self-interest' that make for gift reciprocation. For Mauss, these rules show that even very simple communities are far removed from a 'state of nature' and the obligation to reciprocate takes a 'contractual' aspect. Be that as it may, it is clear that Mauss is primarily concerned with the determinants of the gift's exchangeability (as property of the gift, even if not as quantitative proportion), and seeks those in the moral aspects of the gift relationship.[9]

On the other hand, Malinowski (1922, Ch. 6; also 1935, Pt I), ever a fieldworker, concentrates on providing exhaustive accounts of exchange transactions in the Trobriands. He also strongly maintains that it is impossible to draw a sharp line between gift-type and commodity-type transactions. Evidently he thinks of exchange transactions as a continuum, with pure (i.e. non-reciprocated) gift on one end and pure commodity on the other. Mauss (1925), however, rejected Malinowski's notion of the pure gift (*mapula*). Whatever other reasons might have caused this rejection, it is undeniable that 'pure gift' directly contradicts Mauss' own emphasis on the 'contractual' obligation to reciprocate and effectively denies the existence of the gift's exchangeability. It is particularly significant that Malinowski (1926), in a rare show of deference to criticism, acknowledged the validity of Mauss' strictures and postulated the principle of 'reciprocity' as a foundation for analysis of all early societies.[10] In other words, he admitted that his notion of the 'pure gift' is analytically incompatible with his exclusive focus on exchangeability as the distinguishing feature of gifts and commodities. Strong concern with exchangeability is also evident in Malinowski's (1929, Ch. 3) methodical listing of the series of gift exchanges incumbent upon marriage parties in the Trobriands. The questions that attract his attention are primarily related to gift exchangeability. Does it exist (i.e. is the gift reciprocated)? What forms does it take? How is it different from transaction to transaction? What are its moral and customary constituents? Furthermore, in discussing exchangeability Malinowski (1935, p. 45) takes great pleasure in showing that quantitative ratios among exchanged products can be arbitrary and intransitive. Several other anthropologists have also done this, both before and after him (for instance, Firth, 1959).

Preoccupation with the exchangeability of the gift rests on the largely unspoken assumption that the same property fully captures the character of the commodity. Commodity exchangeability appears intrinsic, complete, and precise: *quid pro quo.*[11] Given this, gifts can be positioned analytically as the properties of different gift transactions approximate the features of exchangeability presumably exhibited by commodity transactions. Thus gifts are not inherently exchangeable, since they are not given as things that will necessarily elicit the return of another. Their ability to do so is circumscribed by a host of non-economic factors – moral, religious and customary. Not least, even when a return gift materialises, there is no precise quantitative equivalence with the original gift. Moreover, gifts penetrate into areas of social life that are not immediately and obviously touched by the market. To give gifts in order to establish a relationship, and in expectation of a reciprocal gesture, is fundamental to interpersonal relations, to family relations, to friendship, to relations at work, and to political and social intercourse.

Gift-giving therefore appears to possess a trans-historical aspect that captures something of the deeper reality of human beings.[12] Given that commodity exchangeability (especially as exchange value and money price) is the province *par excellence* of economics, the appeal of the gift as a vehicle for analysis of the non-market aspects of social life is apparent. The gift can act as terrain and metaphor for analysis of social relations that differ in kind from the cash nexus at the heart of markets. It appears conducive to analysis of social obligation, trust, hierarchy, prestige, solidarity, and so on, in ways not available when the analytical focus is on commodities and markets. Even when important and relevant new distinctions are sought in more recent literature in this field, the analytical contrast between commodities and gifts remains vital. In putting forth the concept of things non-exchangeable, for instance, Weiner (1985, 1992) implicitly assumes that the character of commodities derives from their full exchangeability, while the character of gifts derives from exchangeability that is less complete than that of commodities. Consequently, the character of things non-exchangeable (for instance, religious *sacra* or the crown jewels) is supposed to derive from the complete absence of exchangeability. Hence things non-exchangeable are thought to possess stability and aloofness from the disorder of social relations. In this vein, Godelier (1996) argues that things non-exchangeable act as the true foundation of society; fixed points of reference that provide meaning and continuity to social intercourse.

The literature's close analytical focus on the exchangeability of gifts and commodities is problematic for two reasons. The first is the assumption that what is typical of capitalist commodities is also typical of commodities in general. It is incontestable that a particular type of reciprocity characterises capitalist commodities: they are brought to market as exchangeable things, their exchange value depends overwhelmingly on economic factors, and they bring back a quantitatively precise equivalent. But for this kind of reciprocity to prevail, it is necessary to have capitalist social conditions in production, distribution and exchange, as was shown in Chapter 1. The untrammelled exchangeability of capitalist commodities rests on the institutional framework of capitalist markets (consumers' associations, best practice agreements, and so on), and the combined forces of the law of contract and the law of tort. Fundamentally, however, capitalist commodities are immediately exchangeable and have precise quantitative equivalents because they have been produced by capital in order to make profits. The fully developed exchangeability of the commodity, typically assumed by the commodity-gift literature, exists only when capitalist conditions of production prevail. Moreover, it exists only for produced commodities and not for things generally traded in a capitalist economy, such as land and financial assets. In contrast, for commodities traded in non-capitalist societies, exchangeability has different determinants that are not exclusively economic. Non-capitalist societies typically lack a substantial working class available for wage labour, and hence the substance of commodity value does not have a social existence. By the same token, exchange value is a formal property of commodities. It is not systematically anchored in the underlying material realities of social life, and its determinants are not purely economic. Rather, exchange value depends on customary, ethical and hierarchical factors, and therefore the quantitative equivalents of non-capitalist commodities are far from precise. Thus, to return to Gregory' distinction, while it is certainly true that capitalist commodity exchange represents 'exchange of alienable things between transactors who are in a state of reciprocal independence', this does not hold generally for non-capitalist commodity exchange. Indeed, the exchange value of non-capitalist commodities is heavily influenced by factors that reveal reciprocal dependence among 'transactors'.

The second reason is that the close focus on exchangeability leads to the misapprehension that capitalist economic activity is dominated by commodity-like relations, in contrast to non-capitalist activity, which is presumably dominated by gift-like relations. But capitalist economic activity does not imply the total destruction of the social and personal relations that are characteristic of gift exchange, and nor does it generate exclusively calculating and self-interested behaviour. It is one-sided to focus exclusively on narrow economic motivations and the self-expansion of value when considering the capitalist economy. Capitalist economic activity is also, and irreducibly, the mobilisation and deployment of commodities as useful things, as is shown below. When analysis focuses on use values, it becomes clear that capitalist economic activity necessarily relies on, and continually engenders, non-market social relations. Capitalist economic agents constantly engage in non-market relations of moral obligation, custom, trust and power, which arise purely out of their economic activities. Yet these relations are also stamped by economic considerations at the core of capital's reproduction.

2.3 The role of use value in commodity exchange

Formal analysis of commodity transactions is skewed and incomplete when it ignores use value. For exchanges of commodities to take place at all, use value must exist for each participant in the product of the other. If use value were not present or, rather, if it were not precisely defined and functional for each party in the other's commodity, no commodity transaction would take place. Moreover, if a commodity transaction is to have any content at all, use value must be different for the two parties: commercially exchanging the same type of potatoes makes no sense at all. These points are obvious for direct commodity exchange, but also hold for monetary exchange.

Use value is a source of non-market relations between buyers and sellers in capitalist markets. For the seller, the commodity held has no use value. Whether it counts as a use value for society at large, as well as how it is going to be deployed by the buyer after purchase, are issues that the seller must tackle prior to exchange. The seller typically does so on the basis of general information about social practice and expectations about the future. Sellers, moreover, cannot know in advance whether their anticipations about use value hold true for particular buyers.[13] The most that the seller can do is ensure that enough of the postulated use value has been imparted to the commodity prior to exchange. For the buyer, in contrast, the use value of the commodity acquired must have a precise character deriving from the private use to which it is going to be put after purchase, be it consumption or production. Whether the buyer actually finds the required use value in the commodity, or not, depends on the properties of usefulness imparted to it by the seller in anticipation of sale. It also depends on the accuracy of the buyer's judgement of the commodity's use value at the time of sale. Neither the seller's anticipation nor the buyer's judgement of use value can be assumed to be perfect at the outset (other than as an analytical device for particular purposes). If use value did not fully meet requirements, if it had superfluous aspects, if it needed to be calibrated more accurately for particular buyers, non-market relations would emerge between sellers and buyers involving trust, moral obligation, custom and hierarchical ranking.

Non-market relations deriving from the use value of commodities are apparent between small retailers and consumers. They are the source of various folkloric types in both non-capitalist and capitalist societies (the trusted baker, the garrulous barber, the friendly butcher, the needy widow, and the like). These relations hinge on the need to specify and guarantee the use value of the products concerned. They also arise out of the simple repetition of particular transactions, i.e. the regular purchase of a good or service from a particular outlet. Practices of this kind can lead to habit and a sense of moral obligation among the transacting parties. However, things are very different when large merchant capital dominates the circulation of commodities (supermarkets, department stores, etc.). The sale of finished consumer goods is then affected by standardisation of quality, homogenisation of packing, availability of several ranges of the same product, and display of great variety of goods in large stores. Carrier (1994a, 1994b) has shown in detail that advanced industrial capitalism brings with it the rise of more impersonal retail trade. Imparting use value to the product by the seller and the perception of it by the buyer come to rely on impersonal and arms-length information rather than personal relations between market participants. Even then, however, non-market relations attendant to the use value of commodities cannot be fully extinguished in capitalist retailing.

However, it is not only in retailing that non-market relations emerge between buyer and seller. Profuse non-market relations, hinging on use value, also emerge in transactions among capitalist enterprises involving inputs for the production process. They show clearly that capitalist exchange constitutes fresh terrain for relations of trust, moral obligation and commitment. Moreover, non-market relations among capitalist enterprises are systematically organised and achieve complex institutional forms through the credit system. Despite originally having a non-economic character, these relations acquire economic aspects and prove critical to capitalist profit-making (as is shown in Chapter 4). In any sector of industry, capitalist enterprises are connected with each other in chains of productive activities that spring from the technical and physical characteristics of their products. Thus, cotton-goods makers are naturally linked to cotton-cloth makers, who are linked to cotton spinners, who are further linked to raw cotton producers, and so on and so forth. The division of labour is inevitably based on the characteristics, requirements, and specification of the use value of products, but links originating in the division of labour take commercial forms because of the class structure of the capitalist economy. Consequently, capitalist enterprises as sellers need to anticipate and impart appropriate use value to their products, while as buyers they need to assess use value accurately in line with their private production requirements. It follows that non-market relations emerge among enterprises along lines similar to, but not identical with, those between retailer and customer. At the simplest level, buyers rely on a certain quality of product and service from their sellers, while sellers expect a measure of commitment from their buyers. These relations are important for the credit practices that spontaneously emerge in capitalist markets.

Trade credit (i.e. buying commodities now and paying for them later) is a standard practice in commercial transactions among capitalist enterprises.[14] The normal commercial operations of capitalist enterprises involve the sale of output and the purchase of inputs, not with money but against promises to pay at a given time in the future. Settlement of obligations relies on a complex institutional and legal framework of guarantees, payment practices and clearing. More fundamentally, it relies on non-market relations of trust and reputation among enterprises, in the absence of which it is unlikely to be extended. The reason is that trade credit involves at root the private advance of value (embodied in commodities) against an equally private promise to return value in money later. Parting with value without immediately receiving an equivalent is extremely difficult for a capitalist enterprise, since it contravenes the most essential impulse of capitalist accumulation. Thus, the practice of trade credit tends to arise among enterprises that are already joined by non-market relations of trust and commitment. These are most likely to be created through frequent contact resulting from purchase and deployment of commodities in production. Trade credit could also arise if asymmetric power relations among enterprises imposed the advance of credit on the weaker party. At the same time, the non-market relations necessary for trade credit have a clear monetary dimension. Trust, commitment and power among capitalist enterprises must always result in profit; they must produce an effect on the 'bottom line'. There is no deeper content to relations between capitals. Capitalist credit is built on trust, but aims exclusively at money profit. For this reason, it is inherently noxious and always likely to turn into outright fraud. Extensive institutional mechanisms are necessary to police the edifice of promise and counter-promise that comprises the capitalist credit system.

In this light, consider the role of usefulness in gift transactions. For the commodity seller, as already mentioned, use value does not exist in the commodity held. A gifted thing, on the other hand, might or might not be useful to its giver, without having any appreciable qualitative effects on the gift transaction. The recipient's perception of the usefulness of the gift matters only as far as it affects the giver's assessment of the appropriateness of the gift. The giver alone must ascertain the right degree of usefulness of the gift for the recipient, while also deciding how well this meshes with the symbolic, sentimental and moral aspects of the transaction. This is in sharp contrast with the commodity, for which, if the buyer perceived that use value did not exist, the transaction would not take place at all. Indeed, for the gift, usefulness might derive exclusively from the act of giving itself – for instance, from the prestige and social standing of the giver or past holders of the gift. There is no imperative on the part of the giver to impart usefulness to the gift. Moreover, for the gift giver, assessing the appropriate usefulness of a gift is a perilous and uncertain undertaking. A thing of negligible usefulness is as likely to offend as to gratify the recipient. An eminently useful thing could produce a very different effect on the recipient as the latter's circumstances change. A gifted thing that is typically used by 'the wrong sort of person' (in terms of social standing) is also likely to cause offence (Carrier, 1994b), as is a thing typically used by the 'wrong' age group. Examples of this kind could be easily replicated, reinforcing the point that usefulness is neither a fundamental nor a necessary aspect of the gift although it cannot be extricated from the gift's symbolic and other aspects. While the commodity must be an intensely useful thing or activity, the gift might or might not be so. The precarious presence of usefulness in the gift is a source of uncertainty and danger among transacting parties.

Classical anthropology offers abundant evidence in support of this claim in early pre-capitalist communities. In the marriage-gift exchanges in the Trobriands discussed by Malinowski (1929, Ch. 3), for example, essentially similar things were exchanged, but in different quantities. This meant, above all, raw and cooked food that was not significantly different in kind between the exchanging parties, or might even be in the parties' possession already. The gift's usefulness clearly was a secondary aspect of the transaction. Moreover, it is not unknown in early societies for the very thing originally given as gift to be returned in fulfilment of the obligation to reciprocate, making usefulness insignificant to the transaction. It is, however, easiest to see the limited relevance of usefulness in connection with the great gift-exchange systems studied by anthropology, namely *kula* and *potlatch*. In *kula* exchanges, the items used were clearly specified and of the *vaygu'a* (valuable) type, which meant mostly armshells (*mwali*) and necklaces (*sulava*) of distinctive types. Yet these items were not sought for their usefulness; indeed, they were very rarely used for the purpose of personal decoration for which they were probably originally intended.[15] If they had notable usefulness, it derived exclusively from the system of exchange itself – typically to confer kudos and prestige to their holders as other powerful and important men had held the objects in the past.[16] Similarly, in *potlatch* exchanges (which Mauss, 1925 also discussed), although the items used were clearly specified, such as copper ingots and elaborately woven blankets, the participants primarily accrued kudos and prestige from the process of exchange itself. Indeed, so secondary was the role of the original usefulness of the items involved that the ritual could sometimes take the form of their ceremonial destruction, discussed in the *potlatch* literature for its psychological, moral, and other implications.

It is worth restating that usefulness is not irrelevant to the gift. In societies studied by anthropology, for instance, return gifts are often thoroughly checked by their recipients for their qualities as products, and are sometimes accepted grumpily and with suspicion. The point is that while usefulness (more precisely, use value) is an indispensable aspect of the commodity, it is not so for the gift. Use value engenders non-market relations among commodity sellers and buyers, which are very different to those between gift givers and recipients. Such non-market relations are of critical importance among capitalist enterprises, contributing to the spontaneous emergence of trade credit, with its markets, institutions and assets. The importance of use value for the analysis of capitalist non-market relations can be demonstrated in still broader terms by considering the circuit of capital. Three fundamental flows of value were identified while summarising the circuit of capital in Chapter 1: from money to productive capital (investment); from productive capital to finished goods (production); and from finished goods back to money (sales). In this chapter, analytical focus has so far been on the first and the third of these flows, both of which occur in the sphere of exchange.[17] However, use value is also critically important for the second flow – production – and generates still more non-market relations as capital undergoes its essential motion, as is shown in the following section.

2.4 Non-market relations in creation and deployment of labour power

In the sphere of production, labour power and means of production are brought together at the workplace to produce output for sale. Commodities are used up in production – they are productively consumed. The characteristic use values of the means of production and labour power are fundamental to the analysis of productive capital flows. For our purposes, they reveal a wealth of non-economic relations instrumental to capitalist profit-making. The role of use values in capitalist production lies outside the recent social science literature on use values and individual consumption. In this literature the meanings, symbolisms, and identities of particular products used in individual consumption have been thoroughly discussed, partly due to the influence of post-modernism.[18] The resultant output belongs mostly to cultural theory, and draws conclusions about the cultural aspects of commerce and capitalism. Emphasis has been laid largely on the markets for final consumption, implicitly treating them as typical markets. However, the use values that comprise productive capital (and the markets through which they are obtained) are tenuously related to individual consumption. Yet, they offer insights into non-market relations attendant to capitalist commodities as well as into the world of power, custom, collegiality and trust that capitalist productive activity creates. They are briefly discussed below, focusing mostly on labour power.

The circuit of capital locates the source of capitalist profit in the use value of the commodity labour power, namely in the workers' ability to generate value and surplus value when employed in production.[19] However, creating and maintaining the use value of labour power is a very peculiar process when compared to that of other commodities. Despite the defining role of wage labour in capitalism, the commodity labour power is not produced capitalistically at all. The capacity to work is neither created at a workplace, nor is it the result of a formal labour process. Rather, labour power emerges as a marketable commodity because of non-market processes, both personal and social. On the one hand, labour power results from activities undertaken within the family, such as rearing children and housekeeping. Its use value rests primarily on non-economic labours within the household. On the other, it is created by activities associated with the provision of education, health and old-age care, which might have a market aspect (or even a capitalist one, if such services happen to be provided by capitalist enterprises) but are also strongly non-market in essence and form. State hospitals and schools, for instance, contribute to the creation of labour power, but do not typically produce and sell their services on a capitalist basis.[20] Thus the educational and health-related activities that produce labour power have an irreducible non-market and non-capitalist aspect. Consequently, they are permeated by morality, ethical concerns, mutual obligation, and a sense of duty and commitment that have nothing to do with profit-making. Nevertheless, in the capitalist mode of production the existence of such relations is taken for granted, and they are expected to contribute to creation of labour power.

At a further remove, creating and maintaining labour power requires regular consumption of a range of products (the real wage), which is determined by moral, customary, institutional and historical factors. The real wage is best understood as a social norm of consumption that prevails, with variations, across the working class.[21] This norm certainly has a market aspect, since wages are paid in money that workers use to obtain requisite goods in commodity markets, but it has an equally strong non-market aspect. The overriding concern of workers, both in determining the level of money wages and in spending wages as private revenue, is to acquire the use value of wage goods. From the perspective of workers, the prices of commodities entering the wage basket matter only in so far as they affect the quantities of use values that can be obtained. Concern about market prices and the level of money wages derives purely from the workers' attempts to maintain the consumption norms associated with social customs, moral practices and the requirements of biological reproduction. The opposite holds true for market participation by capitalists for investment purposes. From their perspective, the overriding concern and broad aim of market transactions is to obtain money profits and augment their capital. Use value is important only because it allows for successful creation and realisation of surplus value; it matters to capitalists solely as vehicle for, and source of, value. Hence the use values of investment goods obtained by capitalists have none of the deeper moral, ethical and customary implications typical of the consumption norms of workers. They still engender relations of trust, custom and obligation among capitalists, as was shown in previous sections, but these are geared to profit-making.

Deployment of labour power after its purchase gives rise to further non-economic relations within the capitalist enterprise, which are required for success in profit-making. To create surplus value it is necessary to mesh economic with non-economic relations. This can be clearly seen in relation to determining the length of the working day, i.e. the most fundamental condition for success in profit-making. The number of hours worked daily constitutes an economic datum, but also a social norm. In mature capitalism, the working day is legally and institutionally limited for society as a whole. Defining the standard length of the working day always involves social conflict and compromise, since the issue goes to the heart of exploitation and profit-making by capitalists. Establishing the length of the working day as a norm is equally fraught with conflict and antagonism, given that capitalists have a built-in incentive to prolong the working day, while workers want to shorten it. Whenever the capitalist class has sufficient power and confidence, unpaid overtime occurs as a general social phenomenon. The actual length of the working day is a primary gauge of the balance of power between the capitalist and the working class at any moment in time.

Successful deployment of labour power also depends on the pace of work, on the absence of gaps between completing various tasks, and on the ability of workers to take breaks from the daily flow of work. These are conventions and norms that have evident technological and economic dimensions, but are also determined by non-economic processes. The class nature of capitalist production gives rise on the one hand to a hierarchical structure of command within the enterprise, and on the other to independent workers' workplace organisations. Management structures embody the relations of power and authority necessary to impose exploitation, while trade union organisations rest on the relations of solidarity and collective action essential to resisting exploitation. Norms and workplace practices across capitalist production are determined partly by technical and economic factors, but also by conflict between these inherently antagonistic structures. They reflect local compromises, retreats and sacrifices as well as political, moral and social influences emanating from the broader struggle between capital and labour across capitalist society.[22]

To recap, commodities are not tokens of pure market exchangeability, providing a neat contrast with the reciprocity intrinsic to gifts. Capitalist commodities, in particular, presuppose and give rise to a terrain of non-market relations. These relations embody trust, custom, solidarity and moral obligation in ways reminiscent of the gift, but they also embody hierarchy, power, authority and rivalry deriving from capital as a set of exploitative economic operations. This argument was substantiated above through analysis of the role of use value in capitalist exchange and production. In the realm of the market, the need continually to obtain reliable and precisely calibrated use values leads capitalist enterprises into relations of trust, commitment and custom. These relations are fundamental for the emergence of trade credit, and sustain credit institutions, markets and instruments. However, inter-enterprise relations are also permeated by profit-making, and hence they are precarious and prone to fraud and deception. In the realm of production, the use value of labour power derives from non-capitalist and non-market processes associated with the family and public provision. It is also related to consumption norms that rest on moral, historical and customary factors. The deployment of labour power in production according to the requirements of exploitation leads to relations of authority, top-down power and hierarchy. However, it also creates relations of solidarity and collegiality among workers. Thus, commodities are far more complex than is initially revealed by the simple act of buying and selling. Through their use value, commodities rest on, and give rise to, both economic and non-economic relations.

Part II

Money and credit

3 Money's monopoly over the ability to buy

3.1 The peculiar role of money in capitalist exchange

Money pervades capitalist society, and access to it is normally essential for daily life. However, familiarity with money often obscures its peculiar and contradictory character as an economic asset. The peculiarity of money is briefly indicated below through discussion of three of its aspects: first, money is generally held but not consumed, second, money is universally sought in exchange but never offered for sale, and third, money is plebeian but also undemocratic. It is then shown that the contradictory aspects of money originate in the social and economic relations that underpin it. Money therefore provides a uniquely apposite field of study of the interplay between the economic and the non-economic. Drawing on Marx's analysis of money, it is shown that money has a monopoly over the ability to buy, which derives from the social and economic relations characteristic of commodity trading. Specifically, money acquires its unique ability to buy ultimately because economic agents in commodity markets are independent from each other and absorbed with self-gain. At the same time, however, emergence and generalised use of money also rely on custom and tradition in undertaking commodity transactions and representing wealth. Money presupposes the existence of a thoroughly individualist outlook for commodity traders, but also the presence of social norms among them. Moreover, possession of money confers to its holder power over commodities and, by extension, over people and resources. The power of money is directly social, despite money originating in individual relations among commodity owners. In a capitalist society, organised by market exchange among capitalist producers, money becomes a foundation of social power. The use of money, furthermore, creates its own social norms.

3.1.1 Money is privately possessed but socially consumed

Money is ubiquitously held by those who are economically active in capitalist society, be they capitalists, workers or others. It is an asset that all commodity owners take with them to market, irrespective of their specialisation and demand for particular commodities. Money is also the asset of choice for storing wealth for future purposes, as well as for settling past obligations, commercial or otherwise. Wealth can be stored in other assets, such as land and real estate, and obligations are also settled by means other than money – for instance, by transfer of physical property. However, for capitalist society as a whole, money is the asset that typically performs these tasks, and thus the vast majority of economic agents keep some of their wealth in money, whatever other assets they might also hold. But, the agents who possess money consume it neither directly nor privately. This is a paradox for neoclassical economics, since the calculating 'rational individuals' of capitalist society appear to hold a portion of their earned (or inherited) wealth in an asset that affords no direct consumption. One solution for the paradox might be to claim that the holders of money consume the services it provides – above all, liquidity and storage of value – yet this answer is not immediately satisfactory. The services of liquidity are typically rendered by money at the point of spending, i.e. when property over it is relinquished and money is held no more. The services of hoarding, on the other hand, presuppose complete denial of consumption of money. Thus while other goods provide gratification by being possessed and privately consumed, money provides services by being surrendered to others, or via abstention from active use. It makes no difference in this regard if the holder of money is a capitalist or a worker, since money is not an input in the production process, and capitalists use money formally as individual consumers.

It follows that the usefulness of money to its owner cannot be analysed in a similar way to that of other commodities. Money renders services to its owner by being released into the market, or by being locked up in a safe. Consequently, if only the private relation between an individual and money were taken into account, the usefulness of money would remain deeply obscure. The contrast between money and other commodities is sharp, since the usefulness of the latter has an irreducible private dimension: bread satisfies personal hunger, clothes keep out the cold for their wearer, and cars take their driver from one place to another. However, the benefits from holding money do not result from the private relationship between money and its holder; instead, they are comprehensively social.

3.1.2 Money buys but is never sold

Money is universally sought by participants in capitalist markets. Regularly and customarily, workers offer their labour-power in search of money wages, and capitalists offer commodity output in search of sales (money) revenue. Similar patterns of generalised seeking of money occur in other markets, including those for land and services. The same holds even in financial markets, where the object of trading appears to be money itself.

In these markets (as is shown in Chapter 4), loanable money capital is traded as a commodity that is typically offered for sale in exchange for (more) money. Thus the general principle of trading across the vast network of capitalist markets is to offer commodities for sale and to seek money in return. However, money itself is never offered for sale – it always buys. It stretches the ordinary meaning of words to absurd extremes to claim that a buyer of commodities is a 'seller' of money. There is an evident formal difference between purchase and sale in capitalist markets, which requires explanation. The commonsense view that sale is essentially different from purchase has a valid core: to sell is to offer a commodity for money, while to buy is to accept such an offer by handing over money. In capitalist markets commodities do not typically buy other commodities, nor do they 'buy' money. Only money buys and is never sold.

In this respect, too, money is the most social of assets held by market participants. It acts as a unique purchasing instrument, providing services of liquidity, because of the generally held expectation among traders that money can buy other commodities as a matter of course. This expectation normally fulfils itself, since participants in capitalist markets systematically offer their commodities for sale against money (rather than attempting to exchange them directly with other commodities). Market participants, moreover, typically find that the commodities of others are offered to them in request for money. Thus, in a capitalist economy, the use of money is a social norm established through the collective practice of all participants – namely to offer commodities for sale against money. Commodity owners behave collectively and socially (but without planning) in ways that make it possible for money to operate as money. If the social dimension of money were taken away, only metal discs, pieces of paper and book entries would remain. Money must be immediately and directly social, otherwise it would not be money.

The difference between selling and buying has profound implications for capitalist markets. A capitalist who holds money and intends to buy approaches the market with different capabilities and outlook than does the capitalist who holds commodities and intends to sell. The difference arises because money can buy each and all of the other commodities, while commodities are sold specifically for money. Consequently, it is normally more difficult to sell commodities for money than to use money in order to buy commodities. The capitalist who holds finished output and searches for potential buyers must actively solicit the consent of other market participants to the proposed sale. In contrast, the capitalist who holds money and searches for potential suppliers of inputs is in the commanding position of selecting among offers made by others. These observations naturally do not hold for all markets at all times, and conditions could arise under which the holder of money would find it difficult to obtain commodities while the holder of commodities could easily get hold of money. However, the normal condition of markets – a 'stylised fact' of their operation – is for purchase to be easier than sale. The holder of money normally approaches the market with more power and less trepidation than does the holder of commodities.

3.1.3 Money is undemocratic and hostile to social distinction

Money is the most plebeian of assets. It does not respect traditional rights, and erodes the aristocratic privileges of pedigree and kinship. Money is a great leveller; it does not defer to 'breeding' and catapults the low-born into the same social bracket as their betters.[1] It barely tolerates restraints on its economic and social interventions, especially those deriving from customary practices passed from generation to generation. Money is rude, and disdains established social niceties. It has no regard for intellectual, moral and ideological distinction, and no truck with refined taste in art, fashion and decoration. Pride, duty, glory and service mean little to money, and it elicits the lowest sentiments of humanity – greed, venality and deception. Money is as coarse and vulgar as should be expected from the true spirit of the market. However, plebeian money is thoroughly undemocratic. It does not accept the equality of individual human beings – only the equality of dollars, pounds and francs. Money affords economic, social and political power to those that possess it. Whoever has more dollars also has a stronger presence in the market, and can make his or her will go further in society. By the same token, money denies power to those who lack it. This plebeian paragon despises the poor and leaves them without access to resources. Money creates new distinctions and refinements in art, fashion and conspicuous consumption. It can send children to exclusive schools and buy appropriate spouses. It leads to emergence of fresh privileges in society and, if inherited, it can transfer privileges across generations. Money builds a web of customary practices that perpetuate social divisions and harden social attitudes toward the weak and the needy.

Thus money is deeply contradictory. Market participants possess it but do not consume it, seek it but do not sell it, hold it privately but draw benefits from it socially, and use it to overcome traditional privilege only to create fresh social divisions. To locate the source of these contradictions it is essential to establish what money is, and this task requires explaining money's emergence in commodity markets. The social and economic relations characteristic of markets give rise to money and explain its pervasive and contradictory presence in capitalist economies. Money's spontaneous emergence in commodity exchange is discussed in the rest of this chapter, drawing on Marx's work in Part One of the first volume of *Capital*. Money is shown to materialise out of the social and economic relations of commodity owners. Its emergence is due to market processes, but also rests on social custom associated with markets. Specifically, money emerges as monopolist of the ability to buy, and constitutes a necessary social link among individual commodity owners driven by personal gain. Its unique ability to buy is a purely social property created by the collective and universal action of commodity owners; namely, to offer their commodities for sale in exchange for money. Consequently, the use of money strongly resembles a social norm – money can be money because the action of commodity owners turns it into money. The peculiar and contradictory role of money in capitalist society ultimately derives from the purely social character of money's ability to buy.

3.2 The theoretical problem of money's emergence and the labour theory of value

For Marx, the emergence of money represents a difficult theoretical problem – a 'riddle' or 'mystery'. He was the first among the major economists to identify the problem, and proudly to claim that he had solved it:

> Now, however, we have to perform a task never even attempted by bourgeois economics. That is, we have to show the origin of the money-form, we have to trace the development of the expression of value contained in the value-relation of commodities from its simplest, almost imperceptible outline to the dazzling money-form. When this has been done, the mystery of money will disappear.
>
> (Marx, 1867, p. 139)

However, Marx's writings on money are extensive and – as is frequently the case with thinkers of his breadth – contain a variety of arguments capable of sustaining different views on the origin of money and its economic role. The account of money's emergence presented in this chapter involves a strong interpretation of Marx's analysis of commodity value.[2] It draws on the most innovative aspects of Marx's work on the relationship between value and money in the first three chapters of the Volume I of *Capital*, and puts forth a coherent solution for the 'riddle' of money. Its strength lies in explaining directly the contradictory aspects of money's functioning in a capitalist economy. The solution is also free of the problems that bedevil other theorisations of money's emergence (discussed in Chapter 6).

In Chapter 1 of this book it was shown that commodity value as abstract labour is fully established only under capitalist conditions of production. In the capitalist mode of production there are social processes that make abstract labour a social reality. These processes include workers regularly moving between jobs, work being performed under the discipline of capital, and commodities being systematically exchanged as products of capital (enterprise output). Thus the substance of value is a historically specific social category that occurs under capitalist social conditions. Within the capitalist mode of production, the forms of value (exchange ratios, prices, etc.) can also arise without having a direct connection with the substance of value, as in the markets for real estate and financial assets. Indeed, in contrast to the substance of value, it is not at all necessary for capitalist social relations to exist in order for the forms of value to emerge. Commodities, exchange value, money, prices, interest and lending are commonly observed in non-capitalist societies, including several that have historically predated the capitalist mode of production. However, despite the disjuncture between form and substance of value, the theoretical examination of the forms of value is best undertaken under the assumption of capitalist economic conditions. The reason is that in the capitalist mode of production the forms of value are fully developed and closely related to the substance of value. Consequently, analysis of exchange value under capitalist conditions allows for general conclusions to be drawn about price and market trading.

This argument has important implications for the theoretical demonstration of the emergence of money, one of the most prominent of the forms of value. It is unquestionable that the social role and economic functions of money are fully developed and manifested under capitalist economic conditions. It is also unquestionable, however, that money long predates establishment of the capitalist mode of production, and therefore of the social substance of value. Money, moreover, functions complexly and extensively in non-capitalist societies, despite the absence of the substance of value. Consequently, though capitalist social conditions provide the appropriate terrain for the logical demonstration of the emergence of money, the demonstration should not rely on the substance of value as abstract human labour. The substance of value is a specifically capitalist category, while money's presence in commodity trading is general and not specific to the capitalist mode of production. It follows that money's emergence should be demonstrated exclusively in terms of the form of value. In other words, the roots of money lie in the evolution of the form of value, and they are unrelated to the substance of value. The assumption of capitalist conditions is still vital in this connection because they provide a natural framework for analysis of the relations among commodity owners that are necessary for money to emerge. Specifically, in the capitalist mode of production, commodity owners are mutually 'foreign' and motivated by personal gain, but do not fight each other. These relations are essential for the form of value to develop and money to emerge.

Abstract labour is best left out of the reckoning when explaining money's emergence. The validity of this point can be seen – though negatively – in Marx's own discussion of the issue. At various places in his work (for instance, Marx, 1859, pp. 42–46; 1939, pp. 142–145), he claims that money emerges because of contradictions between the two fundamental aspects of the commodity, i.e. use value and value as abstract labour. Marx's argument can be condensed as follows. On the one hand, commodities as values are homogeneous, perfectly divisible and simple – i.e.

they are general. On the other hand, commodities as use values are heterogeneous, imperfectly divisible and complex – i.e. they are particular. When attempts are made to exchange commodities directly, these two aspects clash because they are bound together in each commodity. The result is a breakdown of the process of exchange. To give a simple example, coats and tables as values (quantities of abstract labour) are homogeneous and general; therefore they are also equivalent with each other at some per unit rate, say, of two to one. However, as use values they are heterogeneous and particular, and thus if the owner of one coat happened to meet the owner of one table, direct exchange would prove impossible despite the abstract homogeneity of the commodities. Suppose now that the two fundamental aspects of the commodity became separated from each other – to put it differently, assume that each commodity appeared in the market in two separate forms: first as the natural thing that it is (i.e. as a use value), and second as value but in the form of another thing. Then the contradiction would be resolved because the commodity would be brought to market as both a use value and a value, but not bound together in one entity. According to this approach, money generates this desired 'doubling' of the commodity. Specifically, money emerges as one commodity that represents value as abstract labour for all others. With money present, all commodities are use values as the things they were produced to be, and also values as quantities of the money commodity. The contradiction between use value and value is immediately resolved and exchange does not break down: the owner of one table simply obtains the equivalent of half a coat in the money commodity.[3]

The ingenuity and elegance of this dialectical argument should not obscure its essential failure to explain the emergence of money in commodity exchange. There are two separate reasons for its inadequacy, both related to value as abstract labour. First, as already noted, the historical emergence of money long predates establishment of abstract labour as social reality. Abstract labour has no bearing on the spontaneous use of money by ancient Summerians, Persians and Greeks or, for that matter, contemporary tribal Polynesians. It does not follow from this that the aim of theoretical analysis should be to produce a timeless theory of money that applies uniformly to all modes of production; the point is, rather, that the theoretical demonstration of money's emergence should not hold only for specifically capitalist money. For the solution of the 'riddle' of money to have general validity, it must also give insights into the emergence of money that is not capitalist but remains recognisably money. This is not the case with Marx's explanation based on the substance of value as abstract labour. The contradictions between use value and value as abstract labour have little meaning for commodities produced under conditions that are not capitalist.

Second, the economic content of Marx's analysis of the contradictions between use value and value is similar to that of standard economic analysis of the 'difficulties of barter'. The argument regarding the 'difficulties of barter' was formulated by Smith (1776), and Jevons (1875) later captured the gist of it with the term 'double coincidence of wants'. In a nutshell, it is maintained that direct commodity exchange would continually break down because commodities are not perfectly divisible, homogeneous, durable, and so on. The 'difficulties of barter' could be overcome if a commodity existed that was generally accepted by market participants. The generally accepted commodity could act as intermediate step in transactions pursued by market participants, allowing eventual completion of the desired exchanges. The generally accepted commodity is money, and it resolves the 'difficulties' by transforming barter into monetary exchange. The weakness of this analysis (explored in Chapter 6) is that it assumes as given precisely what is to be explained – i.e. the general acceptability of money, or its universal ability to buy. Analogously, for Marx, the breakdown of barter is an outcome of the contradictions between use value and value as abstract labour inherent in all commodities. A commodity that represented value generally could resolve the contradictions by virtue of being 'another', or a 'third', between any two commodities. This is the money commodity, which turns direct into monetary exchange. Not surprisingly, this argument contains a weakness. If a general representative of value existed, the contradictions between use value and value as abstract labour would indeed be resolved. However, how do the contradictions themselves lead to emergence of a general representative of value? What are the economic mechanisms through which value becomes socially represented by money as a result specifically of the contradictions between use value and value as abstract labour? There is no answer to this question in this strain of Marx's work on money.

However, Marx also proposed a further resolution for the 'riddle' of money; one that does not rely on the substance of value and is free of the above weakness. This resolution is to be found in Marx's discussion of the form of value in Chapter 1 of the first volume of *Capital*. In the section under the rubric '*The value-form, or exchange value*', Marx focuses on the exchange value of commodities (as distinct from the substance of their value). He examines relations among commodity owners in the course of exchange, and claims that exchange value develops in four stages, which he calls the 'forms of value'. Starting with the 'simple, isolated or accidental form of value', exchange value passes to the 'expanded form', to the 'general form', and finally to the 'money form'. The postulated development of exchange value is also the logical process through which the 'money form' emerges in commodity exchange. By analysing relations among commodity owners in the course of market transactions, Marx shows that money emerges as the 'universal equivalent' – i.e. as the commodity that can buy all others. The general method of his proof is to identify 'defects' existing in each stage which lead to it being overcome and replaced by the next stage, until the 'universal equivalent' emerges.

In the remaining sections of this chapter, Marx's demonstration is reworked and critically interpreted.[4]

3.3 The 'simple, isolated, or accidental form of value'

To analyse the development of exchange value, commodity owners are initially assumed to possess a fixed quantity of one commodity each, and to trade in pairs. They interact at random ('accidentally'), in the sense that any two among them could meet. They are also assumed to be free of social ties created by kinship, custom and moral obligation. The dominant concern of those who engage in trade is to obtain an equivalent for the commodity they bring to market. In short, commodity owners approach each other as mutually alien, independent and essentially 'foreign' individuals, who might not even know each other.[5] Consequently, an opening gambit is necessary between commodity owners in order to establish relations and allow trade to occur. The interpretation of Marx's analysis suggested here is that this opening gambit takes the form of one commodity owner requesting exchange with another by making an offer to sell the commodity possessed. The commodity owner who makes the request is the 'active' party, and assumes the position of the relative. The request made by the 'active' commodity owner puts the other party in the position of being 'passive' or equivalent (Marx, 1867, p. 139), and thus the relationship that emerges between the owners of commodities A and B (who have 'accidentally' met) assumes a definite direction captured with an arrow:[6]

x of A→y of B

The arrow indicates that the owner of A ('relative') requests exchange with the owner of B ('equivalent') by offering x of A for sale against y of B. The two commodity owners play very different roles in this relationship. The 'relative' makes an offer of sale, thus declaring that the exchange value of A is equal to a quantity of the commodity possessed by the 'equivalent', B. The 'equivalent', on the other hand, finds that B can be exchanged directly with the commodity in the possession of the 'relative', A. Clearly, there is no *a priori* reason for A to be the 'relative' and B the 'equivalent' when they initially meet – their 'accidental' relationship could be reversed. However, once the opening gambit is made, the two commodity owners assume positions that are the 'polar' opposite of each other (Marx, 1867, p. 140).[7] The economic content of the relationship between 'relative' and 'equivalent' is important for the eventual emergence of money. Before coming to market the owners could take for granted neither the possibility of direct exchange, nor the quantity of other commodities that could be obtained in exchange for the one held; the exchange value of their commodities was entirely hypothetical. After engaging in the 'relative'–'equivalent' relationship, however, things are different. The exchange value of A is declared unilaterally by its owner to be equivalent to y/x of B. The owner of B, meanwhile, finds out that B could be directly exchanged for A. If the transaction was actually completed, a measure of validity would accrue to both pieces of information.

The important result in this connection for our purposes is that, after an 'accidental' exchange, the 'equivalent', B, acquires the property of direct exchangeability with the 'relative', A. This property amounts to the ability of the 'equivalent' to buy – even if only one specific 'relative'. The property of direct exchangeability, moreover, is not an intrinsic aspect of commodities, but arises purely because the 'relative' has requested exchange with the 'equivalent'. The source of direct exchangeability for one commodity lies in the action of the owner of another, and the property exists exclusively in the context of the market. Commodity B has acquired the ability to buy A because the owner of A offered it for sale against B, but B can buy only A and as long as the 'accidental' form of value prevails. The eventual emergence of money rests on the concentration in one commodity of the ability to buy all others. This process occurs through the collective action of all other commodity owners.

The defect of the 'accidental' form is evident: the relationship established between commodity owners A and B is fleeting, and has no applicability across the market. It has to be established again in the next transaction, but this is neither certain nor predictable. The owner of A might not re-enter the market for a long period of time, or might engage in 'accidental' exchange with the owner of C. Even if they met again, the transaction between A and B might be reversed, making A the 'equivalent'. However, the process through which A and B originally met also offers a way of overcoming this defect of the 'accidental' form of value. The owner of A could, in principle, visit the market regularly and frequently, making offers of sale to any and all other commodity owners. Consequently, a full representation of the value of A as 'relative' necessarily requires an exhaustive list of 'equivalents'. The 'expanded' form of value consists of requests of exchange addressed by one commodity owner toward all others, frequently and repeatedly.

3.4 The 'total or expanded form of value'

The 'expanded' form of value can be written as:

x of A→y of B
x of A→u of C
x of A→w of D
...

The owner of the 'relative' A now declares that its exchange value is given by a boundless set of quantitative ratios relative to other goods, i.e. {y/x of B, u/x of C, w/x of D,...}. Thus, A's exchange value is less partial and fleeting than before, since it is represented by all other commodities. On the other hand, the ability to buy, which was previously restricted to B, is now spread across the market and belongs to all commodities except A. It has become a common property of commodities, even if emanating only from A. Put differently, both the exchange value (of A) and the ability to buy (possessed by B, C, D, etc.) have acquired the aspect of a social norm, because commodity owners recognise them as social realities that apply to exchange as a whole, and which must be incorporated in the practice of trading. However, both are entirely market-based norms and lack deeper foundations in society – above all, in the sphere of production.

The defect of the 'expanded' form arises from the exchange value of the 'relative' being a boundless set of bilateral exchange ratios. The owner of A now offers x for y of B, then x for u of C, then x for w of D, and so on and so forth – hence the terms on which A is offered for sale are irregular and heterogeneous. The exchange value of A applies across the sphere of exchange, but lacks simplicity and therefore generality. Similarly, the ability to buy is spread thinly across the sphere of exchange and applies only in relation to A. Consequently, for B and C to exchange with each other their owners have to go through the 'relative'–'equivalent' procedure afresh, without any advance guarantee that it would result in actual exchange. However, the economic process through which the defect of the 'expanded' form is overcome and the 'general' form emerges is far from obvious, as is shown below.

3.5 The 'general form of value' and the role of social custom

The 'general' form of value consists of the following series of requests of exchange:

y of B → x of A
u of C → x of A
w of D → x of A
...

On the 'relative' side, the exchange value of all commodities is now represented as quantities of A alone. This is a simple and homogeneous representation of exchange value that is generally valid for the sphere of exchange as a whole. Exchange value has become a market norm that applies to all commodities (except A), and commodity owners can expect commodities to be offered for sale on terms that are regular and manifest across the market. On the 'equivalent' side, A possesses direct exchangeability with all others – i.e. it can buy all others. This property of A is not limited with regard to any other commodity, and hence A is already the 'universal equivalent', or money (Marx, 1867, p. 159). Therefore, it is vital to specify precisely the economic process through which the 'general' arises out of the 'expanded' form of value.

Marx (1867, p. 157) suggests that the 'general' is implicitly contained in the 'expanded' form: passage to it is as simple as reversing the 'expanded' to derive the 'general' form. But this is not a persuasive argument, and does not do justice to the economic issues involved in the transition to the 'general' form. The 'general' form is formally the reverse of the 'expanded' form, but its emergence as a stage in the development of exchange value requires deeper argumentation than simply rewriting the relations of the 'expanded' form in reverse. After all, the formal reversal of the 'expanded' form could be undertaken in principle for each and every possible 'relative', and therefore it would generate as many 'universal equivalents' as there were commodities. Reversal of the 'general' form of value on paper alone would turn all commodities into 'universal equivalents', rather than isolating one of them. This difficulty is symptomatic of a deeper analytical problem. When they are considered purely in terms of their exchange values, commodities have no *a priori* advantages or disadvantages relative to each other. Their physical make-up undoubtedly differentiates commodities from each other as use values, but is entirely unrelated to their exchange value. As far as pure buying and selling are concerned, all commodities are undifferentiated traded objects, and there is no reason why the form of value should become attached to one of them differently compared to the rest. From the standpoint of trading, commodities are inherently symmetric relative to each other, and every one of them could be placed in the position of the 'universal equivalent'. However, the establishment of money as a permanent feature of commodity exchange amounts to creating extreme asymmetry: one commodity is permanently placed on the side of the 'equivalent' and all others on the side of the 'relative'. Formal arguments about commodity trading are incapable of producing this universal asymmetry, since commodities are inherently symmetric relative to each other. To establish the universal asymmetry that is characteristic of money, it is necessary to seek recourse to social custom.[8]

In this light, the following claim made by Marx (1867, pp. 182–183) in a separate but related section of *Capital* is worth quoting at length:

> The universal equivalent form comes and goes with the momentary social contacts that call it into existence. It is transiently attached to this or that commodity in alternation. But with the development of exchange it fixes itself firmly and exclusively onto particular kinds of commodity, i.e. it crystallises out into the money-form ... The money form comes to be attached either to the most important articles of exchange from outside, which are in fact the primitive and spontaneous form of manifestation of the exchange-value of local products,

> or to the object of utility, which forms the chief element of indigenous alienable wealth, for example cattle.

This quotation indicates that, for Marx, historical and traditional elements are instrumental to emergence of money. It suggests that some commodities are more likely than others to become 'universal equivalents'; namely those that foreigners bring to a community, or those that a community can most easily trade. The symmetry among commodities is broken by factors extraneous to plain buying and selling. This view accords fully with another claim made by Marx in several different places (e.g. 1867, p. 182; 1894, pp. 447–448; 1939 (see 1973, p. 223); namely, that commodity exchange arose where different communities came into contact with each other, rather than within communities. For Marx, the historical agents of commodity exchange were the 'pure trading peoples of antiquity' (Phoenicians and Carthaginians) existing in the 'intermundia' of the ancient world, and connecting societies for which commerce was a marginal activity.

Our analysis of exchange value is based on the assumption of bilateral exchange among commodity owners who are essentially alien or 'foreign' to each other. Commodity owners are assumed to be unaffected by kinship, hierarchy, authority, religion, and other social ties. Their interactions and relations are guided primarily by the search for an equivalent of the commodity they possess and bring to market. This assumption is easily justified under capitalist social conditions. The capitalist economy is separate from society, and operates with a large degree of autonomy because of the class relations characteristic of it. Capitalist producers are in competition with each other and motivated by money profit alone; hence capitalist commodity owners are naturally 'foreign' to each other. However, the assumption of 'foreign-ness' cannot be immediately justified in non-capitalist societies, since the economy is not separate from society and does not operate autonomously. On the contrary, economic interaction is embedded in a web of power, prestige, kinship and custom. By the same token, the motivations and outlook of economic agents are unlikely to be dominated by personal gain. Consequently, the internal economic relations of non-capitalist societies do not offer appropriate terrain for examining the interaction among commodity owners. Where non-capitalist communities and societies come into contact with each other, however, things are different. Traders from different communities could be essentially 'foreign' to each other, and could develop mutual relations based exclusively on commodity ownership. Thus, the preceding analysis of the development of the form of value could be applied to commercial interaction among separate communities and societies.

From this perspective, it makes analytical sense to associate the historical (not the logical) emergence of money with commercial contact among separate communities, as Marx does in the quotation above. His reference to 'trading peoples' is reminiscent of the following description by Herodotus (1954, p. 307) of Carthaginian trading with 'Libyans' beyond 'the pillars of Hercules' (Atlantic Africa):

> On reaching this country, they unload their goods, arrange them tidily along the beach, and then, returning to their boats, raise a smoke. Seeing the smoke, the natives come down to the beach, place on the ground a certain quantity of gold in exchange for the goods, and go off again to a distance ... There is perfect honesty on both sides; the Carthaginians never touch the gold until it equals in value what they have offered for sale, and the natives never touch the goods until the gold has been taken away.

There is 'foreign-ness' and suspicion of the alien 'other' in Herodotus' description of this form of trade. Grierson (1903) has extensively discussed similar forms of primitive barter, which he called 'silent trade'. The focus of his analysis is on hostility and fear of the stranger, but also on the difficulty of communication between alien peoples lacking a common language.[9] Making an offer of sale constitutes an opening gambit among them, establishing relations and leading to gradual development of the form of value.

The social custom necessary for money's emergence is now easier to specify. Regular and frequent commercial contact is likely to lead to the emergence of chains of traditional transactions containing specific commodities. Transition to the 'general' form of value is more probable within chains of traditional transactions, since they separate specific commodities and bring them into regular contact with each other. Through pure chance a commodity within one chain could attract several requests of exchange, becoming a transient 'universal equivalent'. This need not happen for just one commodity within the chain, not even for the same commodity over time. Passage to the 'general' form can happen for several commodities at once, each becoming a transient 'universal equivalent'. However, once a 'universal equivalent' emerges even temporarily, economic mechanisms are set in motion that lead to self-reinforcement of the incipient asymmetry among commodities. From the analysis of the 'general' form it follows that a commodity that temporarily attracts several requests of exchange also acquires a stronger ability to buy than others. The enhanced ability to buy constitutes an additional use value for this commodity – a specifically market-related property – which Marx (1867, p. 184) calls a 'formal' use value. Consequently, the commodity is likely to attract further requests for exchange purely because of its temporarily enhanced ability to buy, rather than because of its proper use value. However, since its 'formal' use value derives from other commodities being offered for sale against it, the more requests that it attracts, the stronger will be its ability to buy, and still more the requests that will come its way. Transition to the 'general' form of value is set in train.

In conclusion, for the 'general' form of value to emerge, social custom is necessary, giving rise to chains of traditional transactions. Within those chains it is likely that the 'expanded' form would be, by chance, reversed, and probably with regard to heavily traded commodities. Such reversals could take place frequently and with reference to several 'equivalents'. These reversals are self-sustaining in so far as they give rise to a stronger ability to buy, thus attracting further requests of exchange, and so further strengthening the ability to buy. Thus social custom and the market-related property of 'being able to buy' combine to lead to emergence of the 'universal equivalent.' By the same token, the defect of the 'general' form is that, at any moment in time, several 'universal equivalents' are likely to exist, arising spontaneously and continually. Each would be unable to buy some of the commodities that would belong to the set of 'relatives' of another, and therefore exchange would remain compartmentalised and lacking in unity. From the side of the 'relatives', moreover, the presence of more than one 'universal equivalents' means that exchange value lacks a single representation across the market. Thus exchange value is still not a general market norm. Passage to the 'money' form of value resolves these difficulties, but for that to take place further social custom is necessary.

3.6 The 'money form of value'

The money form of value consists of the following series of requests of exchange:

1 of A → u/x of C
1 of B → u/y of C
1 of D → u/z of C
...

This form of exchange value implies that the position of the 'equivalent' has been completely and stably monopolised by a single commodity. The money commodity, C, permanently attracts requests of exchange from all others, and has the unique ability to buy all others. The exchange value of all other commodities has a simple and homogeneous expression, and appears as money price. Put differently, all commodity owners now bring their commodities to market intending to exchange them with money, and expect to find other commodities priced in money terms. Exchange value in the form of money price is a stable market-based norm that holds for all commodity owners. Consequently, the defects of the 'general' form have disappeared. For passage to the 'money' form, however, social custom is still necessary.

Any commodity can be money, but not all commodities are equally suited for the task of carrying the 'formal' use value of being able to buy all others. Durability, homogeneity, divisibility, portability, and other physical properties make some commodities better than others at being money. Ice cream, the favourite example of economics textbooks, would make a rather poor money commodity. The commodities that are physically best suited for the task of monopolising the ability to buy are the precious metals – exceptionally durable, homogeneous, finely divisible and portable. Thus the historical monopolisation of the role of the 'money' commodity by gold is partly due to the physical properties of gold. However, social custom also plays a key role in this connection. Gold and silver have historically been used as costly jewellery and for ostentatious manifestation of wealth. Habituation of people with this role of gold and silver makes it easier to associate the precious metals with representing value and carrying the ability to buy. Gold monopolises buying ability and becomes the independent representative of value partly because of its physical properties, and partly because of the social customs attached to its use. After reaching the position of money, however, the use of gold becomes a social norm in itself. Commodity owners expect the money commodity to be gold, and they also assume that their commodities should be priced in terms of gold. The regular and customary practice of offering commodities for sale against gold fulfils the expectations of commodity owners.

3.7 The specific character of monetary exchange in contrast to barter

In the preceding demonstration of money's emergence, commodities do not buy money and nor do they buy other commodities. Rather, commodities are exclusively sold for money – that is, their owners bring them to market with the intention of exchanging them specifically for money and not for other commodities. When this practice is generalised and becomes a social norm, money is established as a permanent economic phenomenon. In monetary exchange, only money buys and all other commodities are offered for sale against it. Two of the paradoxical aspects of money, discussed in the first section of this chapter, are immediately answered. First, money is necessarily carried by market participants, since they expect others to bring commodities to market with the express purpose of offering them for sale against money. In so far as they wish to acquire other commodities, all commodity owners must hold money. By the same token, the holders of money consume its services in an entirely market-related way, since money's 'formal' use value of being able to buy is itself market-related. The use value of money appears when money is used to acquire commodities. In the absence of the market, neither the holding nor the consumption of money has meaning. Second, money is permanently sought by commodity owners and is never offered for sale, for that is what makes it money. The general norm of other commodities requesting exchange with money is the source of money's 'formal' use value. Should this norm break down or become attenuated through the money commodity being offered for sale, money's monopolisation of buying ability would cease and it would become, at least in part, an ordinary commodity. Money must never be 'sold' but only used to buy, if it is to remain money.

For these reasons, it is fallacious to think of monetary exchange as barter into which a convenient means of exchange has been introduced. When a money commodity is established, ordinary commodities are not brought to market with the purpose of obtaining other commodities. Rather, they are specifically brought to market with the intention of obtaining money. Monetary exchange is a qualitatively different form of trading from barter, and involves the universal request by other commodities to exchange with money. Even if money was actually excluded from particular transactions, as might happen if two commodity owners agreed to exchange directly or through the mediation of credit, that practice would not amount to barter. The commodities involved would continue to express their exchange value in money complying with the general market norm of requesting exchange with money. The transaction would simply be monetary exchange from which money as the means of exchange would have been excluded. The historical ascendancy of credit money in developed capitalism can be seen as the process of limiting money's role as means of exchange – but firmly within monetary exchange.[10]

The fraught issue of the relationship between barter and money can now be seen in a fresh light. Anthropologists emphasise the persistence of barter and the existence of multiple forms of commodity exchange in non-capitalist communities.[11] They also denounce the assumption, often made by neoclassical economics, that barter is a primitive stage of commodity exchange. Nevertheless, what is analytically necessary is not also what is historically or socially accurate. It might be a myth that barter is a stage of commodity exchange that is found among 'primitives', but to establish an economic theory of money's emergence it is necessary to deploy the assumption of direct exchange among commodities. The difficulty lies entirely in using this assumption in a historically specific manner. The analysis of the forms of value in this chapter does not assume that money arises out of a primeval and inefficient state of barter that is overtaken by a 'developed' state of monetary exchange.[12] Rather, money arises spontaneously and necessarily out of the social and economic relations between 'foreign' commodity owners. By the same token, money emerges early in history and as soon as commodity trading attains some regularity and breadth. At the same time, money's emergence is a process that involves social custom as well as economic processes. Money's complete monopolisation of the ability to buy is subject to continuous confirmation, and depends on money's use becoming accepted as the social norm. In non-capitalist modes of production, in which the assumption of 'foreign-ness' among commodity owners might be inappropriate, the norm of money's use is inevitably weaker than in capitalist society. Several 'monies' at different stages of their development are likely to be observed simultaneously in non-capitalist societies. Depending on the particularities of societies and communities, direct exchange may also spring out spontaneously and continuously, co-existing with monetary exchange.

3.8 Money as source of social power

The social relations of commodity owners are instrumental to money's emergence. Essential 'foreign-ness' shapes the private relations between two commodity owners engaging in 'accidental' exchange. Their lack of social ties external to the market keeps non-economic considerations out of account. Market participants, therefore, express both exchange value and the ability to buy purely by means of each other's commodities – i.e. they express both privately. When many commodity owners interact repeatedly and regularly, exchange value becomes a stable market norm, while the ability to buy is concentrated in a single commodity. These developments occur through the collective action of individual commodity owners, and therefore buying ability is expressed socially through one commodity that also represents value. Accordingly, money is an outcome of the essential 'foreign-ness' among commodity owners. It functions as money across markets because commodity owners regularly and frequently meet each other as 'foreigners', thus requiring a monopolist of the ability to buy. Commodity owners require money to provide a social nexus among them. Money is a peculiar way to link human beings, since it subsumes social relations under the ability to buy, but also is an appropriate social link for such extraordinarily estranged human beings as commodity owners. Thus money is not simply a cog, a means of exchanging output across the surface of society and allowing agents to fulfil their consumption plans; rather, it is the glue that holds commodity owners together, the social medium through which they express their volition to each other and to the market as a whole.

Consequently, money affords to its owner power over others. It is misleading to think of the market as a locus of democratic equality because, presumably, commodity owners have exactly the same rights and obligations as each other. In monetary exchange there is no symmetry among commodity owners, as there is no symmetry among commodities. Commodities are divided into a great mass that seeks sale and a single commodity that can buy all others. Money embodies economic power in a world of commodities, since it is the only commodity that can buy all others. The individuals who possess more money can also command more commodities and natural resources and, in the capitalist mode of production, more workers. The economic power of money is the source of its social power, making it possible for the owner of money to impose his or her will on others by advancing or withholding money.[13] In turn, money's power over people and resources allows its owners constantly to establish new hierarchies of wealth and privilege. These are based on money's unique ability to buy, hence they disregard traditional and customary rights or privileges. However, money-based hierarchies are still arbitrary and exclusive. Money affords the means of obtaining superior education, even to those of mediocre mental powers; it allows marriage into 'better' society, even if not warranted by manners, graces and airs; it transfers to children some of the social acuity of their parents, even when they are insipid. Money's social power derives from its unique ability to buy, and hence it is inherently plebeian and comprehensively discriminatory.

4 The social content of credit relations

Credit transactions in a capitalist economy take a large variety of forms: credit card purchases, consumer loans, mortgages, buying 'on tick', bank loans, money market loans, government bonds sales, and so on. Despite the variety of forms, all credit transactions have one thing in common; namely, the absence of immediate exchange of equivalents. In credit transactions value is advanced (even as a mere paper claim) against a promise to return its equivalent later. The lack of immediate exchange of equivalents sets credit transactions apart from regular commodity transactions. Commodity buying and selling is premised on immediate *quid pro quo*: value in the form of commodities is balanced at once with value in the form of money. In contrast, the balance of value in credit transactions is reconstituted at a later point in time. For this reason, the party that advances credit must have trust in the counterparty making the requisite transfer of value in due time. Trust between participants is also necessary in plain commodity exchange, for instance, to avoid violence or robbery. However, the trust required to part with capital value against a mere promise to pay is of different order of magnitude.

The role of trust as the foundation of credit transactions implies that the essential economic relations among capitalists have to be reconsidered. It was previously assumed that capitalists are fundamentally independent, autonomous and in competition with each other. At the same time, they were shown to develop non-economic relations with each other (based partly on the use value of their commodities) and to deploy authority and fiat toward their workers in the course of production. As commodity owners, though, capitalists approach each other as 'foreign' entities linked through the nexus of money. However, the emergence of credit relations is hardly plausible among 'foreign' entities, since value is relinquished against mere promises to pay later. Consequently, it is essential for credit transactions that relations of trust and power are present among capitalists. Capitalists who engage in credit are already complexly related to each other – they are not 'foreign' entities engaged in plain buying and selling. By the same token, credit practices bring out economic and non-economic aspects of relations among capitalists that are not apparent in commodity markets.

It is shown in this chapter that credit is originally a private and subjective relation of trust and power between capitalists, deployed to promote their individual economic activities. However, relations of trust and power are transformed in the course of credit transactions, and gradually acquire a social and objective character. Credit gives rise to a layered set of institutional mechanisms – the credit system – that sustain the capitalist economy as a whole. Relations of trust and power are transformed within the credit system, and acquire an increasingly social content by involving banks, markets, and other credit institutions. The requirements of credit also become increasingly social, especially with regard to the information necessary to support trust. At the same time, the class character of the capitalist mode of production makes itself apparent at all levels of the credit system. Capitalist credit, even in the most developed social forms, is ultimately founded on the ability of industrial capitalists to generate profits through the exploitation of workers. The credit system lends a social and objective aspect to trust and power, but only in order to place both at the service of capitalist exploitation. Thus capitalist credit contains a noxious moral element leading to fraud and deception.

4.1 Trust and the structure of the capitalist credit system

The simplest definition of credit under capitalist social conditions is as the advance of capital value against a promise to return its equivalent later, plus an increment.[1] Credit transactions create relations of creditor and debtor – that is, of assets balanced out by debts. Credit between two capitalists can be differentiated into first, the advance of commodities against a promise to pay later ('buy now – pay later'), and second, the advance of money against a promise to return it later (money-lending). In Marxist economics, the former is termed commercial (or trade) credit and the latter banking (or monetary) credit.[2] The two forms of credit differ significantly in terms their trust requirements, as is briefly shown below.

Commercial credit, since it involves the advance of particular commodities, necessarily occurs between capitalists whose production processes are linked materially, technologically, and even geographically in the social division of labour. The practice of 'buying now – paying later' has no content among capitalists whose activities are not directly connected – for instance, between automobile and textile manufacturers. At the same time, regular economic interactions among capitalists linked through the division of labour provide the necessary background for commercial trust to emerge. Capitalists can acquire confidence in each other's promises to pay in part through regular contact as plain buyers and sellers, discussed in more detail below. Confidence is also strengthened because value is returned to the commercial creditor in the fluid form of money. In principle, commercial credit transactions could have been completed by the creditor receiving particular commodities of a given amount of value, rather than money. This form of repayment would have restored the *quid pro quo*, but at substantial cost to the debtor, who would have had to search for requisite commodities, perhaps stocking them for a period. The basis for trust in the debtor's ability to repay would have been correspondingly narrowed. Furthermore, repayment in the form of commodities could also imply costs for the creditor, since the returned commodities might not be directly appropriate for the creditor's production requirements. The creditor's value-generating activities gain in fluidity and versatility when commercial credit is repaid in the form of money. Thus settlement of commercial credit obligations in money rather than commodities is beneficial to both creditor and debtor, and broadens the basis of trust between them.

In contrast, banking credit operations rely only tenuously on links among capitalists established through the division of labour. For banking credit to take place, there is no need for material, technological, geographical or other connections between borrower and lender. Money is lent, money is returned, and as long as money is somehow generated, use values do not matter at all. Hence banking credit possesses a degree of fluidity that is absent from commercial credit. However, additional fluidity comes at a cost in terms of trust between lender and borrower. Capitalists participating in commercial credit can build trust through regular production and trading contacts – they are already buyers and sellers, or suppliers and customers. Those participating in banking credit lack this spontaneous basis for trust, since there is no reason for them to be linked other than through the act of credit. As a result, the development of banking credit draws partly on the ready-made field of trust established by commercial credit among capitalists.

The credit system comprises social mechanisms, both commercial and banking, that make credit-related trust increasingly social and objective. Credit mechanisms comprise processes of commercial credit, including the issuing of letters of credit and the factoring of trade debt. They rest on institutions that specialise in banking credit, such as commercial, investment, and development banks. They function through credit markets, above all the money market. Finally, they give rise to a profusion of instruments, such as deposits, certificates of deposit, call loans, bills, and commercial paper. The sum total of credit markets, institutions and assets is commonly referred to as a 'system', a term that implies an integral whole observing its own rules of motion. However, in mainstream economics the credit system is not normally theorised as a totality comprising more than the sum of its parts. Instead, the various features of the credit system, such as the hierarchy of activities and interests among its institutions, the relationship between markets and institutions, and the links among credit instruments, are usually examined separately and individually. In contrast, the Marxist approach adopted here treats the credit system as an integral, pyramid-like whole, which comprises successive layers of credit relations and is embedded in historically specific conditions.[3]

At the first and fundamental level, there are commercial credit relations. These arise spontaneously among capitalist enterprises in the normal course of their operations, and provide a direct link between the credit system and capitalist accumulation. Commercial credit relations rest on a field of trust and power between capitalist enterprises that emerges within the division of labour, as already mentioned. At the second level, there are banking credit relations. These also arise spontaneously, but involve the lending of temporarily idle money by one capitalist to another, against a promise to pay it back later plus interest. Transactions of banking credit can arise accidentally and occasionally between any two capitalists. However, to become systematic there must be a regular presence of money available for lending among capitalists. Thus the systematic advance of banking credit presupposes the creation of pools of idle money in the normal course of industrial capitalist accumulation.[4] The credit system contains institutions (banks) that collect idle money, transform it into capital available for lending (loanable money capital), and direct it toward production and the generation of profit. The operations of commercial credit increase the scope for the systematic advance of banking credit to industrial capitalists. Banking credit represents a more developed and social form of credit, compared to commercial.

At the third level there are money market relations, which still involve the lending of money against a promise to repay plus interest. However, money market relations arise among the institutions of the credit system – typically in order to secure reserves for their operations – rather than between financial institutions and industrial capitalists. In the money market, loanable money capital is traded as a commodity among capitalists who specialise in its collection and eventual advance to industrialists, merchants and others. As a result, credit in the money market is homogeneous and strongly social in character. Finally, at the fourth level and apex of the pyramid there are central banking relations. The central bank is the spontaneously emerging bank of banks that dominates the money market. Similarly to money market credit, central bank credit involves the lending of money on condition of repayment plus interest. However, the advance of loanable money capital now originates in the pivotal bank of the credit system, and is aimed mostly at the banks operating in the money market. Consequently, the character of central bank credit is clearly social, especially as the central bank also acts as the bank of the state and holder of the reserve of international money for the capitalist social formation to which it belongs. In the operations of the central bank there are elements of aggregative, social rationality.

The non-economic aspects of credit relations are discussed in detail in the following sections. However, it is worth noting at this point that in developed capitalist economies, the advance of banking credit often takes the form of mere promises or entitlements to value. A bank, for instance, gives credit by issuing a deposit to its borrower – that is, by merely making available to the borrower the bank's own promises to pay. Settlement of the transaction, moreover, simply involves the borrower handing to the bank a countervailing promise to pay by a third party – for instance, a cheque drawn on another bank. Thus credit transactions appear as mere swapping of promises that create a pile of claims and counterclaims with a mysterious ability to sustain themselves.[5] Banks seem able to supply credit purely because they can persuade others to trust them and accept their promises to pay. By the same token, the supply of credit appears detached from material economic reality, a bottomless pit created by institutional arrangements and conventions based on trust.[6] This is a misleading appearance. The supply of credit has a material basis in the processes of capitalist accumulation. Banking credit indeed depends on trust, but the quantities of it that can be made available to capitalist accumulation are not limitless, even when trust between participants is unimpaired. The material foundations for banking credit supply are given on the one hand by commercial transactions among capitalist enterprises, and on the other by creation of idle money in the course of industrial capital traversing its circuit. The institutional edifice of the credit system subsequently provides order and regularity to credit advance and repayment. In Marxist terms, credit is an economic aspect of the circulation of capital and is therefore ultimately dependent on the processes of production.

4.2 Non-economic foundations of commercial (trade) credit relations

Trade credit, as already mentioned, emerges spontaneously among capitalist enterprises. It also gives rise to commercial bills – that is, private promises to pay a sum of money at some point in the future. For capitalists who receive trade credit the benefits are clear, since their purchases of production inputs are financed without using their own capital. Commercial debtors can expand the range and volume of productive activities undertaken by a given capital for a period of time, thus raising its profitability. For capitalists who advance trade credit, in contrast, the benefits are less clear-cut. Commercial creditors economise on the costs of storing finished output and avoid the risks of sudden price fluctuations during the time it takes to sell output, but they also part with capital value against mere promises to pay and hence they carry the risk of delayed (or altogether cancelled) payment. Moreover, by advancing credit they prevent a part of their capital from becoming engaged in the production process, thus lowering the profitability of the whole over any given period of time. In technical terms, commercial creditors lengthen the turnover time of their capital, thus lowering its profitability.[7] It follows that there is an inherent asymmetry in the operations of commercial credit: other things being equal, individual capitalists would benefit if they could sell for cash while buying on credit.[8]

This asymmetry is important for the spread and pattern of the proliferation of commercial credit across the sphere of capitalist circulation. Competitive pressure acts as external force on capitalist sellers, encouraging them to offer commercial credit despite its partial disadvantages. It would be a competitive handicap for an enterprise to refuse to sell on credit while others did. However, given the inherent advantages of selling for cash, trade credit would be refused whenever possible. Slight differences in product quality, or in services attendant to the product after its sale, for example, could lessen the competitive pressure on sellers to offer credit to buyers. A seller who has a dominant market share might also be under less compulsion to offer credit. Last but not least, mere suspicion of lack of creditworthiness is enough to preclude trade credit. The competitive pressure on capitalist sellers to extend trade credit to buyers could be avoided or attenuated. This makes the availability of trade credit in any given market far from homogeneous. There is also variation in the terms on which trade credit is offered – the length of time to repayment, increment over cash price, place of repayment, and so on. Non-economic relations among the counterparties become particularly important as a result of the relative weakness of competitive compulsion to extend commercial credit.

The trust necessary for commercial credit is highly specific and narrowly circumscribed. It was earlier assumed that capitalists entering commodity markets are fundamentally 'foreign', to whom social rank, kinship, custom and tradition are subsidiary to profit making. Their dominant social bond is money. It follows that, if commercial trust developed among them, it would be trust among formal equals – i.e. trust among market agents who relate to each other as commodity owners. Commercial trust is not trust between hierarchical superiors and inferiors, which is typically a broad and diffuse relation that pertains to several aspects of personal life, such as marriage, family, security, and ideology. Hierarchical trust usually provides a social bond conditioned by traditional and customary rights and obligations for both parties, as, for instance, between feudal master and servant.[9] In contrast, commercial trust lacks hierarchical determinants and pivots on one issue alone: repayment of money according to terms agreed. Its most important prerequisite is confidence that the debtor will make the appropriate payment at the time due. Thus, the following two determinants of commercial trust are particularly important.

The first is the debtor's potential for profit generation. This is partly a technical economic issue, since success in profit generation depends on labour skills, technologies, and inputs used by the debtor. For industrial capitalists directly connected with each other through the social division of labour, information about the profit-making activities of a commercial credit counterpart accrues naturally and unavoidably. Information is obtained partly through the physical interdependence of production processes, and partly through regular buying and selling. When a firm uses the product of another as input in its own production process, the use value of the commodity purchased directly conveys information about the other's quality of work, regularity of production, and technological capacity. Moreover, when enterprises regularly engage in commercial transactions with each other, they automatically obtain information about each other's marketing skills and reliability. Thus the physical interdependence of production processes and regular commercial contacts generate a field of trust among industrial capitalists, making commercial credit possible. However, success in profit generation is not simply a matter of the quality of a capitalist's industrial project, nor of the efficient deployment of the forces of production. Profit generation is ultimately the result of exploitation, the outcome of class relations in the sphere of production. Up-to-date technologies and high quality inputs will not necessarily produce surplus value, if relations between capital and labour within the enterprise are not conducive to successful exploitation. Thus the creditor must gauge the ability of the debtor to act as a capitalist employer, rather than simply as technical manager of the production process. The debtor must be able to discipline workers and keep their independent organisations (especially trade unions) sufficiently compliant to ensure generation of profits. The presence of, or potential for, capital-labour conflict in the activities of the debtor is always a prime concern of the creditor. For commercial creditors, regular contact through buying and selling offers a natural opportunity to assess debtors from this perspective.

The second determinant of trust among commercial credit counterparties is access to money. What matters to the creditor is actual payment of the money sum agreed – how the borrower procures the money is ultimately unimportant. If the debtor had sufficient economic, social and political power to guarantee access to money necessary for repayment, his or her economic activities would be irrelevant to the creditor. The debtor could be inefficient or mediocre as a capitalist, without necessarily forfeiting the creditor's trust. The questions that matter to the creditor in this respect are unrelated to the technical and managerial aspects of the debtor's project. Does the debtor enterprise belong to a large group with a variety of interests across several markets? Do its owners participate in formal and informal industrialist groups? Do they possess significant social and familial connections? Do they have political contacts and the ability to elicit help from the state? Power could guarantee repayment of the sums due regardless of the borrower's actual economic activities. Given a sufficiently powerful borrower, it would be rational for the lender to advance value irrespective of success in generating profits. Creditworthiness sustained by power relations is not necessarily worse than creditworthiness based on the quality of the borrower's investment project.

The class element of the commercial creditor–debtor relationship is in this respect apparent. Capitalists relate to each other as equals in the market, but they are not equals within capitalist society. Rank and hierarchy permeate the capitalist mode of production, based partly on access to money. The debtor's social, political and property connections, often with a familial and kinship tinge, afford power and access to money. Consequently, particular enterprises and individual capitalists might be able to obtain commercial credit purely because of hierarchical power relations within the capitalist class. By the same token, close connections with the mechanisms of the state – the most coherent power structure in capitalist society – can secure access to credit. From the creditor's perspective there is nothing irrational about relying on the debtor's broad class standing to guarantee access to money and sustain repayment. Thus the trust requisite for commercial credit derives not only from the economic factors that ensure the generation of profits, but also from broader social factors that guarantee access to money. By the same token, commercial trust has a noxious and precarious character. The overriding concern among capitalists engaging in credit relations is to make more money. No higher aspirations and sentiments challenge the pre-eminence of profit-making, and hence the threat of fraud, swindling and deceit is constantly present. If it were possible for the debtor to keep the creditor in the dark regarding problematic aspects of the investment project, the debtor would probably do so. Outright lies could also be told about future profitability, or the social and political power available to the borrower. Since the foundation of commercial credit is ultimately provided by the ability to repay money, the moral dimension of credit among capitalists is feeble.

Contemporary neoclassical economics acknowledges the unsavoury character of capitalist credit by using the concept of 'moral hazard'. Relations between creditor and debtor are analysed in terms of a non-cooperative game between a principal and an agent. The agent can choose actions that affect the welfare of both agent and principal. Consequently, the principal must design a binding agreement such that the agent has incentives to choose actions that optimise the principal's welfare. This is complicated by the presence of uncertainty about the outcome of the agent's actions, as well as by information asymmetry between the counter-parties. Typically the borrower (agent) is better informed than the lender (principal) about the investment project at hand. 'Moral hazard' arises because the agent could lie to the principal regarding the actual outcome of the actions chosen, and retain a larger share of the proceeds. To confront this problem the principal devises an agreement that takes the form of a standard debt contract, requiring the agent to pay a pre-determined amount of interest. The cost of failing to do so is bankruptcy, and hence the agent has an incentive (i.e. an overhanging threat) not to lie but rather to comply with the agreement.[10]

This is an astonishing view of the moral qualities of capitalists participating in credit transactions. Put plainly, it is assumed that capitalists would renege on the terms of an agreement as soon as they derived a pecuniary advantage from doing so. There is no moral imperative on credit transaction participants either to be honest or to keep their word – each would defraud the other at the slightest opportunity. Consequently, credit agreements have to be specified in such a way that capitalists have a pecuniary incentive to comply with the terms agreed, buttressed by the powers of the courts. According to neoclassical economics, avoidance of the ever-present threat of fraud among capitalists is secured by making it more profitable to tell the truth, provided that a 'debt-enforcer' lurks in the background. This cynical vision is made even worse by assuming that 'moral hazard' flows inexorably from human nature. Apparently 'moral hazard' is a timeless problem that emerges whenever a principal relates to an agent, since human beings are inherently and profoundly amoral.

The neoclassical view of the moral content of capitalist credit is inadequate. Credit among capitalists is a historically specific relation that is based on trust and power with social determinants. Trust between capitalists is certainly a nefarious relationship. However, it is fallacious to assume that it is non-existent, thus creating the need for legal agreements backed by penalties. Fraud is never far away from relations of credit, but this has little to do with the abstractly defined relations of principal and agent among human beings. Morality is thin among capitalists engaging in credit transactions, primarily because they focus exclusively on profit-making. The social relations that sustain credit operations are deep and pervasive, but ultimately translate into dollars and pounds. That is no basis for exulted sentiments. Regular repayment of debt, however, is substantially due to the underlying social relations among credit counter-parties. The law of contract formalises and codifies practices deriving from the fundamental economic relations of society; i.e. it is a distillation of these relations. A party that failed to comply with terms agreed would forfeit the basis of trust and be excluded from future credit transactions, incurring social opprobrium in the process. Economic, social and political power would be brought to bear on the debtor to force settlement. Power as the ultimate source of repayment is apparent in the grubby world of informal finance for the poor, where it may also involve naked violence. Those who are weak and cannot abide by the terms of credit transactions are in danger of life and limb. The formal credit system, on the other hand, contains mechanisms that standardise credit-related trust and power. The legal violence of the state ultimately plays the same role as the freelance violence of the 'debt-enforcer'.

4.3 The role of trust in the operations of banking (monetary) credit

The systematic advance of banking credit and the emergence of financial intermediation rest partly on trade credit relations.[11] To substantiate this claim theoretically, consider briefly the implications of trade credit advance for the creditor (industrial capitalist). The advance of trade credit entails significant disadvantages for the creditor, including the risk of debtor default or late payment, and the cost of keeping a fraction of capital away from the generation of surplus value (slowing down the turnover of capital). Other things being equal, commercial creditors would benefit if they could obtain the return of their capital within the period of trade credit originally agreed. In this respect, the first option open to them is to use the instrument of trade credit (commercial bill) as a means of payment in their input purchases. The holder of a bill could endorse and pass it to his or her suppliers as payment for inputs, provided that the suppliers were prepared to accept it. In effect, possession of the underlying trade debt would be transferred from one capitalist to another, while the bill would function as rudimentary credit money.[12] For this to be possible, a field of trust and power must exist between the creditor and his or her suppliers such that the promise to pay would be acceptable to the suppliers despite having been originally made by unrelated (downstream) capitalists. If the suppliers accepted the bill as payment they would immediately find themselves in a similar position to the original creditor, and consequently they would have to use it again as a means of payment. However, they would now have to persuade their own suppliers to accept the initial promise to pay, and these are capitalists who are even further removed from the original relations of trust and power that supported the bill. Given that all the capitalists involved are, directly or indirectly, linked to each other through their production processes, it could well prove possible for several successive holders of the bill to act as conduits for trust and power, especially by adding their own private guarantees to it. Even so, the bill's acceptability for others remains partial, since it rests on a sum of private assurances given by individual capitalists. At every turn, the bill's ability to act as credit money (and secure return of the creditor's capital) has to be negotiated anew by persuading others of the validity of the original promise to pay and the preceding guarantees.

The second option is to sell the trade bill (more accurately, the debt represented by it) to other capitalists who possess temporarily idle sums of money. Specifically, the bill could be discounted – that is, sold for a sum smaller than that due on repayment – the difference constituting interest. This transaction is qualitatively different from trade credit: it involves the lending of money with the aim of earning interest, and hence it is banking (or monetary) credit. For it to take place, the cost to the seller in terms of interest paid must be outweighed by the benefits from the rapid return of capital. Of greater importance for our purposes is that, once the validity of the original promise to pay is established by its buyer, the seller obtains ready money that can be used freely and generally. On the other hand, since a bill can be sold to anyone who holds money, the purchaser must assess its validity without in principle having the benefit of links with the production activities of the bill's issuer. Therefore, the problem of discounting the bill is far more complex than persuading an upstream capitalist in a chain of production activities to accept an endorsed bill. The issue that must be tackled here is, who are the capitalists that are likely to possess idle money and stand ready to buy instruments of commercial debt?

A distinguishing feature of Marx's approach to banks is the claim that the original providers of banking credit (in exchange for trade bills) are merchant capitalists or, more accurately, money-dealing capitalists. According to Marx (1894, Ch. 16, 19), merchant capitalists are distinct from industrial capitalists because they specialise in the activities of circulation without entering production.[13] Merchant capitalists comprise two groups, namely commercial and money-dealing capitalists. Commercial capitalists specialise in buying and selling commodities. They reduce the circulation time of industrial capital as well as lowering the costs of buying and selling for industrial capitalists. Consequently, they raise the profitability of industrial capital and earn the average rate of profit. Money-dealing capitalists, on the other hand, specialise exclusively in the monetary aspects of circulation, such as transferring money across long distances, safekeeping it on behalf of others, or simply changing it from one national denomination to another. Consequently, they reduce the circulation costs and turnover time of industrial capitalists, and also earn the average rate of profit.

Money-dealing capitalists are naturally placed regularly to purchase commercial bills by advancing banking credit. Their capital is kept largely in the money form (since their field of specialisation comprises monetary transactions), and hence they are likely to possess temporarily idle sums available for lending. More importantly, their normal business affords them knowledge of the relations of trust and power that sustain several particular commercial bills. To transmit money abroad or convert money from one denomination into another, and even to store money, money-dealers must constantly handle commercial bills. It is inevitable that they acquire information about the regularity of payments, the attitude toward commercial obligations, the frequency of transactions and access to money of many other capitalists, despite having no direct connection with the bill issuers' productive activities. Thus money-dealers have relative advantages in assessing the creditworthiness of particular bills offered for sale. They are the capitalists who are most likely systematically to advance banking credit and become banks, though the possibility is open to all capitalists who hold sums of idle money. Even in developed credit systems banks do not lose their original function as money-dealers, and their core activities typically involve foreign exchange transactions and general money-dealing.

The characteristic aspect of the operations of banks, however, becomes clear only after closer consideration of the form in which they normally lend. A bank could make loans out of its own capital, but the scope of its lending would clearly be limited by the size of its capital. A more profitable and radical option for a bank is to make loans in the form of its own promises to pay. If the seller of a trade bill could be persuaded to accept a bank's promise to pay in return for the bill, the bank could draw profits without directly committing any of its capital. The particular form taken by banks' promises to pay depends on the institutional and historical development of the credit system, but there are two generic types; banknotes and bank deposits. Both are promises to give access to money at the holder's behest, and both have become typical forms of credit money in advanced capitalism. Banking proper can be said to emerge when a bank acquires trade bills by issuing its own banknotes and by creating deposits that give the right to withdraw money. Thus the fundamental form of banking credit consists of exchanging one kind of promise to pay (enterprise to enterprise) for another (bank to enterprise). In other words, banks typically acquire assets (i.e. the liabilities of industrial capitalists) by means of issuing their own liabilities. The liabilities of banks represent a higher grade of trust and a superior form of credit instrument compared to the liabilities of enterprises, for reasons discussed below.

An enterprise's promise to pay represented by a trade bill entails two major disadvantages for its holder: first, the turnover of capital is slowed down by the period of the bill to maturity, and second, there are risks of default or delayed payment. If a bank is to be able to persuade the holders of trade bills to sell by accepting the bank's liabilities in exchange, the bank's promises to pay must prove superior to the trade bill in both respects. The answer to the first is straightforward: banks typically issue promises to pay of shorter maturity than the promises to pay made by industrial capitalists.[14] At the limit, bank liabilities are payable on sight, and begin to acquire the aspect of cash. The problem of risk, however, is far more complex, not least because of the solution for the first problem – namely, the tendency of banks to issue liabilities that have a shorter term to maturity than their assets. The acceptability of an enterprise's promise to pay depends on its ability to make payments according to the terms agreed. This ability depends on the enterprise's success in profit generation, and its access to money. The acceptability of a bank's promise to pay similarly depends on its ability to make payments according to the terms agreed, but the substance of the matter is quite different. The profit-generating capacity of an enterprise can be assessed by examining its technology, labour, plant and equipment, as well as its skills in organising production and exploiting labour power. However, banks are neither engaged in production and nor do they produce value and surplus value – banks merely employ their capital in the business of transforming one type of promise to pay into another. Though they also rely on technologies, labour skills and office space, their profitability does not derive directly from these factors, since no surplus value is produced in the banking business. A bank's profits and ability to honour its promises to pay depend overwhelmingly on the validity and prompt repayment of the bank's assets – i.e. on other capitalists' promises to pay. In short, trust in a bank's liabilities derives from the composition and quality of the assets on its balance sheet, which are mostly the debts of others.

Establishing the ability of a bank to honour its promises according to the terms agreed is a qualitatively different exercise compared to establishing that of an industrial enterprise. Two aspects of banking activity are particularly important in this respect. The first is the degree of diversification of bank assets. By purchasing promises to pay issued by several unrelated industrial capitalists, banks can reduce the risk of default posed by the sum total of their holdings. Successful diversification is a matter of practical experience for the banks. Banks can further strengthen their ability to confront default by possessing substantial capital that could be used to write off defaulting assets. The second aspect is the access of banks to reserves. The maturity difference between long-term assets and short-term liabilities is a perilous problem for banks. Banks are faced with the maturing of their liabilities (and hence the need to make payments) at rates faster than the maturing of their assets (which brings in fresh funds). It is evident that if banks were presented with extraordinary withdrawal demands on their liabilities – a sudden rush of demands to honour pledges given – they would be unable to meet requests and go bankrupt. Thus banks must possess an amount of liquid assets, including generally acceptable money, to satisfy recurrent and unusual withdrawal demands. On the other hand, holding liquid reserves brings little or no profit to banks. Banks therefore continually walk a tightrope, learning through experience to keep the minimum level of reserves that allows them to honour their promises to pay in the normal course of business.

It is apparent that the acceptability of a bank's promises to pay has more strongly social determinants than the acceptability of an enterprise's promises to pay. The soundness of a bank's liabilities rests on the quality of its assets, i.e. on the validity of the promises to pay made by industrial capitalists, which the bank has chosen to acquire. By constructing a set of assets a bank brings together a variety of fields of trust and power across several industrial sectors that act as a foundation for trust in the bank's promises to pay. The particular and private trust between capitalists across a broad swathe of industry is subsumed under the bank's own promise to pay. Thus the trust between a bank and a capitalist who accepts the bank's liabilities rests on broader and more strongly social foundations than trust between two industrial capitalists. By the same token, banks' promises to pay are more generally acceptable than those of enterprises. Banking credit can supersede trade credit.

This difference between banking and trade credit corresponds to an inherent asymmetry between banks and enterprises with respect to credit operations.[15] Banks lack the direct contact with their customers provided by production and trading links, but they have specialist skills in assessing commercial and other promises to pay across sectors and industries. Moreover, they develop further skills in collecting and evaluating information about a variety of enterprises across sectors. Banks construct internal mechanisms that allow them to compare one enterprise against another, thus establishing social standards of creditworthiness. In contrast, industrial enterprises are at a disadvantage in assessing the creditworthiness of banks. Enterprises normally lack mechanisms that could allow them systematically to assess the quality of a bank's assets, since their business is to produce and sell commodities. Moreover, it would be prohibitively expensive for industrial capitalists to check the individual quality of a bank's assets, given that these include promises to pay made by many enterprises in several different sectors. Consequently, industrial capitalists base their assessment of banks' creditworthiness on the extent of diversification of bank assets as well as on the size of reserves and bank capital.

The asymmetry between banks and industrial capital is also reflected in the role of power in sustaining their respective creditworthiness. Power available to industrial capitalists (economic, social and political) could guarantee access to money and therefore prompt settlement of promises to pay. Consequently, banks use their information-collecting mechanisms to become acquainted with property links, political and social connections, and even family and kinship relations among their customers. Banks are repositories of knowledge about the technical and social aspects of capitalist accumulation across several sectors; they also accumulate knowledge about the patterns of social and political power relevant to their operations. Banks must also project the image of power, if they are more easily to persuade industrial capitalists to accept their promises to pay, in view of the difficulty of assessing the quality of bank operations. Industrial capitalists acquire confidence in a bank's liabilities partly as a result of the property relations and the social and political standing of the bank's owners. For a bank, extensive political contacts, family connections, the image of wealth, and wide-ranging property interests are part of the banking business.

In sum, banking transcends commercial credit and broadens the basis of trust among capitalists by giving a more social character to credit. Banks specialise in purchasing promises to pay made by industrial capitalists across several enterprises and sectors. Therefore, banks provide a more general basis for trust in their own promises to pay. To undertake their operations, banks must further cultivate their relative advantage in collecting and evaluating information about other capitalist enterprises. Consequently, banks systematically amass knowledge about economic, social and political issues relevant to capitalist accumulation in particular areas (economic and geographical). The interaction of banks with each other in the money market further strengthens the social aspect of credit.

4.4 The social character of money market credit

Money market credit arises spontaneously and necessarily among banks as they attempt to obtain reserves. Essentially it entails the advance of money on condition of repayment plus interest, but trading takes place primarily among financial institutions and does not typically involve industrial capitalists. Reserves are necessary for banks in order to sustain their liabilities. Banks can commit some of their own capital to reserves, but this naturally limits the extent to which they can expand their liabilities, and therefore their profit-generating assets. Alternatively, banks can obtain reserves by borrowing temporarily idle money from capitalists and others (deposits). For capitalists who possess idle money, the evident advantage is that their money is thus transformed into loanable capital earning interest. For banks, apart from obtaining requisite reserves, a further advantage is that a part of the incoming funds could be used to make loans to industrial capitalists. Through this process banks eventually acquire the function of financial intermediation – i.e. the systematic collection of idle money across society, its transformation into loanable money capital, and its channelling back to accumulation. The truly remarkable aspect of financial intermediation is not the lending of money by banks; rather, it is the action of capitalists to deposit idle money with banks on the basis of mere promises to pay. This is an economic act that does not entail transformation of one type of promise to pay into another, but rather represents outright lending by capitalists to banks. For capitalists to take this bold step it is necessary to have sufficient confidence in the operations of banks. Trust is provided through the acceptability of the bank's promises to pay, which is based on its purchases of other capitalists' assets. A bank is able to attract idle funds (borrow) from individual capitalists because it has already created a basis of trust and confidence in its liabilities through its banking credit operations.

When banks obtain funds by borrowing from individual capitalists, it follows that their access to reserves varies according to the particular area (geographical and economic) in which they operate. Depending on the area's characteristics (composition of production, balance of agricultural and industrial activities, profitability of industrial capital, and so on), some banks find it easier than others to obtain idle funds from capitalists. There is no reason in principle for banks across the economy to have similar access to reserves, when they obtain them by borrowing from capitalists in their area. The unevenness of bank access to reserves is the basic reason for emergence of the money market; banks that find it difficult to secure reserves borrow from banks that have abundant reserves and funds to spare. These are transactions of loanable money capital, but occur among financial institutions. The borrowing bank, for instance, could resell assets against a promise to pay by another bank. Alternatively, it could issue its own promises to pay and exchange (sell) them for those of another bank.

In generic terms, however, money market transactions consist of inter-bank borrowing and lending that emerges spontaneously as banks attempt to secure reserves.

Emergence of the money market is of particular importance for the evolution of trust and power within the credit system. In the money market loanable capital is traded among specialist capitalists, typically in large sums and for short periods of time. The asymmetry that characterised the advance of banking credit when it involved banks and industrial capitalists is not present in the money market, since participants are specialists in banking credit. The acceptability of promises to pay issued by banks in the money market is assessed by other banks, rather than by industrial capitalists. Banks continually compare, contrast and evaluate each other's promises to pay, empirically establishing standards of acceptability. However, as was shown in the previous section, the acceptability of a bank's promise to pay draws ultimately on the assets held by the bank – that is, on the multiple private promises to pay that the bank has chosen to acquire and hold. Consequently, in the money market, the various private promises to pay (which are made by particular capitalists and subsumed under a single bank's promise to pay) are assessed as a homogeneous mass. They are compared with the assets of other banks – again assessed as a uniform entity – and an appropriate degree of acceptability is accorded to each bank's promise to pay, valid for society as a whole. The standards applying to bank creditworthiness in the money market are strongly social.

By the same token, the money market turns funds available for lending across society into a homogeneous commodity; that is, it transforms them into loanable capital proper. The money market cuts across economic and geographical areas and makes it possible for idle money funds to acquire a common and general character across society, thereby commanding the payment of interest. Consequently, the rate of interest is established in the money market with precision and society-wide applicability. Given a money market, banks can systematically function as financial intermediaries across society, collecting idle funds, transforming them into loanable capital, and channelling them toward capitalist accumulation. This point is worth emphasising in view of the current neoclassical treatment of banks as financial intermediaries.[16] The underlying approach is to assume that the natural state of economic affairs is for markets to exist in which lenders would directly meet borrowers to trade available funds. The question is then posed, why do financial institutions (banks) emerge? The answer typically is that banks exist because of market imperfections, such as informational asymmetries between lender and borrower, which give financial intermediaries an advantage in collecting and lending funds. Thus financial intermediation emerges fully-formed out of the imperfections of markets. From the approach adopted here the process is the reverse: the interactions of financial institutions create the money market. Once the money market is established, proper financial intermediation becomes possible. Financial intermediation is a function that accrues to banks gradually and as the institutional complexity of the credit system increases.

The ability of banks to honour their promises to pay is subjected to meticulous and detached assessment in the money market. Transacting parties (banks) are typically removed from production and circulation of commodities, while money is both the means and the object of transactions. In establishing a relationship between the counter-parties to money market transactions, therefore, all considerations are subsumed to the imperative of money-making. Economic and non-economic aspects of a bank's activities are precisely assessed from the point of view of securing the repayment of money advanced. To this purpose, credit ratings are established for market participants. Despite its social character, money market credit is still, in every instance, a promise to pay by a particular bank, and hence it retains a private aspect. The private aspect of money market credit is often measured and expressed as a single index (rating) attached to participants. Given the pivotal role of the money market in the credit system, the practices and methods of credit rating spread across the credit system and apply to individual enterprises, persons and even countries. Economic position, social standing, access to power, even the national characteristics and traits of particular borrowers are subsumed under a single index the sole purpose of which is to indicate probability of repayment. The ethical, moral, religious, customary and hierarchical dimensions of borrowing and lending are reduced to a figure that suffices as foundation of trust. In short, in the money market creditworthiness is established as a social property of capital in the objective and 'thing-like' form of an index.

4.5 Central bank credit

The central bank is the apex of the pyramid of the credit system, and emerges spontaneously out of bank interaction in the money markets.[17] Banks operating in the money market could effect substantial cost reductions if they concentrated their reserves at one central point and deployed them as need arose. Concentration would also reduce the size of reserves. The central bank is the money market bank that attracts reserves from all the others – the bank of banks. The central bank's promises to pay (banknotes and deposits) are the main means of payment in the money market. There is constant selling and buying of promises to pay among banks that participate in the money market. These promises require settlement at maturity, and hence they give rise to transfers out of bank reserves. If mutually held and opposite promises to pay were cancelled out, other things being equal, banks would make fewer transfers and keep smaller reserves.[18] The dominant money of the clearing process typically comprises promises to pay by central banks.

The acceptability of central bank promises to pay derives, in the first instance, from the quality of the central bank's assets. Its reserves – which are the ultimate reserve for the credit system as a whole – are fundamental in sustaining trust in its liabilities, and typically include the money commodity (gold). However, equally important is the quality of promises to pay made by others (especially money market banks) that are held by the central bank as its own assets. Consequently it is vital for the central bank systematically to assess other banks' promises to pay, and this involves continuous and meticulous examination of their operations, often on a daily basis. Gathering and evaluating information about others, something that all banks practice, reaches its pinnacle with the central bank, partly because its activities are directed toward other banks. To sustain the acceptability of its banking credit, the central bank must accumulate skills in analysing economic, social and political information, and it must formulate assessments of the capitalist economy as a whole. Analogously, by constantly evaluating and acquiring the promises to pay made by banks in the money market, the central bank homogenises credit even further. Its own promises to pay therefore represent the most social form and highest grade of credit in the capitalist economy. They function as the means of payment of choice in the money market, and become the credit money *par excellence* across the economy. There is an irreducible asymmetry between the central bank and other banks, arising purely out of the money-like aspect of the central bank's liabilities. As long as central bank promises to pay are able to function as a means of payment among banks and capitalists in general, banks are strongly disposed to accept them. The central bank thus performs a delicate balancing act: its credit is the best available in the capitalist economy, allowing its liabilities to function as the money of settlement and trade, but for other banks to be disposed to accept them, its liabilities must continue to function as money.

The social character of the central bank's credit derives from its role in the money market, but is fully established only after two further developments: first, the central bank becomes the bank of the state, and second, it emerges as the guardian of the nation's reserve of means of payment employed in the world market.[19] As the bank of the state, the central bank manages the state's accounts and debts, and makes direct loans to the state. These activities have immediate implications for the central bank's credit. Central bank assets include the state's promises to pay (bonds and bills), which derive validity from the state's ability to tax income. Possession of state promises to pay typically improves the quality of the assets of the central bank and strengthens the acceptability of its liabilities. The state can further attach open social acceptability to the central bank's promises to pay by making them legal tender, i.e. by declaring their acceptance obligatory in discharge of private debts. By proclaiming central bank liabilities as legal tender, the state places its own authority and power behind central bank promises to pay, turning their use as a means of payment into a stable social norm. Consequently, the credit of the central bank reflects directly the state's political power as well as its power to tax. In undertaking international operations, on the other hand, a central bank's promises to pay could become accepted by other nations as a means of payment and elements of international reserves. The credit advanced by a central bank would in that case transcend its national character and assume a global aspect. Central bank credit would then reflect the comparative strength of nations in the world arena.

Central bank credit, because it represents credit that has the most clearly social character in a capitalist economy, affords to the central bank enormous economic and social power.[20] Given that it systematically collects information about the credit system and the economy, the central bank is able to monitor the credit system for moral hazard and fraud.[21] Its unique position within the credit system allows it to impose sanctions on banks, sustained by a battery of professional and legal regulations. By regularly supplying its credit to the money market, moreover, it can influence the terms on which banks lend to each other, altering the level of the rate of interest across the economy. Its liabilities can also rescue financial institutions from bankruptcy and prevent or ameliorate financial crises. Finally, the central bank could, if it wished, intervene in the allocation of credit by banks across industry, thus affecting the performance of particular sectors and even the distribution of income. However, the central bank remains at bottom a bank – i.e. a creature of the capitalist credit system. Its first and overriding concern is to protect the interests of financial institutions and of their most powerful customers. The bias inherent to central bank interventions emerges starkly at times of crisis, as the broader interests of society are subordinated to the needs and demands of the credit system. Nevertheless, deciding which financial institutions are to receive credit, as well as how much of it, under what terms and for how long, also depends on broader considerations. Political power, social connections, wealth, property links, and even family relations, influence deployment of central bank credit in times of crisis.

4.6 Conclusion

In the course of capitalist credit relations, value is relinquished against mere promises to pay it back later. For this reason, credit transactions contain integral non-economic elements. Capitalists engage in credit operations within explicit relations of trust and power, which directly affect the availability and terms of credit. Credit markets are qualitatively different from plain commodity markets in this respect, and the same holds for the give and take of capitalists in credit compared to commodity markets. In credit transactions capitalists are not 'foreign' to each other, their actions being driven primarily by comparison of the value of the commodity they hold with that of their trading partner. On the contrary, capitalists offer and receive credit depending on each other's trustworthiness and power. The counter-parties to credit transactions rely on familiarity due to repeated commercial contacts, as well as on customary practices of exchange, property over resources, access to money, hierarchical position, and each other's broad social relations.

It was also shown above that the non-economic aspects of credit are systematically marshalled by the institutions of the credit system, and placed at the disposal of capitalist accumulation. Banks and credit markets transform the relations of trust and power inherent to credit among capitalists. Credit that emerges as a private and subjective relationship between two capitalists gradually becomes a social and objective relationship that involves the institutions of the credit system. Assessing the creditworthiness of credit counter-parties, therefore, turns into a detached exercise in collecting and evaluating information about economic activities and social relations. However, the influence of property, power, hierarchy and social connections on economic relations formed through the credit system remains vital. By the same token, the class content of capitalist relations is apparent within the credit system, since creditworthiness focuses entirely on the ability to repay money plus interest. The moral content of capitalist credit relations is thin, facilitating fraud, deception and outright cheating.

Part III

Theoretical approaches to the social relations sustaining markets and money

5 Social norms and institutions in the capitalist economy

The neoclassical approach to the capitalist economy is thoroughly individualist. Mainstream economics directs its focus on the 'rational individual', who is motivated exclusively by self-gain and rationally uses all means available to achieve desired ends. In recent years, however, neoclassical economics has started increasingly to deploy concepts that are social rather than individual. In microeconomics in particular, there is systematic and regular recourse to 'social norms' in accounting for economic behaviour. 'Social norms' is shorthand for actions that are regular and predictable, but cannot be explained in terms of the private gain of the 'rational individual'. They have provided the means for neoclassical economics to introduce social concerns into its theoretical analysis, thereby conditioning individual choice. Economic models now typically include norms of trust, solidarity, commitment, etc., thus constraining the instrumental rationality of the economic individual. Deployment of concepts that are social rather than individual has given to contemporary economics a breadth that previous neoclassicism lacked. This is especially apparent in the neoclassical institutionalist and information-theoretic approaches to the capitalist economy, both of which are discussed below. Nonetheless, neoclassical economics remains deeply uncertain about the social component of norms, and refuses to treat society as an independent and valid object of study. Social norms are typically seen as emerging and operating due to the actions and choices of individuals. Institutions and economic information are still theoretically analysed within an individualist framework, leaving out much of their social content as well as the historically specific context to which they belong.

This chapter selectively reviews recent neoclassical theory regarding the impact of social norms, information and institutions on the operations of markets. It then turns briefly to sociological theory of social relations in the capitalist economy. The theories of networks and 'social capital', in particular, focus on social relations as constitutive parts of economic activity, and have become influential in analysing the interaction of economic and social relations in the capitalist economy. The purpose of this chapter, apart from deriving insights from the theories reviewed, is to provide a contrast with the Marxist discussion of social and economic relations in previous chapters. The economic and sociological theories discussed below ignore the class nature of capitalism, and pay no heed to the specific character of capital as economic and social phenomenon. Consequently, they miss the specific character of the interaction between the economic and the non-economic in capitalist society, the overbearing presence of class exploitation and money profit.

5.1 Rationality and social norms in economic analysis

General equilibrium theory, the set of core theoretical concepts deployed by neoclassical economics, was developed through the work of Kenneth Arrow and Gerard Debreu after the Second World War.[1] Using strict assumptions about individual behaviour, general equilibrium provides a conceptually coherent theoretical system within which market exchange and price determination are analysed. The most fundamental assumption is that economic decisions are taken by the 'rational individual', a human being with a very peculiar form of consciousness. The individual is supposed to be interested solely in private gain, and to lack entirely altruism or concern about the collective good. Yet the individual employs neither violence nor power in order to obtain personal benefits. Relations with others occur in markets, to which individuals bring commodities for the purpose of exchange. Private gain for the individual derives exclusively from the goods obtained in exchange. Hence the methods used by individuals to achieve gain are essentially those of commercial trading, i.e. undergoing minimal expenditure to obtain maximum return.

In this light, the choices made by the individual are assumed to be rational in the sense that they do not contradict each other. If an exchange transaction revealed that good x was preferred over good y, the individual would be expected to comply with this ordering in future transactions. Thus, for economic theory, the individual's rationality is primarily a matter of ensuring a coherent ordering of choices made. Moreover, given that to obtain private gain the individual must make an outlay of resources, the rationality postulated by economists is strictly of the instrumental variety: means have to be coherently utilised to achieve ends.[2] This is normally called 'rational choice'. Sen (1976–1977, p. 323, original emphasis), in his outstanding critique of the premises and methods of general equilibrium, put it the following terms:

> This approach of definitional egoism sometimes goes under the name of rational choice, and it involves nothing other than internal consistency. A person's choices are considered 'rational' in this approach if and only if these choices can *all* be explained in terms of some preference relation consistent with the revealed preference definition, that is, if all his choices can be explained as the choosing of 'most preferred' alternatives with respect to the postulated preference relation.

For our purposes, the important aspect of the approach of 'definitional egoism' is that moral, ethical, customary, familial, or generally social considerations are absent. Only economic considerations matter, i.e. those that directly determine private gain.[3] In addition, general equilibrium theory makes further very restrictive assumptions, including possession of full information by all individuals prior to making decisions as well as existence of a complete range of markets in all commodities (including commodities to be produced and consumed in the future). Pure theory also assumes the existence of generalised price taking and the absence of 'externalities', i.e. of side effects on the individual's well-being that are not captured directly by the market, such as pollution. Under this extraordinary set of assumptions, both regarding human motivations and the context within which these are carried out, general equilibrium theory can show that free market exchange is an efficient economic arrangement.

During the last three decades, however, neoclassical economics has started increasingly to accept that economic agents react to various stimuli in ways that cannot be captured by the calculus of individual cost and benefit. These reactions are captured by the term 'social norms'. Thus much of contemporary microeconomic theory starts with the assumption that the 'rational individual' makes decisions based on a calibration of ends to means aiming at the optimal outcome under given conditions, but also admits that the same 'rational individual' could undertake actions that are simply dictated by social norms. These norms are presumably enforced through sanctions that draw on the approval or disapproval of other members of society. As Elster (1989) notes, the individual actions entailed by norms cannot be explained away as 'in reality' promoting self-interest (or even the common interest) without the individual thinking through or realising their effect. There are norms, for instance, that result in harm for all individuals that follow them, such as the vendetta in Southern Europe. There are also norms that bring no discernible benefit to society or the individual, such as sexual norms, or norms of social etiquette. The implications for economics are profound. If individual behaviour is conditioned by social norms, it follows that there are economic phenomena which result from a combination of economic and non-economic (social) factors.[4]

Consider the following examples of how social norms can be understood to affect economic decision-making. It could be assumed that there is a widespread social norm in favour of 'working', established through imitation of those who have been successful at work as well as through the actions of family members and others instilling habits of work into the young (Elster, 1988). At the same time, it could be postulated that the welfare state in modern society provides handouts to individuals as a right and reduces their economic incentive to work. Consequently, a tension seems to exist between the social norm of 'working' and the incentive to 'laziness' that is created by the welfare state (Lindbeck, 1997). On this basis, economists are able to develop a rational choice analysis of the individual decision to enter employment or claim welfare benefit, in view of taxes to be paid and the total number of claimants. A similar approach can be used in relation to the universal presence of money in commercial exchange. General equilibrium theory postulates that 'rational individuals' draw benefits from the goods they possess through consumption. However, money is an asset that is never privately consumed, despite being constantly used. Why, then, would 'rational individuals' choose to hold some of their wealth in money? To answer this question, contemporary neoclassicism assumes the existence of the social norm of believing that some commodities are more generally acceptable than others (as discussed in Chapter 6). Given this belief, rational choice analysis can show that individuals choose to hold some goods that they do not wish to consume but might be of use in procuring the goods they actually desire – that is, they hold money.

The additional explanatory power given to neoclassical theory by inclusion of social norms should not be underestimated, as can be seen in relation to the work of the Nobel prize winner Gary Becker. Long before the importance of social norms was explicitly acknowledged by economic theory, Becker (1996, p. 1) deployed rational choice theory with the aim of accounting for social phenomena that have traditionally lain outside the normal remit of economics.[5] Becker's method is resolutely to apply the theoretical principles of economics – understood as maximisation of private gain, stable individual preferences and tendency to equilibrium – to all social issues regardless of their context (Becker, 1976, p. 5).[6] Thus choices and decisions made within the family are analysed by Becker (1991) by treating the family as if it were an economic unit operating in several markets.[7] In earlier work, Becker (1965) treated the allocation of an individual's private time along the same lines. Most famously, he has employed this approach to analyse skills, education, training, aptitude and suitability for work as 'human capital' (Becker, 1993). Throughout, Becker has assumed that the preferences and tastes of the individual are given and generally applicable across society, i.e. they are not determined by an individual's social position or interaction with others (Stigler and Becker, 1977).[8]

However, other economists, even some firmly wedded to general equilibrium, were aware that Becker's approach could lead to absurdity (Akerlof, 1990). For them, rational choice should not be used indiscriminately to explain all social phenomena. Social norms and customs are hardly susceptible to standard economic analysis, yet they appear to shape economic activity. Thus Arrow (1974a, Ch. 1), doyen of contemporary neoclassicism, assumes that there is a systematic difference between individual and social good (i.e. a tension between society and the individual) and considers different forms of economic organisation with respect to resource allocation. He concludes that social norms are very important for the efficient performance of free market capitalism. Arrow (1974a, p. 23) is particularly insistent on the significance of the social norm of trust, and is worth quoting at length:

> Now trust has a very important pragmatic value, if nothing else. Trust is an important lubricant of a social system. It is extremely efficient; it saves a lot of trouble to have a fair degree of reliance on other people's word. Unfortunately this is not a commodity which can be bought very easily. If you have to buy it, you already have some doubts about what you've bought. Trust and similar values, loyalty or truth-telling, are examples of what the economist would call 'externalities'. They are goods, they are commodities; they have real, practical, economic value; they increase the efficiency of the system, enable you to produce more goods or more of whatever values you hold in high esteem. But they are not commodities for which trade on the open market is technically possible or even meaningful.

Explicit inclusion of social norms into the apparatus of neoclassicism, therefore, has opened new theoretical vistas for mainstream economists. Among leading neoclassicals, Akerlof has been deeply committed to acknowledging and analysing the role of social norms in economic phenomena, but firmly within the confines of neoclassicism. Thus, for Akerlof (1980), unemployment arises because firms refuse to hire cheaper unemployed workers. The reason is that the social norm of 'solidarity' among employed workers makes it impossible for new (cheaper) entrants to integrate with existing workers. Individual workers refuse to accept and train newly hired workers, since the norm of 'solidarity' implies that they would lose 'reputation' among their fellow workers already in employment. Akerlof (1982) has also suggested that workers perform unpaid overtime in return for firms behaving paternalistically toward them. The norm of reciprocal obligation, characteristic of gift-giving, is here deployed to account for the widely observed practice in developed and developing economies of working beyond the legal term prescribed by the employment contract. Similarly, Akerlof (1983) has argued that norms of loyalty and honesty result in benefits for the individual, and hence it should not be assumed that economic man is unflinchingly selfish.

A purely technical factor that has contributed significantly to the rise of non-economic concepts within neoclassical economics is game theory, associated with the gifted mathematician and Nobel prize winner in economics, John Nash. Prior to the spread of game-theoretic techniques, economists generally assumed the existence of the 'rational individual', and subsequently dealt with the ends–means problem as a technical issue of optimisation, given the individual's endowment of assets. Economic decision-making appeared as a rational response to objective circumstances confronting the individual, and equilibrium was reached when the individual's plans were fulfilled. Without disturbing these fundamental premises, game theory contributed to economic theory its own characteristic analysis of systematic interaction between the players of a game.[9] In any game for which the rules, means and ends are given, there will be patterns of action and counteraction by the players. These lead to the formation of strategies (guides to action) enabling players to confront all possible actions taken by the opposite party. Possibly, but not necessarily, in a given game there are also strategies that are not susceptible to change in view of any possible counteraction by the opposing party. Adoption of such strategies by the players results in a state of 'Nash equilibrium' for the game. This concept currently dominates equilibrium analysis in microeconomics.

There is nothing inherently 'economic' about the game-theoretic approach to human action; much less anything inherently 'social'. It could be applied, and indeed has been, with equal facility and appropriateness to any game, or to anything that can be perceived as a game – from backgammon to military rivalry. It is simply a technique of analysis within a certain framework of rationality. Thus to apply game theory to economics it has to be assumed at the outset that the players are distinct economic agents – for instance, two commodity owners, or an employer and an employee, or a lender and a borrower. Definite rules of the game have to exist in advance, such as abstaining from violence, or applying the principle of *quid pro quo*. The techniques of game theory could then lead to patterns of action and counteraction between economic agents, the emergence of strategies, and possibly to 'Nash equilibria'. Despite being inherently asocial, this method of analysis has proven vital to bringing social factors into economics. Game theory makes economic interaction appear as steps taken by individuals in mutual engagement, and hence stands in contrast to analysing decision-making as individual optimisation under given conditions. It brings to the fore the interpersonal, and therefore implicitly social, aspect of economic activity.[10] Furthermore, in game-theoretic analysis, games could be played repetitively. Consequently, players could engage in acquiring and accumulating information, as well as in cooperating with each other. These concepts have obvious social counterparts, and have been used extensively by economists to analyse economic cooperation and the conflict between collective action and private interest.[11]

The techniques of game theory cast a social shroud over economic decision-making because players are assumed to be specific economic agents (commodity owners, lenders, borrowers, employers, and so on) repeatedly interacting with each other under certain constraints. The modern microeconomics of finance, for instance, analyses the relationship between lender and borrower as a non-cooperative game. One player holds money but has no investment project, while the other holds an investment project but has no money; the aim of both is maximum private gain. Several possible strategies then emerge: outright sale of the project, joint ownership, or advance of money to finance the project on condition of return plus interest. Each would result in a different economic configuration between the players, with different social results. Under the assumption that the players do not possess the same information regarding the project, a theoretical solution emerges showing that the two agents enter into a relationship of money-lending (as was discussed in Chapter 4). Theoretical results of this kind are evidently conditional on the initial assumptions about the social characteristics of the players, as well as the background against which they undertake their actions. If the techniques of game theory were applied to, say, backgammon, there would be nothing social about the analysis and its results: action and strategy would be a private affair between the players. However, if, as in the case above, the game is stipulated as money owner meets project owner with the aim of maximising personal gain, the analysis and its results acquire a veneer of political economy.

In sum, social norms are now explicitly incorporated into neoclassical theory, without breaking with the assumption of the 'rational individual'. Neoclassicism openly acknowledges the social dimension of economic and other phenomena, while retaining the 'rational individual' as its point of theoretical reference. The theory of rational choice has gradually assumed a broader aspect, which might in future prove more appealing to other social sciences compared to Becker's unrelenting application of the principles of optimisation. In a series of incisive papers, Fine (1997, 1998a, 1999a, 1999b) called this development a 'revolution' comparable to the very emergence of neoclassicism in the last quarter of the nineteenth century. For Fine, economics is now more able to 'colonise' other social sciences by imposing its techniques, methods and concerns. As Fine also stresses, the outcome of the interaction between economics and other social sciences is not predetermined, and depends on intellectual resistance to neoclassical 'colonisation' in the longer term.

At the same time, the methodological individualism found at the core of neoclassical economics continually hampers analysis of the deeper determinants of social norms. In particular, the social content of the various norms incorporated into economic analysis remains obscure. Why, to use an earlier example, is there a norm of solidarity among workers? What exactly are the social constituents of the norm of trust among capitalist enterprises? To begin to provide answers to such questions, a broader outlook is required than that of neoclassicism. It is important to treat society as an integral whole and subsequently to place economic agents within aggregate, social economic activity. The motivations, practices and customs of individuals could then be assessed in an appropriately broad context. The Marxist framework put forth in Chapter 1 is naturally suited for this purpose. Its differences from neoclassicism concerning the analysis of social relations in the capitalist economy can be shown sharply through discussion of institutions and information in contemporary economics.

5.2 Institutions and markets

The emergence of neoclassical institutionalism is associated mostly with North and Williamson (both mentioned briefly in Chapter 1). Institutions and their impact on economic activity have provided great scope for incorporating social relations into neoclassical economic theory. For North (1990, p. 4):

> Institutions include any form of constraint that human beings devise to shape human interaction . . . Institutional constraints include both what individuals are prohibited from doing and, sometimes, under what conditions some individuals are permitted to undertake certain activities. As defined here, they therefore are the framework within which human interaction takes place. They are perfectly analogous to the rules of the game in a competitive sport.

Thus institutions are taken as conventions (formalised external impositions on individual behaviour) that shape the choices of economic agents. They weigh upon economic equilibrium because they have an effect on the costs of transacting. The nature of the costs of transacting is not immediately clear but, for North, they are mostly the costs of striking, keeping, and enforcing an agreement between two individuals. Thus the cost of a transaction would vary substantially from community to community, since the social conventions and norms constraining individual behaviour also vary. Consequently, institutions matter greatly for decision-making and economic efficiency. A similar role is played by organisations, which can be political as well as economic. North (1990, Ch. 9) defines organisations as sets of rules that significantly reduce the uncertainty surrounding human interaction. They affect transactions costs, but can also induce institutional change in society.

This view of institutions and organisations provides theoretical backing for North's earlier analysis of the role of the state in economic development (North, 1981). Economic and political organisations presumably exist to maximise the gains drawn by individuals from market exchange, which is assumed to be the fundamental form of economic interaction. Thus, according to North (1981, p. 21):

> [a] state is an organisation with a comparative advantage in violence, extending over a geographic area whose boundaries are determined by its power to tax constituents.

The state derives revenue through taxes, which are clearly a cost on economic transactions. Remarkably, North assumes that the revenue of the state is a source of gratification for those who run it. However, he also suggests that the state offers services, which are mostly the provision and supervision of property rights over economic goods. The state's ability to provide these services ultimately rests on its command over violence. At the same time, the services provided by the state lessen the costs of transacting in the economy. Consequently, North concludes that there is a constant tension between the state's taxation practices and the services it provides. In later work, North (1999) offers a theory of historical change that essentially amounts to postulating two underlying processes. On the one hand, there is spontaneous economic change occurring through accumulation of knowledge and growth of population. On the other, the state continually imposes changes on property rights and the institutional structures of the economy. This fundamental view of historical change is supplemented by the notion that ideology and beliefs critically influence the institutions and organisations of society. Hence historical change ultimately rests on the systems of beliefs characteristic of different societies.

Along similar lines, though not directly concerned with history, Williamson has focused on the transactions costs of exchange. Institutions and organisations play an important role in lessening transactions costs and hence improving market efficiency. In his most seminal work, Williamson (1975) argues that the capitalist firm is itself an institution constructed by exchange participants in order to reduce the transactions costs attendant to exchange. The firm relies on non-market, and even non-economic, relations such as hierarchy, authority and power.[12] Direct command by management over workers and resources allows the firm to complete economic activities within its own boundaries, and with lower transactions costs. Thus, firms allow for more efficient completion of economic activities compared to what would have occurred had the same activities been articulated with each other through exchange in the open market. The origin of this notion, as Williamson accepts, lies in the work of Coase (1937, 1960), who has also received the Nobel prize. Williamson (1979, 1985, 1996) has deployed it in order to account for the existence and economic role of a huge range of institutions and norms, including contracts, property rights, and mechanisms to enforce both contracts and property rights, as well as the existence and provision of public goods. In short, institutions are social arrangements that frame individual choice, thus reducing transactions costs.

The underlying approach of both North and Williamson, however, is still rational choice. Individuals who naturally relate to each other as economic agents through the market enter into further social relations through institutions and norms. The additional relations generally improve the benefits drawn by individuals from economic interaction through the market. Thus social relations are brought into economic theory, but on a strictly individualist basis. From the perspective of our discussion in Chapter 1, this approach is narrow and produces poor results in explaining the character of institutions and norms. A minimum prerequisite for the theoretical treatment of social relations found in institutions, norms, practices and customs is to treat society as an entity separate from individuals. The social is properly approached at the level of society as a whole, and on its own terms rather than those of individual choice. The Marxist approach elaborated in previous chapters is able theoretically to distinguish between the economic 'base' and the social 'superstructure' because it first identifies the social (class) relations permeating the economy. These relations have nothing to do with individual choice, and can only be postulated at the level of society as a whole. The institutions, norms and customary practices in capitalist society are subsequently marked by the class relations of production. This was demonstrated in previous chapters, especially for the social norm and institutions of trust, which contemporary neoclassical economics deems fundamental to performance of the economy. Trust was shown to have a specific character based on money-making, which becomes increasingly social through the profit-seeking activities of credit institutions. In contrast, the abstract treatment of trust as a necessary lubricant of 'rational decision-making by economic individuals' simply states the obvious.

The weakness of neoclassical individualism is also clear in North's definition of institutions as 'any form of constraint that human beings devise to shape human interaction', quoted above. Constraints on individual behaviour within society are not institutions, and even less devices to make things run smoothly. Rather, constraints on behaviour are the substance of social intercourse, the molecules of society itself. To think that all constraints are institutions is to imagine that individuals are 'islands' meeting in the market and, in principle, able to interact without constraint. However, whenever two individuals meet for purposes of trade they have already accepted social constraints on their behaviour: they do not apply violence, steal from each other, or openly cheat. Indeed, the act of trading is itself a constraint on behaviour, or an 'institution', according to North's own definition. Where, then, does the 'institution' of trading come from? For neoclassical theory, trading ultimately emanates from human nature, it is perhaps a defining characteristic of human beings. In contrast, for the Marxist approach adopted here, commodity trading is an outcome of the social (class) relations of production. The social character of the norms and institutions of commerce is thus made apparent, without seeking recourse to abstract generalisations about human behaviour.

5.3 Information-theoretic analysis and neoclassical economics

The rise of social concepts within mainstream economics has also been helped by the spread of information-theoretic analysis, typically in conjunction with game theory. The original motivation for adoption of the information-theoretic approach to economics was clearly stated by one of its originators, Akerlof (1984, pp. 2–3), namely to relax the restrictive assumptions of general equilibrium in order to account for deviations from the ideal model observed in the real world. Such deviations from general equilibrium are often economic phenomena that are widely prevalent and very significant in a capitalist economy.[13] Money, as has already been mentioned, is one of the most intractable deviations from general equilibrium observed in the real world. Banks and other financial intermediaries are also deviations. Why are there economic institutions that collect money from some agents to lend it to others? It would make greater economic sense for fully informed agents to lend directly to each other in open markets. There are many other economic phenomena that are also poorly accommodated within general equilibrium: involuntary unemployment, frequent emergence of excess supply in some markets, and the regular presence of excess demand in others. Neoclassical theorists are typically interested in squeezing these awkward phenomena into the framework of general equilibrium, since the latter is assumed to be the most valid theoretical representation of the economy. The assumption that information is asymmetrically distributed among economic agents has been a godsend in this regard.[14]

The starting point for the theoretical transformation of economics wrought by asymmetric information can be dated with reasonable accuracy to the publication of Akerlof's (1970) paper on 'lemons' (poor quality secondhand cars). Hard on his heels, Spence (1973, 1974) used information asymmetry to account for practices in the labour market. Stiglitz, on the other hand, deployed the notion to account for a broad variety of economic phenomena, ranging from share-cropping (Stiglitz, 1974), to practices in insurance markets (Rothschild and Stiglitz, 1976), to the absence of efficient equilibria in financial markets (Grossman and Stiglitz, 1980), to self-rationing of lending by financial institutions (Stiglitz and Weiss, 1981), to the role of efficiency wages in labour markets (Shapiro and Stiglitz, 1984), to disparities in economic development (Stiglitz, 1989), to the role of the state in financial markets (Stiglitz, 1994). In 2001, Akerlof, Spence and Stiglitz were jointly honoured with the Nobel prize for their contributions to economic theory.

The core of this approach is simple, and essentially unchanged across the several cases to which it is applied. It is first assumed that the economy comprises rational, self-interested individuals interacting across a range of markets. The question is then posed: how would the results of general equilibrium be altered if these individuals possessed different degrees of information about markets, commodities and productive activities? Information is typically understood as factual knowledge about the possible uses of a commodity, the quality of an investment plan, or the productivity of a worker. It can be passed among individuals, and can also be traded. This view of information ignores the context specific and socially based character of much economic information (the importance of which was made apparent in the discussion of credit-related information in Chapter 4). However, it provides a major advantage for neoclassical economics because it allows for a simple formulation of the notion of information asymmetry: one individual has a dollop of factual information, while another does not. If these two individuals entered into a market-related transaction aiming exclusively at private gain, it is intuitive that the party in possession of the information could use it to obtain unfair advantage. The other party could be fooled (or simply lied to) resulting, for instance, in unfair division of the material outcome of the transaction. Alternatively, the informed party could keep the other in the dark, securing a higher price for the commodity provided.

If, furthermore, economic interaction between individuals was interpreted as a game, strategies could emerge that would systematically disadvantage the uninformed. This could imply that markets were generally not as efficient as stated by general equilibrium and, in limiting cases, that they might collapse, or even fail to emerge. In Akerlof's original 'lemons' essay, for instance, the sellers of secondhand cars are assumed to have more information about the quality of their vehicles than potential buyers. This asymmetry of information leads to inefficient functioning of the secondhand car market. Put simply, buyers do not know the quality of cars offered in the market, and cannot differentiate between good and bad cars. Consequently, they are unlikely to pay the higher price that is required by the sellers of good quality cars. However, potential sellers of good cars would then abstain from trading, leaving secondhand car markets dominated by sellers of 'lemons'. It is even possible that secondhand car markets might collapse altogether. Analogous results can be obtained in analysis of labour markets, where 'good' workers cannot signal to their potential employers their superior productivity compared to 'bad' workers. Similarly, 'good' users of land might not be able to communicate to landlords their superior merits compared to 'bad' potential users. Finally, money owners might not be able successfully to differentiate between 'good' and 'bad' investment propositions, since they are inherently ignorant about the nature of all investment projects.

The implications for neoclassical theory are profound. If markets are not to collapse or operate inefficiently, institutions and norms must emerge that allow for information asymmetry to be ameliorated, or for its problematic effects to be curtailed. By the same token, institutions and customary practices in the capitalist economy could be seen as either facilitating or obstructing information diffusion among economic agents. Indeed, there is no limit to the social and economic phenomena that could be analysed in these terms, given that factual knowledge is typically distributed asymmetrically in capitalist society. Information-theoretic economics contributes to the explanation of the existence of debt contracts in terms of a putative informational asymmetry between a money owner and an investment project holder. It accounts for the presence of agencies that systematically collect information in a variety of markets, as well as accommodating the role of best practice conventions, self-regulation agreements, and credit ratings. It can rationalise the prevalence of behavioural norms among employers and employees in terms of informational asymmetry regarding effort at work and quality of skills. It could also justify state intervention in the economy, if that were to lessen information asymmetries and therefore improve the functioning of markets.

However, information-theoretic economics challenges neither the essential presuppositions of general equilibrium, nor its pre-eminence as a theoretical framework for analysis of capitalism. It still rests on the 'rational individual', whose optimising behaviour, drawing on a calculus of means and ends, is not in doubt. The supposedly optimal properties of markets are not questioned when the ideal assumptions are met. The capitalist economy, with its extensive array of markets, is assumed to be the most efficient way of organising society's economic affairs. The aim of information-theoretic economics is, rather, to accommodate widely observed institutional and customary practices of the capitalist economy within the abstract framework of neoclassicism. At the same time, information-theoretic economics makes market failure and inefficiency the core of its analytical endeavour. Consequently, it does challenge the belief that free markets are automatically and naturally the optimal way of organising economic affairs. Information asymmetries mean that markets also fail, collapse, or are altogether absent. This view has given fresh impetus to attempts to control and direct markets, and has had an impact on macroeconomic policy. Its influence on growth theory has been even more pronounced, allowing for novel analyses of convergence and divergence of growth paths. Not least, information-theoretic microeconomics has offered post-dated support for the work of neoclassical institutionalists, since institutions and social norms can be seen as rational responses to informational asymmetry.

Despite its prominence, information asymmetry offers precarious foundations on which to base the economic analysis of capitalism and its markets. Information and knowledge are complex and multifaceted notions, interwoven with the social position of economic agents. Economic information has social context and sources, and is inherently contained in the actions and assets of agents. It was shown in Chapter 4, for instance, that credit information is created by and incorporated into the institutions of the credit system. Moreover, the content of financial information is altered as the layers of the credit system are traversed, becoming less private and heterogeneous and increasingly social and homogeneous. Thus the social and context-specific character of economic information becomes clear when society is treated as an integral whole. The class character of production relations cannot be detached from the information that is relevant to, say, investment or lending decisions. Much of the content of economic information is lost when the social relations of the economy are not taken explicitly into account. Thus to discuss the economic role of information it is necessary to engage in the political economy of capitalism as an historically specific society, rather than the political economy of who knows more than whom about what.

Contemporary neoclassical economics lays much emphasis on social norms and systematically incorporates them into its theoretical analysis of the capitalist economy. However, neoclassicism does not challenge the methodological individualism at its core, and meticulously avoids class-based notions. The results it obtains are correspondingly partial and narrow. To pursue this point further, the preceding discussion of social norms can be counter-posed to some recent work in economic sociology. The theoretical approaches of 'networks' and 'social capital' demonstrate, even if sometimes negatively, the importance of treating the social as an autonomous and independent object of study.

5.4 The 'embeddedness' of the capitalist economy in social relations

Sociology has long treated the creation and operation of institutions and norms as its own special terrain that sets it apart from economics.[15] Talcott Parsons, pillar of mid-twentieth century sociology, claimed that society is an integral whole comprising a number of relatively autonomous subsystems.[16] The economy is one subsystem, while economics is understood as the discipline that specialises in its analysis. But presumably only sociology can articulate a theoretical view of society as a whole, with economics merely providing an input for it. When it comes to formation of tastes and preferences, for instance, the economist typically assumes them to be given, while the sociologist develops theoretical explanations, drawing on the complex interrelations between upbringing, employment, social position, the dominant system of beliefs, and so on. Parsons' claims grated with the sensibilities of economists accustomed to thinking that sociologists lack the theoretical principles necessary for examining the rational kernel of individual decision-making. Duesenberry (1960, p. 233) famously quipped that '[e]conomics is all about how people make choices; sociology is all about how they don't have any choices to make'.

In recent years the chasm between economics and sociology has narrowed, especially since neoclassical economics has started increasingly to accept that social norms and institutions supplement individually rational decision-making.[17] Nevertheless, for economic sociology, analysis offered by institutionalist and information-theoretic economics continues to underestimate the depth of the social character of norms and institutions. The approach of 'embeddedness', associated primarily with Granovetter, has been very influential in this respect. Granovetter (1985, pp. 484–485) rejects the 'over-socialised' view of economists who incorporate norms and institutions into their analysis, but treat their operations as the mechanical outcome of social compulsion. For Granovetter (1985; see also 1994), economic behaviour ought to be analysed as 'embedded' in networks of 'social relations' – by which are meant personal relations between individuals taken in pairs. The commonest relevant 'dyadic social relation' among economic agents is friendship. Economic decision-making remains rational, but is shaped by the requirements, impositions and possibilities opened by 'social relations' such as friendship. Granovetter (1974) has studied empirically the role of social contacts and friendships in the labour market, and has shown that economic analysis draws deficient conclusions about the practices of hiring and firing because it ignores the role of 'social relations'. Moreover, the activities of formal economic institutions are also 'embedded' in 'social relations' which condition their behaviour. Thus the actions of individuals are constrained by norms, conventions and collective practice, while institutions are also embedded in networks that reflect the perceptions, values and interests of individuals.

In a little more detail, the economic actions of both individuals and public bodies cannot be separated from the social context (understood as interpersonal relations) within which decision-making takes place. Decision-making units (private and public) typically belong to various networks that constitute integral wholes in geographical as well as social space. Networks affect the actions of particular decision-makers, whether by facilitating or constraining them. It is incumbent upon the scientist to specify the nature of each network by ascertaining the dominant actors, the 'thickness' of the relations among actors, and the network's territorial scope. 'Thickness' can be taken to refer to the density of interactions among actors, and has to be adjusted for the strength and cultural content of these interactions. Intuitively, it is one thing for the families of two businesspeople to meet regularly for lunch; quite another for the head of the local council and the chief executive of a construction company to meet regularly at a gentlemen's club. Granovetter (1973) has also differentiated between 'strong' and 'weak' ties among actors. 'Strong' ties keep information within small tightly-knit groups of agents, preventing general diffusion across the network and hence encouraging malpractice. 'Weak' ties, on the other hand, make it easier for groups of actors within the network to be connected to each other, facilitating flows of information among them and resulting in superior performance. Power is also a fundamental aspect of networks, flowing from the exchange relations among network members and facilitating the achievement of results. Coalition building, negotiation and the direct exercise of power through command over resources are integral to network operations.

The approach of 'networks' or 'embeddedness' typically assumes that trust is a vital norm among economic agents, facilitating efficient decision-making. Presumably, trust emerges when agents have regular contacts with each other in networks of social and cultural relations. This approach has resulted in much empirical and theoretical work in the field of finance, since trust is the foundation of credit.[18] A relevant example is Uzzi (1999), who focuses on the 'middle-market' for finance in the USA – that is, firms with up to 500 employees, and the banks that serve them. Uzzi claims that bilateral relationships and networks among participants in this market are important in determining who obtains credit and on what terms. Firms that have a stable relationship with one bank tend to 'embed' their economic transactions within 'social relations'. In contrast, firms that have commercial transactions with several banks usually maintain arms-length relations with their creditors. Embedded ties encourage firms and banks to share information and other resources, while arms-length ties facilitate access to public information regarding the terms of credit. Thus when firms operate within networks that can synthesise the benefits of different types of ties, they can obtain credit on better terms. 'Embeddedness' can also encourage firms to devote extra effort to production, thus raising individual and social welfare.

Uzzi's work is relevant for our purposes because it examines financial relations on sociological grounds but without demonstrating any tension with the core analytical premise of neoclassicism, that is, individual maximising behaviour. This holds generally for network analysis, which offers a sociology of finance that does not directly challenge the assumptions of rationality characteristic of the economics of finance. The validity of economic rationality is accepted, but also conditioned by specifying the social context within decisions are made. 'Network' theory has no fundamental quarrel with the economics of neoclassicism, which it accepts as standard economics.[19] However, if society is to be treated as an entity that provides a context for market activities, economic analysis must also adopt different principles and methods to those of neoclassicism. The relations between borrower and lender, for example, are more fully analysed on the basis of the circuit of capital, the motivations and dynamics of which are given independently of individuals. Thus relations of power, trust, morality, information collection and fraud between borrower and lender are placed directly within the appropriate social (class) context.

Focusing on the class structure of society need not lead to what Granovetter (1985) has termed 'over-socialised' analysis, i.e. explaining the behaviour of agents as a result of social compulsion. Rather, the 'dyadic' relations of both borrowers and lenders acquire further relevant content in view of the class relations of the economy. The underlying social relations of who owns resources, who works for whom, and who has property rights over the finished product are directly relevant to the 'dyadic' relations identified by network theory. The manager of a large car-manufacturing company and the owner of a small subcontracting firm, for instance, might approach the market as plain trading agents, and they might even be personal friends or acquaintances. However, they also have very different economic and social power, access to information, and ability to confront unforeseen events in the market – all of which are likely systematically to affect their 'dyadic' friendship. Similarly, an individual worker enters the labour market as an independent seller of the capacity to work, and might even be on friendly terms with the individuals who make decisions on hiring and firing. But he or she also has a deficit of power and authority compared to an individual employer, which is again likely systematically to affect 'dyadic' relationships. Finally, the professional lender of money has a different class position and outlook compared to an industrial capitalist. Relations of trust, power and honesty among them derive partly from the different ways in which they secure return of their capital and accrual of profits (as was shown in detail in Chapter 4). To establish the sources of these systematic differences, however, it is necessary to examine the political economy of capitalist production. It is not enough to show that social relations imply different patterns of behaviour to those postulated by neoclassicism, thus super-adding the social onto neoclassical analysis. The point is to adopt altogether different economics.

5.5 'Social capital' and the capitalist economy

The concept of 'social capital' has also risen meteorically to prominence in recent years, offering to social theorists a tidy way of capturing the influence of social relations on the actions of economic agents.[20] In its current form, 'social capital', is associated with the work of Coleman, who believes that rational choice is a fundamental requirement of sociological analysis (Coleman, 1994).[21] For Coleman (1990, p. 302; see also 1988 and 1993), 'social capital' refers to 'social–structural' resources that are inherent to society and operate as capital for the individual in the sense that they can facilitate individual rational action. Moreover, social capital is a public good, and can also shape the actions of public actors. The social–structural resources that constitute social capital usually amount to 'internalised norms' that help individuals act in accordance with collective interests, forming the basis of collective action (Leonardi, 1995). Typical internalised norms are trust and mutual confidence among economic agents (private and public). A society with a substantial stock of 'social capital' is presumable permeated by a climate of trust, confidence, reliability, and moral obligation among its members.[22] Consequently, individuals can take economic decisions that chime with the collective interest. In a well-known study, Putnam (1993) used the approach of social capital to account for differences in the growth performance between northern and southern Italy. Apparently, northern Italy possesses greater volumes of social capital embodied in clubs, associations and other social institutions, which explain its superior economic performance compared to the individualistic and family-dominated south.[23] In similarly influential work, Putnam (1995a, 1995b) argued that social capital is declining in the USA. Americans have lost civic contact because they participate less in associations such as bowling clubs and watch more television.

Putnam (1993, p. 172) assumes reciprocity to be important for the existence and formation of social capital.[24] He contrasts balanced to generalised reciprocity, the former referring to an immediate exchange of *quid pro quo* and the latter to the practice of granting something now and creating a moral obligation to repay later. Generalised reciprocity across society is evidently a norm, an internalised practice of behaviour that cannot be fully captured by narrow commercial interactions. When generalised reciprocity is abundant, social capital is large and there are good prospects for individual action to lead to public benefits. Moral hazard, opportunism, dishonesty and other problematic practices are correspondingly limited. Thus, the social and political institutions of a country are fundamental to establishing generalised reciprocity as well as to increasing or decreasing it. More specifically, social capital appears to be created out of synergies between the economy, the state and various organisations that belong to 'civil society' (i.e. organisations independent of the formal mechanisms of the state). However, the quantity and quality of social capital also depend on the nature of the 'state' and of civil society, particularly on whether the former is centralised or decentralised and the latter strong or weak. It is even possible that 'bad' social capital could prevail in a country – that is, there might be dense networks between social actors, creating an environment of favouritism, cronyism and corruption that goes against the collective good.

The ground here is treacherous. On the one hand, the advocates of social capital are defending the importance of the social and the non-economic in economic life. Norms, collective action and the common good are assumed to be constitutive factors of economic life. Moreover, it is claimed that neoclassical economics insufficiently examines the social character of the institutions that establish trust within markets. The door is opened, therefore, to other social sciences to make a strong input in economic theory and policy-making. On the other hand, social capital derives from a conceptual framework that fully accepts the validity of rational choice, especially in analysis that is considered strictly 'economic'. The methodological foundations of neoclassical economics are deemed to be valid but partial in so far as they leave out of account the influence of social factors on economic phenomena. Consequently, social capital reconstructs the economic effect of norms, institutions and collective action, but in terms deriving from the choices and predilections of the 'rational' agent. Despite the emphasis laid on all things social, the theory does not consider the 'social' to be a qualitatively distinct aspect of society, an object of study that requires its own analytical and methodological principles separate from the 'private'.

Precisely because of the individualist approach adopted with respect to the 'social', the term 'capital' is rendered devoid of meaning. For neoclassical economics, capital can mean any set of relations or any set of assets that simply reproduces itself. An individual can have 'physical' capital, meaning property in durable goods or in means of production; 'human' capital, meaning mostly education and training, 'political' capital, meaning contacts and an inside track in political decision-making, 'cultural' capital, meaning familiarity and skill at complying with cultural norms, and so on and so forth. By the same token, social capital is understood as being any set of social relations outside the economy that can sustain and reproduce itself. A country's social capital exists in its sports associations, community self-help schemes, Rotary Clubs, informal neighbourhood arrangements for punishing wrongdoing, communal sanctions for dishonesty and fraud, the spirit of solidarity and social belonging, and so on. In this light, social capital could mean almost any social relation actually observed, as Fine (2001, Ch. 7) has pointed out. But then it means nothing.

To interpret the cultural, educational, familial, hierarchical and other relations of capitalist reproduction as so much capital at society's disposal is to create a false analogy with capital at the disposal of the individual. While capital is certainly a set of social relations, some of which are economic and some non-economic, not everything is capital. There is an irreducible economic content to capital, i.e. a permanent motion in search of profit that gives rise to distinct flows and stocks. The cultural, institutional, legal, and ideological relations that permeate capitalist society might derive their characteristic features from capital, but are also separate from it. Similarly, economic and non-economic relations within the family are important for the functioning of capital, but do not belong to it. When social relations are indiscriminately collapsed into 'capital', the result is that nothing is capital, especially not capital as a set of exploitative and authoritarian relations. Thus despite the best intentions of many of its advocates, social capital often ends up supplementing contemporary neoclassical economics – as can be seen from the influence of social capital on the intellectual and policy output of international economic organisations in recent years.

Development theory and policy during the last two decades has been dominated by the so-called Washington Consensus, which demanded macroeconomic stability, free markets domestically, and openness to international trade and finance.[25] Its main purveyors to developing countries have been the International Monetary Fund and the World Bank. Unfortunately, the results from policies inspired by the Washington Consensus have been very poor, while financial and economic crises have become commonplace. Partly as a reaction to policy failures an alternative approach began to take shape in the second half of the 1990s, often called the post-Washington Consensus. This alternative relies heavily on the work of Stiglitz, and accepts that asymmetric information among economic agents leads to market failure. Markets are seen as the only realistic and efficient way of delivering growth, but state intervention is also necessary to sustain, supplement and create markets. For the post-Washington Consensus, state intervention should facilitate market operations by dealing with market imperfections and creating markets. This was the message that Stiglitz (1998a, 1998b) disseminated widely as chief economist of the World Bank for a brief period in the late 1990s. Thus the post-Washington Consensus provided a congenial environment for a flowering of social capital. For what can be a greater market imperfection than different volumes of social capital available to different societies? Social capital has consequently become a point of convergence between economists and other social scientists within international economic institutions (Fine, 2001, Ch. 9). Suppose, for instance, that Indonesia and South Korea were to present systematic differences in their growth performance over a period of time, despite broad similarities in macroeconomic policy. These could be plausibly adduced to differences in the volumes (and quality) of the social capital available to the two countries. If plain economics of development (i.e. the Washington Consensus) is unable to account for growth divergences, things could perhaps improve if the sociology of development (i.e. social capital) was also taken into account.

With this in mind, and given the diffuse and arbitrary nature of social capital, there is no limit to the empirical research that could be undertaken to specify exactly how social capital differs between countries. Networks among local businesspeople could be described, links between the local and the national state examined, cultural and ethnic specificities identified – the list of factors could be extended at will, the researcher assigning to them whatever significance he or she chose. Moreover, broad policy prescriptions could also be made, if a country's social capital was deemed deficient. These would typically take the form of the unarguable requirement to create an environment of trust, confidence and probity sustained by social norms as well as formal institutions. As a result, social capital has broadened the scope of the policy prescriptions of the international organisations: development is no longer only a matter of changing economic relations, but also of altering the non-economic norms and institutions surrounding the economy.[26]

For those who want to criticise the Washington Consensus without directly taking issue with the class character of the capitalist economy, social capital has evident appeal. It is supposed to help markets work better, despite not being economic in character; it offers grounds for state intervention, but not of a kind that might discomfit participants and agents in capitalist markets; it avoids focusing on price controls and the regulation of private capitalist activities. Policies to improve social capital, however specified, could be interpreted as eliminating or ameliorating information asymmetries, and thus being conducive to the more efficient operation of markets. Social capital is tailor-made for critics of capitalism who accept its fundamental efficiency but are troubled by its 'imperfections'. Thus the international organisations are able to advocate fundamentally conservative economic policies that promote capitalism while shrouding them in talk about the social foundations of markets and their inadequacies. The freeing of markets and the unfettered operation of private capital can be demanded from impoverished countries, while concern is expressed about their lack of social capital to make markets work efficiently.[27]

To recap, analysis of social norms and relations in the capitalist economy is heavily one-sided when it ignores capital as a set of specific social and economic relations. Capital has class foundations deriving from access to and control over resources. It is also exploitative and motivated fully by money profit. For the character of capital to emerge clearly, society has to be considered as an integral whole. However, it is a fallacy indiscriminately to include all kinds of social relations into capital. Trust, honesty, confidence, integrity, reliability and the like are not capital, and they might be generated in contexts that have nothing to do with the economy. Yet they are also capable of acquiring a specific character that derives from capital and pivots on money-making. The result of collapsing capitalist social relations into social capital is to obscure the character of these relations, rather than broaden the analysis of the economy.

6 The emergence and functioning of money

Money's emergence and functioning are phenomena that relate uniquely to the interaction of the economic with the non-economic in society. The Marxist treatment of the 'riddle' of money in Chapter 3 specified the economic relations and social norms that sustain the evolution of the form of value from the accidental to the money form. A process was outlined through which money comes to possess a monopoly of buying power over other commodities, and hence also to play a pervasive and contradictory social role. The present chapter discusses other theoretical treatments of money's logical and historical origin. These are divided into two approaches, each having far-reaching implications for the analysis of monetary phenomena and non-economic relations in capitalist society. The first approach, typical of neoclassical economics, analyses the emergence of money as a process endogenous to markets, and focuses especially on money's function as means of exchange. In brief, it is postulated that money emerges in the course of market trading as the function of means of exchange accrues spontaneously to a single commodity. The second approach accounts for the emergence of money by relying on factors outside the market, i.e. by denying that markets spontaneously give rise to money. The function of money most often stressed in this connection is unit of account, while the preferred non-market factor is usually state authority. This approach tends to be favoured by anthropologists and sociologists, but is also strongly represented within economics. Both approaches are selectively discussed below and are contrasted with the treatment of money in Chapter 3.[1]

The chapter concludes by considering some recent sociological research on the multiple social functioning of money.[2] This work draws on the fragmented and varied functioning of money in capitalist society – means of exchange, means of hoarding, representative of wealth, symbol of iniquity, instrument of power, token of social bonding, and so on. It is then claimed that money lacks a unitary character, and indeed that capitalist society possesses several qualitatively different 'monies'. Without ignoring the insights offered by this work, it is argued that money's ability to function as medium, symbol and representative of a broad spectrum of social relations derives precisely from its unitary character. Money is able to bear, reflect, and symbolise widely different social relations in capitalist society because it has a bland and uniform character as the monopolist of buying ability.

6.1 Money as means of exchange

6.1.1 Classical and neoclassical analysis of money's emergence

The view that money emerges spontaneously as a means of exchange has a natural affinity with the belief that trade is timeless and universal. Adam Smith (1776, p. 17) thought that 'to truck, barter, and exchange one thing for another' is a fundamental disposition distinguishing human beings from animals. The hypothesis underlying Smith's analysis of market trading is that the path of development of humanity matches the evolution of commerce from barter to capitalist monetary exchange. Economic progress ('the wealth of nations') occurs because the evolution of exchange promotes the division of labour, and hence increases the productivity of labour. Smith's approach was, by and large, taken for granted by classical political economy – savages engage in direct exchange of goods in the primeval forest, but civilised human beings sell commodities for money. For progress to take place trading has to evolve from barter to monetary exchange, and for that a means of exchange has to emerge. The emergence of money appears to be a decisive step that transforms barter into monetary exchange, and encourages growth of the productivity of labour.

However, the classical economists did not offer a logical account of the process and mechanisms through which barter endogenously induces the emergence of money as means of exchange. Smith (1776, Vol. I, Ch. V), for instance, is content to list the evident problems confronting anyone engaged in barter, and subsequently to state that a generally accepted means of exchange would solve these problems at a stroke. Specifically, commodities are perishable, imperfectly divisible, heterogeneous, and available at inconvenient times. Thus traders engaging in direct exchange are not generally able to match accurately the commodity they hold with the commodity they desire, leading to continuous breakdown of trade. Smith then claims that 'prudent' traders would carry a commodity accepted by everyone that would function as means of exchange, i.e. as money.[3] This claim seems plausible, but it does not actually prove that money necessarily emerges in exchange. It is evident that commerce which deployed money as a means of exchange would be free of the problems of barter. Yet the problems of barter in and of themselves reveal nothing about the endogenous mechanisms that give rise to a commonly accepted means of exchange. To put it differently, if a generally accepted commodity was in existence, market participants would accept it in exchange for their commodities. They would then use it to obtain the commodities they actually desired for consumption, instead of seeking to exchange their commodities directly with those they desired. But how and why does one commodity become generally acceptable as a result of the problems of barter? On what grounds can rational traders assume that others would generally accept a given commodity, and so decide to hold it even though they would not wish to consume it themselves? The classical economists did not provide an answer to this logical conundrum.

Neoclassical economics considered afresh the problem of money's existence in commodity markets. The founding fathers of neoclassicism – Jevons, Walras, and Menger – broadly accepted the classical view that commodity exchange is a timeless and intrinsic aspect of human society. Exchange, moreover, is assumed originally to take the form of barter. For barter to proceed smoothly, however, there must exist a 'double coincidence of want' among participants (Jevons, 1875). Nevertheless, Jevons did not provide an answer for the problem of the endogenous transformation of barter into monetary exchange. Walras (1926, p. 189; see also Ch. 29) on the other hand, in the course of developing the mathematical foundations of general equilibrium analysis, explicitly postulated the presence of money as unit of account and means of exchange. But money for Walras is an abstract theoretical entity, the functions of which have no concrete dimension. Money appears in his analysis as the medium that abstractly renders commodities into commensurate magnitudes, i.e. it is the 'numeraire' that assigns prices to commodities. Walras' analysis implicitly assumes that market participants have perfect information and that there are no transactions costs. After equilibrium prices are worked out to the satisfaction of participants through the mediation of an imaginary 'auctioneer', all trading takes place at once. It follows that there is no need for money concretely to *act* as means of exchange: all trade is effectively barter.

The most powerful neoclassical answer for the question of money's emergence came from the Austrian current, above all, Menger (1871, 1892). Until fairly recently, the Austrian approach to money's emergence lacked influence among general equilibrium theorists, partly because the Austrian School and general equilibrium have significant differences despite their common neoclassical pedigree.[4] In particular, Austrians theorists do not accept the concept of equilibrium, and have a characteristic view of the economic individual as source of radical dynamic change in economic life, instead of simply as rational utility maximiser. Austrian theorists also reject the mathematical accoutrements of Walrasian modelling. The absence of mathematics probably contributed to a lack of appreciation of the sophistication and subtlety of Menger's analysis of money among contemporary general equilibrium theorists. However, things have changed drastically since the 1980s, especially since the widespread adoption of game-theoretic techniques by economic theorists. The main elements of Menger's analysis have now been introduced into technical general equilibrium modelling. Yet, mathematical accomplishment has wrought no improvement to the conceptual content of Menger's argument.

Menger's explanation of the origin of money is properly understood in the context of the *Methodenstreit*, a fierce methodological debate that took place in the Germanic world at the end of the nineteenth century and the beginning of the twentieth. On one side stood the Historical School (Schumpeter, 1954, pp. 807–824) denying the possibility of theoretical thought in social science and especially in economics. For the Historical School, money was associated with non-market processes such as nation-building, and was seen as an abstract claim upon goods. On the other side stood the Austrian neoclassicals, led by Menger, who were uncompromising on the need for abstract theoretical analysis of economic processes, based on the formal rationality of absolute subjectivism.[5] For the Austrians, money had to be shown to emerge through endogenous market processes and rational individual decisions, rather than through arbitrary intervention by the state, or other non-market factors. It also seemed to Menger (1892) that a theoretical demonstration of money's emergence had to focus exclusively on money's function as means of exchange. His aim was to show that a barter economy spontaneously becomes a monetary economy by creating a universally accepted means of exchange through market processes alone. Thus Menger's theoretical demonstration of money emergence out of market processes bears the hallmarks of his exclusive focus on money as means of exchange.[6]

To achieve his aim, Menger (1871, p. 248; 1892, p. 243) introduced the concept of 'saleableness' or 'marketability' of commodities. Commodities are economic goods intended for sale, but afford to their owners different degrees of facility in obtaining the requisite economic price.[7] This facility is defined by Menger as the marketability of commodities, and depends on the volume and intensity of demand, on the geographical spread of the market, and on the duration of demand (Menger, 1871, pp. 241–247; 1892, pp. 243–245). For Menger, commodities are differentiated among themselves prior to exchange, as some are more marketable than others. Marketability is a property that commodities have independently of their physical properties, and serves as a foundation of Menger's demonstration of money's emergence. Yet marketability is a very peculiar property. There is no doubt that commodities have several properties that belong to them intrinsically and flow from their ability to satisfy human needs and desires. These properties exist independently of the process of commodity exchange – knives cut and needles sew, whether they are exchanged or not. In contrast, Menger's property of marketability is clearly social and not physical, since it is attached to things because they are bought and sold in the market. But then it follows that economic theory should also demonstrate the social processes through which things (tangible or not) come to acquire this property in the market. Social conditions ought to be specified under which things become commodities, and might then acquire marketability. Menger offers no such discussion. He simply lists the factors on which the strength of marketability depends, such as volume and intensity of demand for the commodity, and geographical spread of the market. Operating within the bounds of Austrian individualism, Menger assumes that commodities already possess the property of marketability when they are brought to market.

Given the assumption of differential marketability among commodities, it is reasonably straightforward to demonstrate the emergence of money, provided one more critical assumption is made. Specifically, a mechanism must be postulated through which the marketability of commodities becomes recognised by market participants. This is a necessary step, since marketability is not a physical property of commodities and is therefore neither immediately acknowledged nor intuitively understood by exchange participants. Menger proposes the following mechanism, the essentials of which have become standard fare for Austrian economic analysis. He postulates the existence of a small number of gifted economising individuals, who realise that the high marketability of a given commodity can rebound in their favour, even though they might not want directly to consume it (Menger, 1871, pp. 210–261; 1892, pp. 248–249). How the realisation comes to them is left unexplained – it occurs like a shaft of light from heaven. However, the benefit that accrues to those who have this insight is clear: a commodity that is more marketable than the one actually held allows for easier acquisition of the desired object of eventual consumption through further exchanges. The difficulties of barter can be overcome because the highly marketable commodity can act as means of exchange. For Menger, the knowledge afforded to the few by their miraculous insight subsequently spreads to the many, as all repeatedly enter the market and undertake exchanges. Emulation of others as well as the habits associated with exchange create a social custom out of seeking more marketable commodities, even though the latter might not be wanted for consumption. The social conditions within which this vital social custom emerges are not specified by Menger, but it is clear that the social custom is self-reinforcing since the more likely it is that others would accept a commodity the more strongly it would then be demanded in exchange, and the stronger its marketability would become (White, 1984, p. 703). Eventually one commodity emerges as the most marketable of all, and functions as a universally accepted means of exchange.

To recap, Menger derives money out of market processes as the means of exchange that overcomes the problems of barter. He relies on absolute individualism – that is, on the benefits that accrue to individual traders and guide their concomitant actions. To establish the putative benefits and corresponding actions Menger makes two vital assumptions, both of which have social determinants that are not explicitly discussed. First, commodities are assumed to have the property of marketability, and to a different degree from each other. Second, the knowledge of marketability emerges among a few traders and then spreads to the others in the form of social custom deriving from repeated market practice. Menger's analysis is the foundation of contemporary neoclassical demonstrations of money's emergence, discussed briefly below.

6.1.2 General equilibrium analysis of money's origin

General equilibrium analysis, in its pure form that assumes full information, no transactions costs and a full range of contingent markets, leaves no room for a commodity that is held universally and facilitates the acts of exchange without being directly consumed. General equilibrium is fundamentally a theory of barter and not of a monetary economy.[8] This is deeply unsatisfactory for a theory that purports to analyse capitalism, the most thoroughly monetary economy in history. More specifically, general equilibrium analysis finds it difficult to assign to money a special role commensurate with its evident peculiarity as a commodity. The unusual role of money in the economy was formulated by Clower as: '*Money buys goods and goods buy money; but goods do not buy goods*' (1967, p. 5; emphasis in original). This statement implies that money stands apart from other commodities in a monetary economy, i.e. that there is a profound asymmetry between money on one side and all other commodities on the other. Clower did not prove this proposition, but put it forth as a conjecture (an aphorism) that has to be imposed on theoretical modelling if general equilibrium is to be able to incorporate money.

If Clower's conjecture were tacitly accepted, money could be introduced into general equilibrium models in a variety of ways connected with its function as means of exchange.[9] Clower (1967), for instance, proposed 'cash-in-hand' models by arbitrarily making the sum total of gross purchases in an economy equal to the amount of money available at the start of trading. Hahn (1971, 1973) suggested that transactions costs and sequential trading should be introduced into economic analysis, with the result that money could then act as a means of transferring purchasing power from one period to the next. Niehans (1969, 1978) proposed that money acts as a means of exchange that reduces the costs of multilateral trading among commodity owners.[10] There is, however, a fundamental issue that these abstract models leave unanswered, especially in view of general equilibrium's claim to be a theory of the economic relations of market economies. If a generally acceptable means of exchange were available, it is clear that market traders would benefit from using it instead of exchanging their goods directly. But how does a means of exchange emerge endogenously in a market economy? And what is its relation to Clower's conjecture?

In recent years, general equilibrium theorists have begun to confront this issue directly. Jones (1976) made an early contribution, and further developments have been added by Iwai (1988) and Oh (1989). Perhaps the most influential writings in the field, however, are those by Kiyotaki and Wright (1989, 1991). In all these models, analysis focuses on money's function as means of exchange and draws explicitly on Menger. However, in conceptual terms the recent work does not represent progress for the neoclassical approach. Commodities are assumed to differ in terms of marketability, a concept that is borrowed directly from Menger, but without even his theoretical substantiation. Market agents are supposed to take marketability into account when they devise their trading strategies. High marketability benefits traders, since it allows them more cheaply and easily to acquire the desired object of their consumption. Suppose now that a generally held social belief (a social custom) existed that one commodity possessed superior marketability. It would follow that traders would begin to accept this commodity, even though they might not want to consume it. Evidently, the more they accepted it the stronger would be the commodity's marketability, leading to further strengthening of its acceptability. In short, a social belief in the 'moneyness' of a commodity, presumed to hold because of unexplained social custom, would become validated as the commodity was actually used as money. Thus the conceptual core of the contemporary mainstream analysis of money's emergence derives wholesale from Menger. However, while Menger discusses marketability and social custom extensively (even if problematically), contemporary theory exhausts its rigour in game-theoretic formalisations. Social custom, in particular, operates as a black box that allows the theoretical argument to proceed.

Finally, the recent models openly admit that Clower's conjecture is not fully answered (Kiyotaki and Wright, 1989, p. 945). Even if a generally accepted means of exchange had emerged along lines postulated by contemporary general equilibrium theorists, it would not be clear why 'goods would not buy goods'. In these models, should commodity owners meet under a 'double coincidence of wants', money would be bypassed and direct exchange would occur. Thus the underlying assumption remains that a commodity is brought to market with the aim of obtaining another commodity. If its owner happened to come across another who held 'money' the commodity would be exchanged for money, but if the owner came across another who held the required object of consumption the resultant transaction would be direct (and not monetary) exchange of commodities. Thus the type of economy postulated in the models is still inherently different from a monetary economy, for the key feature of the latter is that commodity owners bring their goods to market with the express purpose of selling them for money (see Chapter 3).

6.2 Money as unit of account

The view that money emerges as an abstract unit of account has a long pedigree in economic theory. It gave rise to the mercantilist myth of the *macoute*, an imaginary gold bar that was presumably used by the natives of West Africa to measure the value of commodities exchanged, but was never deployed as means of exchange (this function was supposedly fulfilled by cowries, slaves and other money commodities). A clear early formulation of money as unit of account was given by Sir James Steuart, a contemporary of Adam Smith. Steuart (1767, Vol. II, Bk III, Ch. 1, 2) differentiates between 'money of account' and 'material money'. Money of account is an arbitrary invention, a scale devised to measure values and set prices of 'things vendible' (Steuart, 1767, Vol. II, p. 270). This money is entirely abstract, an ideal construct of the mind, such as the legendary *macoute*. It establishes abstract accounting prices in the same way that other abstract magnitudes, such as metres and kilograms, establish abstract lengths and weights.[11] The money of account, in other words, is a pure numeraire that creates an abstract accounting system of prices. 'Material money', on the other hand, is money that is in actual use. For Steuart (1767, Vol. II, p. 279), material money is derived purely as a physical approximation of the ideal unit of account. Evidently, material money need not have the same nomenclature as money of account, or even be made of the same substance as the ideal money of account. Being an approximation of the money of account, however, it establishes actual prices that can never fully coincide with abstract prices. The analogy with physical measurement is very close, since an abstract length is merely approximated by the application of a tape measure. Thus for Steuart money is a product of social convention in two separate ways. First, it is an ideal and arbitrary construct that renders commodities commensurate by measuring their values and establishing prices. Second, it is a practical means of exchange that circulates commodities by approximating their abstract prices as closely as possible and then realising them through exchange.

The notion that money originally emerged as an abstract unit of account has persisted doggedly in economics and social science more generally. It appears to offer far broader scope that Menger's austere formulation of the means of exchange arising out of market processes. It also seems to allow for fuller discussion of social conventions implicated in the emergence of money, not least by bringing in the state. For what could be a better authority than the state to establish the ideal scale of accounting units used by the whole of society? 'Chartalism' or 'nominalism', though not directly descending from Steuart, postulates that money is an arbitrary creation of the state that provides a numerical form to purchasing power, a material claim on wealth. The chartalist view, the main rival of Menger in the German–Austrian debates, received its sharpest expression in the work of Knapp (1905), for whom 'Money is a creature of law' (Knupp, 1905, p. 1). Chartalism became influential in the Anglo-Saxon world because Knapp's work impressed Keynes. The issue of money's emergence was put in the following terms by Keynes (1930, p. 3):

> Money of Account, namely that in which Debts and Prices and General Purchasing Power are expressed, is the primary concept of a theory of money. A Money-of-Account comes along with Debts, which are contracts for deferred payment, and Price lists, which are offers of contracts for sale and purchase. Such Debts and Price lists, whether they are recorded by word of mouth or by book entry on baked bricks or paper documents, can only be expressed in terms of a Money-of-Account.

The 'baked bricks' in Keynes' pithy paragraph are a reference to ancient Summerian and Babylonian cuneiform tablets. In those tablets, several objects are rendered commensurate (and could be added up) by being expressed as equivalent to other objects, typically barley and silver. Reference to the tablets is vital to Keynes' argument, because it lends a historical air to the claim that money emerges as a unit of account unrelated to means of exchange. The point is important. The view that money emerges as a unit of account would gain in kudos if it could be demonstrated historically that money has been deployed as unit of account without ever having been a means of exchange. This is not the same as showing that in some society or community the unit of account is unrelated to the means of exchange in use. Indeed, it is a fairly common occurrence for the two functions to be performed simultaneously by different forms of money – for instance, prices to be accounted in dollars but commodities to be bought with roubles. Rather, what is necessary is historically to pinpoint money operating purely as an abstract unit of account and having no connection with means of exchange. Note that for the Summerians and Babylonians of Keynes' text, it is not evident that the function of barley and silver as units of account was unrelated to their function as means of exchange. On the contrary, it is possible that they functioned as units of account because they were also means of exchange.[12]

The theoretical importance of this point is best appreciated in the context of anthropological work critical of the neoclassical association of money with barter. Anthropology often rejects the neoclassical view of direct exchange as an abstract schema that is unrelated to the realities of early communities, and seeks broader explanations of money's origin detaching it from market processes. In other words, because the neoclassical derivation of money is based on the assumption of barter, which is rightly seen as a caricature of direct exchange, the conclusion is drawn that social theory should abandon altogether the effort to relate the origin of money to trade.[13] This typically means that money is associated with the function of unit of account. Einzig (1949, p. 367), for instance, after a sophisticated discussion of barter, states that:

> In a large number of instances the units serving as a standard of value could not possibly have been used as media of exchange, for the simple reason that they were merely ideal units without any concrete existence. Admittedly it is possible that in the remote past those abstract units were represented by concrete objects serving as media of exchange. It is, to say the least, conceivable that some units of account at any rate were purely imaginary at the outset.

Only to continue:

> What seems much more likely is that many objects with real existence were chosen as units of account to facilitate barter, not because they had acted as media of exchange or even as media of barter, but for non-commercial reasons ... Human nature being what it is, there must always have been a natural desire to compare the size of the wealth of one chief against that of another chief.

However, there are at least three reasons why seeking the origin of money outside the process of commodity exchange is problematic for theory. The first reason is that the view that money was originally a purely abstract unit of account requires fuller empirical substantiation. Specifically, it must be firmly shown that units of account have existed that were not also, or originally, functioning means of exchange. It is unsatisfactory to reject the mythical schema of barter as the source of money only to replace it with nebulous tales of units of account unconnected to actual means of exchange. The typical unit of account in history is also (or has been) a means of exchange.[14] The second reason is that, if the unit of account for prices is established outside the processes of commodity exchange, its value is likely to be detached from the values of commodities. The value of money would then appear to derive from decisions of the state, or from legal and social conventions. It follows that money's value would not be a proper subject for theoretical economic examination, since it would not result from the interaction of economic and non-economic forces that typically determine the value of other commodities. By the same token, theoretical analysis of the relationship between the value of money and the prices of commodities would be significantly hampered. However, a theory of money's origin that does not facilitate analysis of the two-way interaction between money and commodity prices is seriously deficient.[15]

The third reason is that, if the unit of account is seen to emerge outside exchange, commercial transactions are unlikely to provide the original terrain for commensuration of disparate things. Theory would then be forced to seek other social mechanisms to act as processes of commensuration thus assigning the form of value to disparate things. However, other social mechanisms do not have the same coherence and plausibility as commerce in this respect. Codere (1968), for instance, puts forth a complex anthropological derivation of money identifying it with measurement while separating it from market functioning. She stresses the symbolic role of money in society, and draws an analogy between money and language. Money is posited as a symbolic order that allows social communication, relating things to each other and providing order to the diverse aspects of social life. But Codere does not specify how the common symbolic order was devised or first emerged. A more influential attempt to identify the required, non-market, processes of commensuration can be found in Grierson's (1977) numismatic work. For Grierson, money emerges as a unit of account, but not out of market trading for the following two reasons. First, there are no natural units of commodity value (unlike units of length or size for natural objects), and second, commodities are extremely varied physically. Thus, Grierson suggests that money emerged in the practice of *wergeld*, that is, payment of compensation for social and individual wrongs.[16] Drawing on the tribal laws of Anglo-Saxons, Celts and others, Grierson claims that money emerged as public assemblies commensurated injuries against one's person and determined compensations. The principles employed were those of assuaging anger and making good the loss of reputation (Grierson, 1977, pp. 20–21). This social procedure was presumably free of the logical difficulties of commensurating disparate commodities in the market. From such origins the use of money spread to other practices, such as bridewealth, and hence to commodity exchange. However, it is hardly a persuasive argument that 'injuries' are less varied than 'commodities', especially for ancient communities in which the variety of commodities used could not have remotely approached the present. Grierson's own list of 'injuries' includes different types of murder, rapes, several instances of personal insult, and so on.

Further implications of considering money as originally a unit of account can be seen in relation to post-Keynesian economics.[17] The focus of post-Keynesianism has been on the deficiencies of the neoclassical analysis of time and uncertainty. For Davidson (1972, 1989, 1990), one of the prime exponents of post-Keynesianism, uncertainty is far deeper than mere risk, and expresses the essential impossibility of knowing the future. Time, moreover, is irreversible, and decisions taken now weigh upon actions that shall be taken in the future. It is then postulated that, to confront these fundamental realities of the human condition, society has devised money and money contracts (Dow, 1984). Agents form expectations about the future, and use both money contracts and money in order to bridge decisions taken now with decisions taken in the future. This appears to be a far deeper and more complex role for money than as a mere means of exchange.[18] It also has no truck with the notion that money originates in direct exchange or barter. Consequently, the post-Keynesian view chimes well with anthropological work that consciously detaches money from the market, associating it with broader social processes.[19] The post-Keynesian approach also allows for money to be associated with the prior emergence of credit – that is, it makes credit relations, with their attendant social baggage of trust, obligation and reputation, the foundation of money. It is assumed that the original economic relations between transacting parties are based on 'buy now – settle later', rather than the immediate exchange of equivalents.[20] Money is the unit of account that makes possible the practice of 'buy now – settle later', as well as dealing with residual balances among parties, once mutual obligations have been cancelled out. Thus money in general appears to be credit-money – that is, a balance sheet entry that allows transactions to proceed (Wray, 1990, p. 13).

The attractiveness of the post-Keynesian approach is increased in no small measure because the vast bulk of modern capitalist money is bank-created credit-money. Post-Keynesian macroeconomic analysis of capitalism relies heavily on the spontaneous creation of credit money as banks make loans to capitalists, i.e. on the 'endogeneity' of credit-money.[21] Thus from the claim that the dominant money of advanced capitalism is 'endogenous' credit money, post-Keynesians move to assert that all money is rooted in credit relations. This aspect of money is assumed to fit with humanity's strivings to surmount uncertainty and irreversible time. In short, while general equilibrium theorists treat money as a plain and simple means of exchange, post-Keynesians turn it into the cornerstone of all analysis of society. However, as already mentioned, there is no clear evidence of a unit of account having existed prior to and independently of the function of means of exchange. There is even less evidence that credit and debit relations expressed in entirely abstract units of account ever occurred spontaneously within historical societies. There is, in this respect, a curious analogy between general equilibrium and post-Keynesianism. Neoclassicals, keen to demonstrate the emergence of money as means of exchange out of the timeless processes of the market, postulate a highly abstract state of barter. Post-Keynesians, keen to show the emergence of money as a unit of account out of processes broader than market exchange, postulate the equally abstract existence of units of account, credits and debits.

Recapping, the theoretical attempts to associate money's origin with either means of exchange or a unit of account stand in sharp contrast with the Marxist discussion of the issue in Chapter 3. Both single out one of money's functions, trying to show that it constitutes the original and defining aspect of money, and both suffer as a result. The neoclassical approach, especially Menger's analysis, has logical coherence but limited purchase on money's broader social and economic functions, as well as on the social custom that sustains money's emergence. Moreover, it rests on an ahistorical and abstract view of barter as the original process out of which money emerged. The alternative approach acknowledges money's broader social and economic functions, but lacks the logical coherence of the neoclassical demonstration of money's emergence. In addition, it rests on the hypothetical existence of money as an abstract unit of account, perhaps related to credit processes among economic agents. In contrast, the analysis of money's emergence put forth in Chapter 3, postulates that money emerges out of processes of direct exchange, without also assuming the existence of an abstract state of barter in the deep recesses of human history. Moreover, money is logically derived as the universal equivalent, i.e. the monopolist of buying ability. Money is not associated with any one of its functions, but with a property that creates an inherent asymmetry between money and the rest of commodities. Nevertheless, money emerges as monopolist of buying ability due also to social custom and the social underpinnings of markets. Money as a universal equivalent, furthermore, stands for power over resources and people. Despite starting from exchange processes, Marxist analysis of money's emergence can offer insights into the social phenomena that surround money's use, capturing the broad functioning of money in capitalist society.

6.3 'Multiple' markets and money

Theoretical analysis in this and previous chapters has focused on what markets have in common. Thus, starting with commodities produced under capitalist social relations, the form of value was distinguished from value's substance (abstract labour). On this basis markets were differentiated among themselves, including markets for capitalistically produced commodities, for labour-power, for land, for financial assets, for non-capitalistically produced commodities, and even 'pretend' markets. Money was similarly pursued as something that markets have in common, defined by its monopoly over the ability to buy. The essentials of this approach are Marxist, and were partly developed as a critique of orthodox economic theory. In recent years there has been research on markets and money within economic sociology which is also sharply critical of mainstream economic theory. This research typically assumes that the capitalist economy is located within a network of social relations which actively determine economic behaviour, not least through perceptions and symbolisations imposed on economic categories.[22] The aim of much of this work is to show that those who engage in market-related economic activity also create social relations to which they assign their own meanings and symbolisations. The implications for the social theory of money and markets in capitalist economies are significant, especially because they are strongly critical of neoclassicism. Within this work, Zelizer's (1983, 1987, 1994) empirical and theoretical output is worth considering in detail for two reasons. First, it represents a broad and penetrating challenge to neoclassical economics, and second, it adopts a perspective on markets and money that is in key respects the opposite of the perspective proposed in this book. The contrast with Zelizer's work can make our earlier claims on markets and money stand in sharper relief.[23]

Zelizer (1988) pivots her analysis on the heterogeneity of markets and money, and the consequent difficulty (or even impossibility) of constructing a general theory for both. She considers and lays aside as deficient two theoretical views of the market. The first is what she calls the boundless market, according to which the market relentlessly invades all aspects of social life. For the 'boundless market' approach, of which Simmel and Marx are taken as prime examples, the market undermines the moral, ethical, personal and other content of social life with its own commercial outlook. The second approach Zelizer calls the 'subordinate market'; this opposes the 'boundless market' and rejects the notion that the market is all-conquering. Furthermore, it refuses strictly to counterpose economic to non-economic concerns in society. Instead, the subordinate market approach focuses on the social relations that provide the necessary framework for market activities. It might also allow for market participants to construct their own meanings and perceptions out of market-related activities. The work of Granovetter on networks and embeddedness (discussed briefly in Chapter 5) is an example of the subordinate market approach. Zelizer leans toward the subordinate market approach, but wants a stronger focus on the independent impact of social, historical and cultural factors on economic life. She also wants further to stress the interactive relationship of economic and non-economic aspects of capitalist society. Thus she proposes the approach of 'multiple markets', according to which any attempt to develop a general theory of markets is pointless. The reason is simply that the economic aspects of social life are influenced by the non-economic in ways that differ qualitatively from market to market and activity to activity. Hence there can be no grounds for theoretical generalisations about commercial trading and, at a further remove, about money.

To establish this point, Zelizer (1983, 1987) has undertaken systematic empirical studies in widely different markets. The commercial sites that she has chosen to examine have all been unusual – life insurance, establishing the 'value' of children for commercial purposes, and the uses to which money is in practice put by individuals. Zelizer has concluded that non-economic factors play a pivotal role in establishing the 'value' of a life, or the 'value' of a child for commercial purposes. These factors include, above all, sentimental concerns and moral imperatives that vary qualitatively from market to market. By this token, no pure theory of markets, such as neoclassical general equilibrium, can hope to capture the extreme range of markets, each with its own qualitatively distinct interaction of economic with non-economic factors. It is a natural step from here to claim that no pure theory of money is possible, and Zelizer (1994, 1996, 1998) has taken it. Despite appearing homogeneous in form and function, money is variegated according to the non-economic purposes of its use. Thus Zelizer (1994) proposes a theory of 'multiple monies': money that is used domestically is qualitatively different from money that is used as a gift, which is different from money used in relation to formal institutions of the economy, which in turn varies from money used for religious purposes, and so on and so forth. Delicate meanings and symbolisations are in practice attached to money, which reflect the complex social relations involved in its various uses. Money earned from prostitution, for instance, is very different from money given as a gift by a favourite aunt, from money earned as a salary, or from money received as a bribe. The upshot of this argument is that money does not homogenise social intercourse, turning it into a uniform practice of commercial buying and selling. On the contrary, people 'humanise' money and attach widely different aspects to it according to the social relations relevant to each of its uses.

Zelizer's conclusion is partly intended as a critique of the 'boundless market' approach to money, especially Simmel, who claimed that money has a homogenising effect in society. Simmel (1900) identifies money as 'the pure form of exchangeability', while exchangeability is assumed to be an aspect common to all economic objects. Consequently, Simmel (1900, p. 130) advances a 'pure theory of money', in which money is what makes things 'economic'. Money's essence is to act in a homogenising way across modern society, assigning an 'economic' dimension to everything that it touches. By this token, money is the enemy of 'distinctions' that were typical of pre-capitalist society, i.e. money makes for elimination of customary privileges and rights (Simmel, 1900, p. 394). Money also destroys mutual obligation and undermines moral and ethical concerns in modern society. It becomes an 'end' for people, leading to greed, avarice, extravagance, social disorganisation and disorder. Thus Simmel is a prime exemplar of what Zelizer has designated the boundless market view. For him, advanced capitalism is a society dominated by money, the latter permeating all aspects of social life and transforming all sentiments and concerns into search for money profit. Zelizer also lumps Marx with Simmel as a leading exponent of the boundless market view. Though less thoroughly discussed, he is assumed to have put forth a 'pure theory of money' in which money is treated as a levelling and homogenising force within capitalist society. In the Marxist view of the world, presumably, money lends a strong commodity character to everything that it touches, resulting in advancing commodification of social life. This is in evident contrast with Zelizer's own view of the humanisation of money.

The inclusion of Marx together with Simmel in the so-called boundless market current represents a caricature of Marx's political economy of capitalism. The parallel between Marx and Simmel in this connection is misleading. In Simmel's work there is no attempt to relate 'economic value' to production and the material aspects of life. Money, therefore, is unrelated to the underpinnings of society, and if it becomes a social 'end' that is only because of the autonomous development of culture. In complete contrast, Marx's political economy starts with the class structure of society, particularly in relation to production. 'Economic value' has a specific meaning resulting from production relations. Moreover, the social relations that define capital are fundamental to understanding the role of money in advanced capitalism. If money becomes a social 'end' that is because capital inherently aims to extract money profit. Consequently, it is also misleading to designate Marx as an exemplar of the boundless market approach. The commercial aspects of capitalist social life cannot be examined separately from the capitalist nature of relations of production. Markets indeed act as social organisers of the capitalist economy, but that is not because of any extraordinary properties of markets themselves. The proliferation of markets is an outcome of the class structure of society – if the capitalist mode of production is organised by markets, that is because of the class relations characteristic of capitalist production. By the same token, the homogeneous character of money and its pivotal role in the capitalist economy emanate from the social relations of production, which imply that capitalists and workers regularly visit the market as atomised, 'foreign' individuals.

By ignoring the role of production relations in shaping the character of markets and money, Zelizer also weakens her own argument. The markets that she has chosen as exemplars of the multiple markets approach, such as insurance, are typically markets in which there is no production of value. In these markets the form of value is detached from its substance, and the influence of economic factors on price determination is limited. It is inevitable that customary, traditional, ethical and moral elements impinge heavily on price formation (as discussed in Chapter 1). In capitalist markets for produced commodities, on the other hand, the reverse holds true regarding the form of value: economic factors predominate and the non-economic play a secondary role. By the same token, the meanings attached to commodities and money might indeed be different from market to market, but that does not imply that markets lack common aspects that make theoretical analysis possible. Workers, for instance, approach markets for means of consumption with the underlying aim of obtaining use values. Capitalists, on the other hand, approach intermediate and final goods markets with the aim of obtaining money profits. Money in the market for land cannot have the same moral and ethical content as in the market for labour. Similarly, financial markets – including foreign exchange, money markets and stock markets – are markets directly related to money capital in circulation rather than capital engaged in production. Distance from value production inevitably affects the outlook of financial market participants, especially their attitude toward money.

The variety of capitalist markets (including 'pretend' markets) and the variable moral and ethical weights attached to money are not problematic issues for Marxist political economy. On the contrary, by establishing the common character of markets and money, the balance between economic and non-economic elements in the various markets can be theoretically assessed. Commodities are things of use and things of value, but not all markets deal in commodities. Non-economic factors weigh heavily on the form of value, particularly in markets where there are no produced commodities. In this light, money is the monopolist of the ability to buy, and this is the reason why money can reflect different moral and personal relations in the markets in which it functions as well as creating relations of power and hierarchy. Establishing the common character of markets and money allows for theoretical understanding of the variety of money's social roles.

6.4 'Limited-purpose' and 'general-purpose' money

Zelizer's treatment of markets and money is strongly reminiscent of the work of the 'substantivist' school of anthropology, except that her analysis and conclusions apply to developed capitalist society. A brief reconsideration of the substantivist–formalist debate of the 1960s and 1970s can help shed more light on the unity as well as the variety of markets and money. For the substantivists, belonging to the tradition of Polanyi, economic phenomena should be analysed only after due attention has been paid to qualitative differences in the structure of societies, especially between 'primitive' and 'advanced' societies.[24] In primitive society, norms, customs, religious and magical practices are inextricably meshed with economic practices, especially because economic activity is neither strongly commercial nor market-related. Indeed, markets and haggling have been marginal to economic life for the greater part of historical time. In contrast, economic practices in advanced society are clearly and closely associated with commerce and the market, thus admitting of analysis by pure economic theory. Polanyi (1944) was the first to propose the concept of 'embeddedness' of the economic in the non-economic. For Polanyi, economic activities are embedded in social relations, but these are broad relations of distribution and power, not of personal friendship and contact. In this light, the chief characteristic of capitalism is that the market becomes the foundation of society. With the market as its foundation, capitalist economic activity is 'disembedded' from social relations for the first time in human history. The market imposes its commercial priorities on society as a whole, i.e. the culture of haggling, with disastrous effects for communal solidarity. Be that as it may, it follows that for Polanyi and the substantivists there can be no economic theory that applies across societies, and certainly none that applies to both primitive and modern societies.[25]

In contrast, the formalists stressed the similarities of form between economic phenomena across vastly different societies. Commodities, money, prices, interest on money, economising on time spent in production, and so on, are found in primitive as well as advanced societies. Moreover, production, distribution and commodity exchange appear to have a general character that admits of systematic analysis across societies. It seems plausible that people engaging in activities that lead to emergence of such phenomena, in whatever society, necessarily employ elements of instrumental rationality before taking decisions. Consequently, formalists sought general economic theories applicable across societies. They came inevitably to rely on the ahistorical and apparently universal concepts of neoclassical economics – markets are markets and money is money irrespective of historical and social context.[26]

In line with his underlying theoretical view, Polanyi (1957) distinguished between 'general-purpose' and 'limited-purpose' money, and the distinction was further developed by Dalton (1965). In brief, money does not have a single essence, and should be distinguished as general-purpose or limited-purpose. The former is characteristic of advanced societies, being uniform in quality and lacking 'personality', while the latter is typical of primitive societies, since it is heterogeneous and often has 'personality'.

> To concentrate attention on what all monies have in common is to discard those clues – how monies differ – which are surface expressions of social and economic organisation ... In sum, money has no definable essence apart from the uses money objects serve, and these depend upon the transactional modes that characterise each economy: as tangible item as well as abstract measure, money is what money does.
>
> (Dalton, 1965, pp. 61–62)

For the substantivists, limited-purpose monies are not interchangeable. Even more strongly, individual limited-purpose monies are not able to operate as money across the whole of society. They are used only in clearly demarcated areas (economic and geographical) to which they become specific, and from which they draw particular characteristics that prevent them from becoming interchangeable with each another. In contrast, advanced money can be universal, applying to the whole of society and across activities. The ultimate reason for the qualitative difference between the two types of money is that advanced society has become thoroughly permeated by the market and the haggling mentality that attaches to it. On the other hand, product exchange in primitive society is far less common and is certainly not driven by narrow commercial motives and practices. Hence primitive money is strongly particular.[27] The similarities with Zelizer's treatment of money are evident, though her aim is to reject precisely the universality of 'advanced' money.

The relevance of the debate between substantivists and formalists to the issue of the historical specificity of theoretical analysis is apparent. It has been strongly argued in this book that analysis of markets and money should commence with the capitalist commodity – that is, a commodity produced through the employment of wage labour. Consequently, the relations of property, power and hierarchy that underpinned commodity production were assumed to be specifically capitalist. By the same token, the moral, customary and ethical parameters within which economic life occurred also had a capitalist character. Therefore results, conclusions and concepts from the analysis of advanced capitalism do not apply wholesale to primitive society. However, capitalist markets and money can act as templates for analysis of markets in other societies, provided that the distinction between substance and form of value is appreciated fully. Analysis of the form of value is capable of producing a general theory of money, without lapsing into the ahistorical generalities of neoclassicism. There is no need to argue that advanced capitalist money differs qualitatively from primitive money. Rather, the form of value develops further as exchange becomes more regular and widespread, with a corresponding monopolisation of the ability to buy by money. Money as monopolist of buying ability can, and does, emerge independently of advanced capitalist society. The theoretical paradox is that this observation can make theoretical sense only after studying the fully developed exchange processes of advanced capitalism.

7 Money as unit of account and means of exchange in a socialist society

It has been shown in earlier chapters that money looms large over the capitalist non-economic sphere because, first, disparate things and relations are traded as commodities even when they are intrinsically different from commodities, and second, personal incomes normally accrue in the form of money through market operations. Money as monopolist of the ability to buy facilitates formation of non-economic relations and lends a pecuniary character to trust, power, hierarchy, and moral obligation. Capitalist non-economic relations are stamped with the imprint of money and are placed at the service of profit making. However, the exceptionally important role of money in capitalist society springs ultimately from its class structure, rather than from money's intrinsic qualities. The underlying relations of production between capitalists and workers imply that markets act as organisers of the capitalist economy. Money as monopolist of buying ability is the social nexus of capitalist society because commercial exchanges are inherent to social relations between the capitalist and the working class, lending an aspect of 'foreign-ness' to all economic agents. By the same token, if the underlying class structure of society was altered, money's economic and social role could become far less prominent. To conclude this book, therefore, it is important to consider some of the theoretical consequences of a socialist transformation of society for the role of money. Some implications also follow for the currently prominent Local Exchange Trading Schemes (LETS), which aim at reforming capitalism and its markets.

7.1 Socialism as the conscious ascendancy of the non-economic

Socialism has taken many guises during the two centuries of its existence as an ideology, a political practice and a form of social organisation. It has been 'utopian', as in the activities and writings of Owen (1813–1814), who built model industrial communities in the hope of acting as inspiration to others and gradually subverting capitalist society through superior performance. It has been 'scientific',[1] as in the work of Marx and Engels, drawing on a theoretical analysis of the capitalist mode of production that demonstrates the inherent nature of opposition between capitalists and workers and calls for revolutionary transformation of society. It has been social-democratic, as in the political practice of the Second International, playing down the severity of class divisions between capitalists and workers and seeking to improve worker conditions by reforming capitalist society.[2] It has also been a tyranny established over the ruined dreams and aspirations of the Russian Revolution – a hierarchical society, dominated by party bureaucrats and driven by a quest for industrial development and military might. While the vicissitudes of socialism lie beyond the scope of this book, it is possible to cast some light on the interaction between economic and non-economic relations in a socialist society.

The *Communist Manifesto* suggests a vision of communism as a society of associated producers that would liberate the non-economic sphere from the shackles of profit making and money.[3] Cultural development, familial duty, education and women's participation in society would emerge free of the shadow of hard cash (Marx and Engels, 1848, pp. 501–502). The vision of the *Communist Manifesto* could be interpreted as a return to an older, pristine state of relations among human beings, based perhaps on the regular creation of mutual obligations and gift giving. But for Marx and Engels the purpose of socialist transformation is not to shed the flam of the market in order, presumably, to restore a primordial purity to human relations. Rather, socialism is supposed consciously to transmute non-economic relations by altering the economic foundations of society. A socialist society would liberate the non-economic sphere from the impositions of money and profit-making, and give a communal content to trust, morality, power, solidarity, and so on. A pre-condition for this, however, is appropriate transformation of the class relations of production, distribution and exchange. With socialist relations of production there would be no rift between economy and society, and both would be permeated by a communal spirit. Two aspects of this issue are relevant here.

First, the most fundamental change in the underlying economic relations is the abolition of exploitation. This requires eliminating capitalist property relations, i.e. abolishing the exclusive property rights held by capitalists over the means of production and final output. The form that socialist property rights would take and the processes through which they would be created are not directly relevant in this connection. It is important to note, however, that abolition of exploitation does not also mean that a surplus would stop being produced over cost. Under socialist conditions of production, surplus labour would still be performed, in excess of what is strictly necessary to replace means of production and necessary goods for workers. The point is, rather, that economic surpluses would be produced on a cooperative basis, belonging to the direct producers collectively. Consequently, the disposal of surpluses – either through increased consumption or through net investment in the means of production –

would also be subject to the collective decisions of the direct producers. It would not be left to the private choices of individual owners of resources mediated by the mechanism of markets, as in the capitalist mode of production.

Second, and partly following from the first, socialist transformation of the economy would have profound implications for the market's role as social organiser. This issue has been intensely disputed throughout the past century. In the 'socialist calculation debate' of the inter-war years, precipitated by Austrian neoclassicals, arguments focused on the feasibility of achieving rational prices for capital goods under socialist planning in contrast to the free market.[4] Controversy re-emerged in the 1980s, originating with Nove (1983), who claimed that socialist planning is excessively complex and costly, thus making markets indispensable for resource allocation in a socialist economy. Mandel (1986, 1988) opposed Nove on the grounds that markets play a limited role in modern capitalism, since large capitalist corporations use planning methods internally. There are parallels here with the recent neoclassical debates regarding transactions costs (see Chapter 5).[5] The Austrian concept of 'entrepreneurship' has also been prominent in the latest bout of controversy (Lavoie, 1985). The 'entrepreneur' presumably innovates and combines resources in ways that are not initially obvious to others, while innovations are subsequently adopted more generally.[6] In this light, capitalist private property and freely operating markets are necessary to provide incentives and means to the entrepreneur. Adaman and Devine (1996) have rejected this view on the grounds that innovation depends on mobilisation of social rather than individual knowledge. 'Market socialists', meanwhile, have discussed property relations in connection with enterprise 'governance' (Bardhan and Roemer, 1992). Using a principal-agent framework, proposals have been made to extend individual worker property rights over the means of production, while developing appropriate mechanisms of control to ensure efficient operation of enterprises within markets. These proposals include a role for banks and capital markets as monitoring agents over enterprises (Bardhan, 1993; Roemer, 1993).

Without directly entering this fraught debate, it seems clear that a socialist economy would be obliged to exercise controls over the operations of markets, often negating them altogether. It was shown earlier that capitalism is not tantamount to networks of markets, nor simply to commercial buying and selling, but comprises a particular set of exploitative class relations of production. The organising role of markets in the capitalist economy is a result of capitalist class relations, while market processes allow the capitalist economy to stand apart from society. The economy is separate from the non-economic sphere in capitalist society, and is not constrained by traditional and ideological imperatives. At the same time, organising the economy through market processes gives rise to non-economic relations that are stamped by profit making. In contrast, socialism promises to reintegrate economy and society, making it possible for the economy to interact openly and transparently with ethics, morality and custom. The non-economic sphere would become free of the tyranny of money, and exercise a directing influence on the operations of the economy. In short, socialism promises the conscious ascendancy of the non-economic over the economic. However, organising the economy through freely operating markets is conducive neither to the reintegration of the economic with the non-economic, nor to the ascendancy of the latter. Free markets rest on relations of essentially 'foreign' participants motivated by the search for precise equivalents for their commodities. A society organised spontaneously by the impersonal market would inevitably loosen the links between the economic and the non-economic spheres as well as imposing the imprint of money on social relations. To integrate economy and society, while ensuring the ascendancy of non-economic relations, a socialist society would have to exercise direct control over market processes.

The implications of this claim are clear as far as disposing of the spare resources of a socialist society is concerned. In a capitalist society, spare resources are directed to productive tasks on the basis of private decisions made by individual capitalists and put into effect through the market. The motivation for investment is profit-making, while non-economic factors (fairness, equality, culture and so on) play a negligible role. Similarly, non-economic outcomes of investment (pollution, social dislocation, etc.) are irrelevant to private decision-making, because they do not directly translate into money and profit. A socialist society, since it promises to integrate the economic with the ascendant non-economic, would be obliged to draw on a fuller range of motivations in order to make investment decisions. Economic concerns would remain integral to investment plans, since no society could ignore efficiency in the use of available resources, especially the skills, time and energy of its workers. However, non-economic concerns would also weigh heavily on decision-making, including consideration of the environmental, familial, moral, and ethical implications of resource use. These concerns cannot be entrusted to private individual decisions effected through freely functioning market mechanisms. Social institutions would have to be created that would plan investment for society as a whole, even if such planning referred merely to volumes and preferred sectors. It would then be possible systematically to include non-economic considerations in making investment decisions. A socialist society would have to control the operations of markets as far as directing investment is concerned. Far-reaching implications follow for the functioning of money, especially as a unit of account and means of exchange, considered briefly below in relation to the notion of labour money.

7.2 Labour money

In a capitalist economy, money functions as a unit of account for the output of disparate enterprises and sectors. The value of commodities is given by abstract labour, a social substance created as workers regularly move between jobs; authoritarian discipline is generally applied at the workplace, and finished products are systematically sold. Thus products that contain labour of longer duration, greater complexity and more intensity than others also contain more value. However, commodity value takes the form of money. Frequent and repeated sales of commodities result in money prices that exhibit regularity across markets, despite local variation. The output of different enterprises and sectors is perforce rendered comparable, and a universal measure of enterprise efficiency is supplied by the money rate of profit. Enterprises or sectors that are more efficient than others in using resources also make higher profits. As capital seeks the highest profit rate, abandoning less profitable enterprises and sectors, reallocation of resources ensues.

It could be inferred, therefore, that output in a socialist economy could be rendered commensurate by being measured directly in terms of labour time instead of a money commodity. Socialist money could be denominated in hours of labour instead of dollars, pounds, and euros – it could be labour money. The output of socialist enterprises would then be accounted for in hours of labour, establishing easy and direct comparability across sectors and industries. In this light, it appears plausible to reform the capitalist economy by simply introducing labour money into its markets. Specifically, ordinary money could be replaced by socially accepted fiat instruments that would be stamped with a given number of hours of labour. Products would then be rendered commensurate on the basis of the hours of labour taken to produce them, rather than through money prices. Similarly, surpluses over cost for capitalist enterprises and sectors would be calculated as hours of labour, instead of appearing as money profits. Aggregate accounting and the distribution of income would be transparent, and directly based on hours of labour – i.e. on the very activity that provides the foundation of society. The material and social underpinnings of production would become more transparent, facilitating the reintegration of economy with society. Thus, adoption of labour money as a unit of account appears to be a plausible socialist reform of capitalist society.

The idea of introducing labour money into the capitalist economy was originally associated with Ricardian socialism, and emerged soon after Ricardo died. In Ricardian economics, the value of commodities is determined by labour embodied in the course of production; wages correspond to the value of commodities that workers must receive to maintain themselves. Profits accrue to capitalists as a residual after workers and landlords have received their income as, respectively, wages and ground rent.[7]

Ricardian socialists, on the other hand, claimed that capitalists obtained profits because they did not pay to workers the full equivalent for the labour performed during the working day.[8] Workers sold to capitalists the time for which they were contractually obliged to labour – equal to the length of the working day – but received wages that were less than the full equivalent. This was defined as exploitation, the remedy for which seemed simple: workers should be paid in labour money and in amounts equal to the number of hours actually worked. Workers could then obtain consumption goods of value exactly equal to the labour performed. The introduction of labour money was strongly supported by the socialists Owen and Proudhon (separately and independently) because of the apparent prospect of abolishing exploitation. Labour money was to be used in conjunction with labour exchanges, the latter being markets in which labour-power and goods would be exchanged at prices accounted directly in labour-time. Labour exchanges were instrumental to utopian socialist ideas, and were established in Britain by Owen as part of the cooperative movement.

Marx (1847; 1939, pp. 136–145) was scathing about the reforming potential of labour money.[9] He rejected the notion that workers sell to capitalists the time during which they are contractually obliged to labour. On the contrary, workers sell their ability to labour – their labour power – but only for a definite period of time. For Marx, the value that is received by workers as wages is not systematically less than the value of the labour power they sell in the labour market. Workers enter the labour market as ordinary commodity owners (though of a very peculiar commodity), and normally receive a proper equivalent for the labour power they sell. Marx's theoretical innovation was to claim that workers are obliged to perform more labour than strictly necessary to counterbalance their wages, despite wages representing a full *quid pro quo* for labour power sold. This happens because relations of production are characterised by power, authority and fiat running from capitalists to workers, and dictate time and conditions at work. Exploitation is indeed a fundamental aspect of capitalism, but it takes place in production, rather than in exchange, due to class relations between capitalists and workers. From this perspective, it is absurd to aim at eliminating capitalist exploitation by simply paying workers the full equivalent for labour performed. Equally, capitalism cannot be fundamentally transformed by replacing ordinary money with labour money but without altering the social relations of production, distribution and exchange. Indeed, as is shown below, the reverse is true: for labour money to be used generally as a unit of account and means of exchange, the social relations of production, distribution and exchange must undergo socialist transformation.

For money to be generally used across the capitalist economy, there must be appropriate ratios of equivalence between the products of enterprises and sectors, as well as comparability between concrete labours of different intensity and skill.[10] Comparability of labours and ratios of equivalence among products are attained through automatic and spontaneous economic processes that result in ordinary money prices. Use of labour money, however, implies that comparability and ratios of equivalence among products are expressed directly in units of labour time. Value is accounted directly in units of its substance (labour time), instead of being measured in physical units of a commodity (gold). However, for this to take place, commodity owners should stop systematically meeting each other as 'foreign' individuals who seek to exchange equivalents in free markets. For, if they continued to meet in a context of 'foreign-ness', a money commodity would spontaneously emerge that would act as monopolist of buying power and account for commodity value. Thus generalised use of labour money requires that commodity owners approach each other as members of a community that are bound together by a multitude of explicit social links. Moreover, they must act in full awareness of their social relations, especially regarding the allocation of the community's available labour time across the division of labour. Consequently, it would be necessary for commodity owners collectively to gather information about products and activities, to assess costs and labour inputs, and to establish ratios of equivalence for labours and products. This is an extremely complex task, especially when commodities are produced with substantial fixed investment and large numbers of workers. To ascertain appropriate exchange ratios among products, commodity owners would also have to make collective decisions on worker remuneration and returns to investment. Moreover, if the use of resources across the economy is to be efficient, commodity owners must also have the collective power to alter the allocation of resources and the distribution of money incomes. In short, to deploy labour money fully as a unit of account, commodity owners would be obliged collectively to organise production and distribution. If they also aimed at eliminating exploitation through labour money, they would have to alter property rights over the means of production in favour of workers. A full-scale socialist transformation of society would have to occur.

If society underwent a socialist transformation, the functioning of labour money as means of exchange would be deeply affected. Since socialist society would rest on a complex division of labour, it would require a technical means of facilitating the accrual of income and the acquisition of goods and services by individuals. At the most basic level, the operation of a socialist means of exchange would resemble that of raffle tickets or lunch vouchers, formally rationing goods and services. Capitalist money behaves similarly, since it facilitates the distribution of goods and services among individuals and enterprises. However, it functions as a rationing device because it possesses a universal ability to buy, and therefore commodities are offered for sale against it as a matter of course. In contrast, labour money would not possess unlimited power to buy, since products would be swapped on terms set by the collective organisation of production, distribution and exchange. Its power to buy investment goods would be restricted either absolutely, if direct transfer of investment resources occurred according to a central plan, or relatively if enterprises were partly allowed to trade investment goods under price controls and quantity quotas. Its ability to purchase labour power would also be restricted, since a socialist society would impose legal and customary restrictions on the labour market, especially on the right to hire and fire workers.[11] Finally, labour money would have limited power to buy consumer goods. Since controls are to be imposed on the labour market, it follows that the provision of means of consumption to workers must also be regulated. The purchasing power of labour money over food, clothing, education, housing, health and transport would be constrained. Provision of key consumer goods would be hedged by social regulations over prices and quantities to ensure adequate access for all as a right and as normal practice. A socialist society would construct a comprehensive system of welfare provision for health, housing and education, supplementing it with price and quantity controls for food, transport, and other consumer goods. Labour money's buying power would be correspondingly reduced.

This discussion has a direct bearing on the practices of Local Exchange Trading Systems (LETS), which aim at replacing capitalist money and have recently proliferated across the developed capitalist world, especially in the USA and Canada. LETS schemes have several characteristics in common. A circle of members is created, with different skills but generally within a compact geographical area. There is typically a committee that administers the circle, and a set of detailed conditions for membership. Ordinary money is excluded, and a new unit of account and means of exchange – LETS money – is used in transactions within the circle. Members supply each other mostly with services, but also with goods, by accumulating debits and credits denominated in LETS money. LETS schemes typically maintain a notional rate between the value of their money and that of ordinary money. The link facilitates arriving at prices for services and goods, which are typically negotiated freely between participants in transactions. The accounts of members are usually open to inspection by all, and transfers of credits are occasionally allowed.

The emergence of LETS belongs to the tradition of attempting to confront the ills of capitalism by reforming money, of which labour money is the best-known example. LETS schemes are exchange mechanisms parallel to the dominant capitalist markets, which implicitly aim at preventing money from becoming the monopolist of buying ability.[12] Their explicit aim, on the other hand, is to establish fair and equitable relations among members, doing away with the 'foreign-ness' and individualism characteristic of capitalist markets. LETS schemes promote a spirit of community, of belonging, of open moral bonding among members. They are also critically disposed toward capitalist profit-making and strongly concerned with the social and environmental problems created by capitalist economic activity. Thus the emergence of LETS is evidence of spontaneous opposition to the spirit and moral attitudes of capitalism. At the same time, LETS schemes remain aloof of production, limiting themselves to the exchange of goods and services for final consumption. However, capitalist society rests on the labour market as well as on enormous markets for investment goods that are dominated by the pursuit of profit and money as a universal equivalent. If LETS money is to become the unit of account generally used by enterprises, the existing concerns of LETS circles regarding morality and alternative ethics will have to be combined with economic efficiency across the economy. Without confronting directly the determination of returns to investment and the level of real wages, LETS schemes will remain unable substantially to affect economic and social life as a whole. For that to happen, however, the economy will have to be managed as a whole, investment will have to be directed, hiring and firing of labour restricted, and capitalist property rights altered. In short, socialist measures across the economy will have to be put in place. Existing LETS schemes, in contrast, are parochial, focusing narrowly on local communities. Not surprisingly, they also have a short life – LETS schemes typically grow rapidly, generate enthusiasm, and then grind to a halt.

LETS aim at confronting the unfairness and selfishness of capitalist markets by creating local exchange processes permeated by the spirit of community. Individualism and selfishness are to be replaced by trust and moral obligation, but without creating grassroots democratic mechanisms that control society and hold it together. Yet LETS schemes do not confront capital as social and economic relation, and nor do they take into account the conflicting interests of capital and labour. Consequently, LETS usually have a narrow vision of the alternative communal values needed to replace capitalist individualism and selfishness. For a socialist transformation of society, in contrast, workers have to be directly involved in running both economy and society. Individualism must be dissolved into collective organisations with society-wide appeal, while trust and moral obligation would emerge from new relations of production. In that context, money would naturally find a new and limited role.

Notes

1 Social relations underpinning commodity markets

1 This claim derives from the logical structure of Marx's (1867, Ch. 1) mature analysis of capitalism and its markets, which commences with the commodity.

2 By explicitly introducing behavioural norms, economists tone down this assumption, as is shown in Chapter 5. However, the inclusion of norms does not challenge the fundamental assumptions of economics regarding the individual's motivations. Norms merely change the framework within which individual rationality can unfold.

3 Appadurai (1986, p. 9, emphasis in original) states the following: 'Let us start with the idea that a commodity is *any thing intended for exchange.* This gets us away from the exclusive preoccupation with the "product", "production", and the original or dominant intention of the "producer" and permits us to focus on the dynamics of exchange.' Appadurai then considers the 'life history' of commodities, the social relations of exchange that make and unmake commodities out of things. However, his definition of the commodity is inadequate, bearing in mind the qualitative differences among traded objects – cars, paintings, real estate, financial services, insurance, haircuts, goodwill, and so on, the list is endless. On what grounds could they all be treated as 'things'? Far from being a constraint, the link with production makes it possible to analyse commodities systematically.

4 See, for instance, Sahlins (1974) and Cashdan (1989). The problematic aspect of Smith's approach, however, is not due to the absence of anthropological work in his day. Smith, after all, was well versed in history. Rather, the problem emanates from Smith's assumption of a 'natural' disposition to trade, of attempting to derive results that are beyond history and society.

5 Braudel (1981, 1982, 1984) provides the most penetrating historical account of the relationship between trade and capitalism.

6 Marx's methodology and his use of dialectics have concerned Anglo-Saxon Marxism ever since publication of Rosdolsky's (1977) outstanding book. In recent years, especially, there has been much emphasis on Hegel and his influence on Marx. A current of 'new dialectics' has emerged, associated mostly with Murray (1988), Smith (1990, 1993), and Arthur (1993). They have attempted to show, in different ways, that Hegel's use of dialectical logic is instrumental to understanding Marx's mature work on commodities and capital. An excellent presentation and critique of this current can be found in Saad-Filho (2002). Interestingly enough, the rise of the 'new dialectics' has been mirrored by the emergence of a very different approach, mostly associated with Meikle's (1995) sophisticated work, that aims at showing the influence of Aristotle's formal logic on Marx's work. It is worth remarking that

arguments about Marx's method are ultimately persuasive only if they are actually applied to particular social phenomena, producing results that are more powerful than those of non-Marxist theory.

7 On this topic I am heavily indebted to Itoh (1981, 1988), both through his writings and through personal discussion and communication. That does not mean that he would also adopt the same approach. A debt is also owed to Sekine (1980, 1997, 1998), who strongly defends the Hegelian aspect of Marx's logic, and holds trenchant views on the failure of western Marxists fully to appreciate the importance of the dialectic in Marx's economics. However, the treatment of use value in Chapter 2 of this book, in particular the claim that use value reveals non-economic aspects of capital, is unlikely to find much favour with Sekine, for whom capital totally subsumes use values. The latter are totally submerged, so to speak, under the elemental movement of capital as self-expanding value. For a broad discussion of the Uno school, particularly the Sekine current, see Albritton (1991, 1999).

8 See Althusser (1969), Althusser and Balibar (1970), Poulantzas (1973, 1975).

9 See Fine and Harris (1979, pp. 8–12) for discussion of production as determining aspect of the capitalist economy.

10 Aoki (1988) made a penetrating attempt to deal with horizontal relations at the workplace in a strictly 'economic' way, in the context of Japan. Horizontal relations of equality and group membership, typical of Japanese firms, are thought to facilitate information flows about production and hence to improve efficiency. Vertical relations of authority, typical of US firms, on the other hand, could hamper information flows and reduce efficiency. Two points should be made about Aoki's analysis, even in passing: first, it is not clear which parts of it are specific to Japan and which could apply to capitalist firms in general, and second, it leaves out of account the exploitative class content of Japanese company relations.

11 This danger is ever-present for Marxist theory that stresses the related concept of 'alienation'. Capitalist producers appear to be 'alienated' from the products of their labour, since these products assume an independent life as commodities and dominate their producers through the operations of the market. Thus, the underlying essence of human beings, their fundamental humanity, is overwhelmed by commerce. One strain of Marxism, associated with Lukacs (1971), has claimed 'alienation' as the dominant feature of capitalism extending to all areas of social life because of advancing commodification. This has clear political implications: socialism appears as the overcoming of 'alienation', which would arrive when the working class realised the true nature of the capitalist social order. In contrast, Althusserian Marxism rejected both 'alienation' and 'fetishism', stressing instead the importance of structural 'ideological mechanisms' within the capitalist mode of production to sustain the dominant position of the capitalist class (Milios *et al.*, 2002, Ch. 4).

12 Fine (1975) captured the circuit in an original way through a circular flow chart. Foley (1982, 1986) developed more complex and sophisticated models of the circuit. A formalisation of the circuit that focuses on its money aspects can be found in Lapavitsas (2000).

13 By the same token, markets cannot be treated as being essentially alike simply because they contain processes of buying and selling. The formal similarity of markets conceals significant qualitative differences among them. This is an important premise for the analysis of 'commodification' in the capitalist mode of production, i.e. of the transformation of things, assets, activities, sentiments, and so on, into traded objects.

14 This is one of the main sources of obscurity in Marx's analysis. Contemporary

theoretical research offers strong support for the view that Marx implicitly assumes capitalist conditions; see Saad-Filho (2002) and Milios *et al.* (2002).

15 Both as a social phenomenon and as a concept in social science, abstract labour affords tremendous insight into the social relations that lead to its emergence. Concrete labour, by contrast, reveals little of the social relations of those who undertake it. In itself, concrete labour is simply a set of natural and physiological processes, see Fine and Lapavitsas (2000).

16 See Saad-Filho (2002, Ch. 5) for a discussion of homogenisation, normalisation and synchronisation of concrete labours under capitalist conditions of production.

17 Relative prices are 'based on' and not 'proportionate to' ratios of abstract labour content. Political economy has known since the time of Adam Smith that the labour theory of value does not provide a precise theory of relative prices. This is precluded by formation of a general rate of profit among capitalist enterprises (and by rent paid for property in land). Without wishing to enter the murky waters of the 'transformation' problem, the position adopted here is that the value content of commodities sets limits but does not precisely determine their relative price.

18 This issue is more fully discussed in Fine and Lapavitsas (2000).

19 See Mohun (2003) for a lucid discussion of labour that does not produce value.

20 Kopytoff (1986) offers insight into 'commoditisation' by studying the 'life histories' of particular commodities.

2 Commodities and gifts

1 More recent views can be found in James and Allen (1998).

2 Economists such as Boyd and Richerson (1992), Guttman (1996) and Binmore (1998) have also attempted to formalise reciprocity within groups, in contrast to self-interest and egoism. Some of this work is breathtakingly bold. Bowles and Gintis (2001), for instance, aim at explaining the path of development of *Homo sapiens* since the late Pleistocene era through the interplay of reciprocity and egoism. From a Marxist perspective, it makes no sense to devise a theory of interpersonal or social relations that applies to *Homo sapiens* irrespective of history. It is absurd to assume that the (largely imagined) behaviour of hunter-gatherers in the remote recesses of historical time is capable of revealing the motivations of contemporary human beings.

3 See Fine (2001, pp. 66–79) for discussion of the links between Blau's and Homans' 'social exchange' and Coleman's 'social capital'.

4 In Hyde's (1983) influential analysis of the gift, *logos* (reason) drives commodity exchange and the market economy, while *eros* (attraction) permeates the swapping of gifts and the gift economy.

5 The gift can also stand for relations of power, since the person who makes it creates an obligation that can be acutely felt by the person who receives it. See Harrell-Bond *et al.* (1992) and Voutira and Harrell-Bond (1995) for analysis of refugee camps based on gift-related power.

6 The best-known use of the concept of the gift in relation to welfare was made by Titmuss (1970), who discussed blood donation as gift to society that earns reciprocal welfare rights for donors.

7 What truly distinguishes a capitalist society from others in this respect is the gradual emergence of economic institutions that place non-market relations systematically at the service of capitalist profit-making. The most extensive and characteristic set of such institutions comprises the credit system – a unique feature of the capitalist mode of production – examined in detail in Chapter 4.

8 Firth (1929) showed that Mauss misinterpreted the Maori text. Nevertheless, Mauss' argument that the gift must be returned because it remains linked to the person of the giver hinges less on the interpretation of *hau* and more on personal and social relations between giver and recipient.

9 For Mauss, society is a system of rules with moral content, and gift exchange symbolises acceptance of and compliance with the rules. Who participates in a gift exchange and on what terms are partly prescribed in advance. In this respect, the exchangeability of the gift is also determined by established rules prior to gift transactions.

10 Malinowski (1926) makes a systematic attempt to turn 'reciprocity' (based on naïve psychological foundations) into an economic principle that disproves 'primitive communism'. In effect, he transforms the *quid pro quo* of capitalist markets into a universal principle.

11 'Appears' is the operative word. Commodity exchangeability is neither immediately complete nor precise, but must continually become so, even under developed capitalist conditions. Seeking sale is always fraught with uncertainty, and there are periods (commercial crises) in which commodities fail to be exchanged *en masse*. This is without even considering the theoretical problems posed by the nature of fully developed exchangeability (exchange value), discussed in Chapter 1.

12 In this vein, analytical analogues have been sought between gift-giving and language. For a well researched attempt, see Caplow (1982, 1984).

13 Custom-made commodities confirm rather than negate this statement: use value is stipulated in advance by the buyer, relieving the seller of the need to arrive at a forecast.

14 See Itoh and Lapavitsas (1999, Ch. 4).

15 Malinowski (1922, Ch. 4) had an ill-disguised contempt for the aesthetic qualities of *vaygu'a*, and appeared to think that they had no usefulness at all. However, if the original use to which a thing is put has become submerged under some other, it does not follow that it has disappeared. A ceremonial axe (*beku*) is still an axe even though it might not be used to cut wood.

16 See Weiner (1988, and 1992, Ch. 5).

17 The extensive non-market relations engendered by money in the sphere of exchange (more accurately, by its use value of universal buying power) were disregarded here, since they are the main topic of analysis of the second part of this book.

18 The *locus classicus* is Appadurai (1986). For a penetrating discussion of the literature on consumption, see Fine (2002, Ch. 3). An original analysis of the social construction of use values and the systems of provision of goods for consumption can be found in Fine and Leopold (1993).

19 The difficult question of how it becomes possible for labour power systematically to enter the calculus of use values is here left aside. This is an issue that naturally lends itself to analysis of the interplay of economic and non-economic relations in society, since it amounts to the very emergence of capitalism.

20 For systematic analysis of the labour market and a review of labour market theories from a Marxist standpoint, see Fine (1998b).

21 See Fine *et al.* (2004, forthcoming).

22 The concept of the gift is ill-suited to analysis of non-market relations at the workplace. There are no exchanges between capitalists and workers at the workplace, be they commodity- or gift-like. Akerlof's (1982) attempt to press the concept of the gift into service in explaining unpaid overtime has an air of unreality. Presumably workers make a gift of unpaid labour to the firm in exchange for paternalistic treatment by management. This formulation

ignores the fact that unpaid overtime can occur regardless of paternalistic treatment of workers by the firm. Non-economic factors are indeed vital to explaining unpaid overtime, but such factors are more likely to be hierarchical authority and power on the one hand, and solidarity and collective action on the other. Davis (1992, Ch. 5) is rightly sceptical of Akerlof's argument.

3 Money's monopoly over the ability to buy

1 Simmel (1900) offers the classic sociological discussion of the levelling, 'plebeian' aspect of money.
2 See also Lapavitsas (2002).
3 More accurately, the contradictions are 'pacified' or reproduced at a higher level, since monetary exchange creates the possibility of disequilibria between on the one hand the output offered for sale, and on the other the effective demand directed toward it.
4 Along lines suggested by the Uno tradition, see Itoh (1976).
5 It is arguable that, under such conditions, war would take place rather than trade. Indeed, war is never very far from the practice and language of trade. But markets also succeed in banishing open violence from their midst, though they certainly retain a role for power and authority, as is shown below.
6 Marx uses equalities in order to capture this relationship, yet at the same time he insists on the 'asymmetry' between A and B (Marx, 1867, p. 140). The problem is that equalities are inherently symmetric and therefore inappropriate for analysis of 'asymmetry'. An arrow is better suited to discussing the 'polarity' between 'relative' and 'equivalent', see Sekine (1999) and Lapavitsas (2002).
7 Commodity owners are assumed to possess an indivisible quantity of a single commodity at the outset, making bargaining over relative prices impossible. However, bargaining *per se* is not a problem in this connection. Nothing would change in the fundamental relationship between the 'relative' and the 'equivalent' if, in the example given in the text, B responded to A's offer of sale by suggesting a ratio of physical quantities other than y/x.
8 Neoclassical theory of money's origin is fully aware of the problem created by the inherent symmetry of commodities. Menger (1892), the pillar of the neoclassical approach to money, postulated that commodities are inherently differentiated in terms of their 'marketability'. This is a property that commodities appear to have *a priori*, and the stronger it is, the greater the benefits for the commodity's owner. Menger further argued that, through a combination of rational economic calculation and social custom, a commodity with superior 'marketability' would become money. Menger's analysis is considered in detail in Chapter 6.
9 See also Herskovits, 1940 (1952, pp. 185–187).
10 Discussed in Lapavitsas (1991).
11 See, for instance, Humphrey (1985, 1992), Orlove (1986); Humphrey and Hugh-Jones (1992).
12 Chapman (1980) unfairly attacks Marx's use of direct exchange relations in the analysis of money, because she is not aware of the distinction between form and substance of value. Her assertion that barter could and does occur in every society is not damaging to the theoretical analysis of the form of value.
13 Power is treated here purely in the sense that Hobbes, 1651 (see 1968, Pt I, Ch. X) uses the term.

4 The social content of credit relations

1 Finance, however, is a broader concept than credit, and involves all forms of acquisition of money funds by capitalist enterprises, including the issuing of shares. Shareholding involves outright property relations (equity) that convey the right to receive a stream of dividend payments in the future. Evidently, relations of equity differ qualitatively from relations of credit. The distinction between finance and credit is pursued at greater length in Itoh and Lapavitsas (1999, Ch. 4, 5).

2 For instance, Hilferding (1910, see 1981, Ch. 5); DeBrunhoff, 1973 (1976, pp. 77–98).

3 See Aybar and Lapavitsas (2001), which also offers a brief discussion of the role of information at each level of the credit system.

4 See Lapavitsas (2000).

5 The shroud of mystery surrounding credit was apparent to classical economists, but to none more vividly than Steuart (1767, Vol. III, Bk IV, Pt I, p. 138), who explicitly discussed credit as a relationship of confidence. It is worth quoting at length: 'Many political writers in treating of credit, represent it as being of very mysterious nature; owing its establishment to a confidence not easily accounted for, and disappearing from the slightest unfavourable circumstances ... That credit, in its infancy, is of a very delicate nature, I willingly allow; as also that we have many examples which confirm the sentiments of those who believe it to contain, in itself, something very mysterious: but this proves no more, than that, in such cases, credit ... has not been properly established. The cause of confidence has had nothing in it but opinion, and when this is the case, credit is but a shadow; and like a thin vapour, it may be dissipated by the smallest breath of wind.'.

6 This is often found in macroeconomic models that include a banking sector supplying credit to buttress aggregate demand; by supplying credit, banks ensure sale of output, realisation of profits, and thus repayment of their own advances. The ability of banks to influence the performance of the economy appears to derive from their limitless ability to generate credit, rather than from the processes of accumulation itself. Models of this kind are characteristic of post-Keynesian economics; see Lapavitsas and Saad-Filho (2000).

7 For analysis of turnover time and profitability, see Foley (1986); Lapavitsas (2000a).

8 The ultimate cause of it is the asymmetry that exists between commodities and money, discussed in Chapter 3. Capitalists who possess money benefit from its unique ability to buy and generate additional profits.

9 Homage and fealty between the feudal lord and his vassal are an example of hierarchical trust. They imposed broad and mutually conditioned obligations on both superior and inferior (aid and protection) (Bloch, 1961, Vol. 1, Ch. 1, p. 16).

10 The original theoretical formulation, as far as the optimal contract is concerned, goes back to Townsend (1979). The principal–agent framework has become standard within contemporary microeconomics of finance. Influential papers in this vein include Gale and Hellwig (1985), for whom the borrower can cheat the lender because of superior information possessed; Hart and Holmstrom (1987), for whom the principal is unaware of the circumstances leading to the agent's actions; and Innes (1990), who makes essentially the same assumption.

11 Schumpeter (1954, pp. 729–730) calls this approach to banking credit the 'Commercial-Bill Theory of Banking', and associates it with the Banking School, but he is also glibly dismissive of it.

12 For further analysis of the emergence of credit money through this process, see Lapavitsas (1991) and Itoh and Lapavitsas (1999, Ch. 4).

13 For a clear presentation of Marx's distinctions, see Fine (1985–1986).

14 This is the well-known issue of maturity transformation effected by banks, whereby their liabilities typically have a much shorter term to maturity than their assets (Sayers, 1938, Ch. 2; Goodhart, 1989, pp. 104–113).

15 This asymmetry currently provides neoclassical economics with a standard approach to banking, associated with Diamond (1984). Banks are 'delegated monitors'; that is, they possess a comparative advantage in collecting and evaluating information about borrowers, and hence monitor them on behalf of bank depositors.

16 Important contributions in this vein include Leland and Pyle (1977); Bryant (1980); Diamond and Dybvig (1983); Diamond (1984); Ramakrishnan and Thakor (1984); Boyd and Prescott (1986).

17 See Lapavitsas (1997).

18 The complex links between clearing and central banking are discussed in Timberlake (1984), but from a perspective that sees central banks as 'unnatural' in a capitalist economy.

19 Evidently these developments occur for reasons that are not simply economic. They rest on domestic political considerations as well as on international relations in the world market.

20 This power has increased substantially in recent years as central banks were proclaimed legally independent of the elected government. For further discussion of central bank independence, see Lapavitsas (1997).

21 Goodhart (1985) has argued that this function of central banks is the reason for their existence.

5 Social norms and institutions in the capitalist economy

1 For the assumptions, structure and results of general equilibrium models, see especially Arrow and Hahn (1971).

2 Simon (1955, 1959, 1978) has made a very influential critique of instrumental rationality from within the mainstream. His argument, tagged to what he termed 'bounded rationality', stresses the restricted cognitive powers of human beings when confronted with complex situations. For Simon, the processes of decision-making, the searching and learning devices employed in coming to rational decisions, are as significant as the internal consistency of the decisions. 'Bounded rationality' is important to contemporary neoclassical economics since institutions, norms and customs are now acknowledged as integral parts of the processes of decision-making.

3 In Hirschman's (1970, 1977, 1982, 1984) work can be found a sustained critique of the simplistic assumptions made by neoclassical theory regarding the motivations and preferences of the individual. His erudite discussion of 'passions' and 'interests' offers insight into the gradual emergence and eventual ascendancy of the typically capitalist motive of private monetary gain (Hirschman, 1977).

4 Economic factors are, of course, also social. However, in order to avoid pedantic disputes and conform with general usage in the literature, the term social has been used in this book to indicate non-economic aspects of social life.

5 A point stressed in Febrero and Schwartz (1995), a volume in honour of Becker's 65th birthday.

6 Economists might be sceptical or dismissive of Becker's claims, but they have little doubt regarding the superiority of the analytical techniques of economics, which typically amount to individual rational choice. Thus: 'What

gives economics its imperialist invasive power is that our analytical categories – scarcity, cost, preferences, opportunities, etc. – are truly universal in applicability. Even more important, is our structured organisation of these concepts into the distinct yet intertwined process of optimisation on the individual level and equilibrium on the social level of analysis.' (Hirshleifer, 1985, p. 53).

7 This approach to the very complex social phenomenon of the family has made even economists deeply uneasy (Ben-Porath, 1982).

8 Posner (1977, 1981) has enthusiastically applied a similar approach to historical and non-economic issues, including the law.

9 As shown in Luce and Raifa (1957).

10 The instances in which game-theoretic analysis brings out the social content of economic phenomena are legion. A particularly clear example is Lindbeck (1995).

11 Olson's (1965) discussion of the prisoner's dilemma and free-rider issues is fundamental to contemporary analysis of the problem of collective action. Axelrod's (1984) analysis of cooperation in repeated games is a more recent and very influential work.

12 Hierarchy is accepted by the individuals concerned, first, because 'bounded rationality' makes the established rules of the firm a preferred framework for decision-making compared to a long series of contracts, and second, in order to mitigate the dangers of 'opportunism' – that is, the pursuit of self-interest through deceiving and fooling others.

13 It seems plausible, therefore, that such phenomena are not 'deviations' but the actual form and content of reality. However, for economic theorists trained to think that general equilibrium is the most developed theoretical abstraction regarding capitalism, they appear as deviations simply because they cannot be explained within general equilibrium.

14 Information and knowledge are far from new concepts in economic theory. Among the neoclassicals, Arrow (1974b, 1984, especially Ch. 11, 12) has written extensively on the role of information in economic interaction as well as on knowledge and uncertainty. Knight's (1921) work on risk and uncertainty remains a standard reference, while Keynes (1921) considered his own stab at probability to be his most important contribution to theory.

15 See Smelser and Swedberg (1994) on present-day economic sociology, and Piore's (1996) review of their book from an economist's standpoint.

16 A view laid out systematically in Parsons and Smelser (1956).

17 See Swedberg *et al.* (1987); also Ingham (1996), who concludes however that the methodological differences between the disciplines remain too great for true convergence to take place.

18 A selective list includes Baker (1984, 1990), Stearns (1986), Mizruchi and Stearns (1994a, 1994b), Petersen and Rajan (1994), Abolafia (1996), DiMaggio and Louch (1998).

19 Granovetter has been critical of neoclassicism, but also seems to accept that economics is neoclassicism, and that the rational individual is an appropriate point of reference for economic analysis. A powerful (if now dated) statement of the virtues of the analytical approach of sociology can be found in Oberschall and Leifer (1986).

20 Analysis in this section owes a heavy debt to Fine's (2001) excellent critique of 'social capital'.

21 'Social capital' is also associated, though very differently, with the work of Bourdieu (1986, 1996). As discussed by Fine (2001, Ch. 4), Bourdieu's social capital draws on Marxist thinking. There are many types of capital for Bourdieu, including economic, cultural and symbolic, that capture a variety of relations in capitalist society – from money to education to rank and prestige. His

social capital is a highly fluid notion, which refers to social reproduction rather than rational individual choice (see also Calhoun *et al.*, 1993).

22 It did not take long for 'social capital' theorists to exploit the evident affinities with 'network' theory. Evans (1996a, 1996b), for instance, locates social capital in network ties, while Paraskevopoulos (2001) treats the two as complementary concepts in his analysis of regional development.

23 Puttnam's methods and recourse to Italian history have been subjected to heavy criticism by Tarrow (1996).

24 See also Ostrom (1998).

25 This issue is discussed at length in Fine *et al.* (2001).

26 Fine (2001) provides an extensive review of this large and changing literature. Important readings are Grootaert and van Bastelaer (2002) and Woolcock (1998).

27 Nevertheless, even this mild radicalism was too much for the adherents of the Washington Consensus. By his own admission (interview in the *Financial Times*, 13/14 July 2002), Stiglitz was pushed from his position as chief economist of the World Bank because of pressure by highly-placed US government officials. His vitriolic attacks on the mode of operation of the International Monetary Fund, and on the professional and moral competence of its staff, have been the stuff of several stories in the international press.

6 The emergence and functioning of money

1 In von Mises' (1934) terms, they are the *catallactic* (exchange-related) and *acatallactic* (non-exchange) theories of money's origin. Von Mises decisively rejected the latter.

2 Especially Zelizer (1983, 1987, 1994, 1996, 1998).

3 Essentially the same argument was also put forth by Mill (1848, Ch. VIII).

4 For an informative discussion, see Ioannides (1992).

5 Weber (1968, Vol. I, Ch. 2) discusses 'formal' and 'substantive' rationality in economic activity, broadly in the spirit of the Historical School. His methodical listing of money forms, and general sympathy for Knapp's (1905) systematic exposition of the view of money as claim on goods (despite occasional criticism), rest on the assumption that money is associated with the diktat of the state.

6 See Lapavitsas (2002).

7 'Economic' has a strict and technical meaning in this connection. It means the price that is compatible with the general economic situation, that is, endowments, productivities, and tastes.

8 A problem expressed with clarity by Hahn (1965, 1982).

9 See Ostroy and Starr (1990) for a review and discussion of this voluminous literature.

10 It is also possible to introduce money into overlapping generations' models by focusing on money's ability to store value (Samuelson, 1958; Wallace, 1980). These models do not openly rely on money's function as means of exchange, and seem unrelated to Clower's conjecture. However, the store of value function cannot be separated from money's unique ability to buy, as is discussed in more detail in Lapavitsas (2000b). The special character of money still has to be tackled whether the analytical focus is on the store of value or means of exchange.

11 Steuart (1805) wrote an entire treatise on physical measurement, an issue that he approached along the same lines: an abstract unit of measurement is first established, and an approximation of it is used in practice.

12 'Babylonia provided a characteristic instance of the existence of a dual system

of currency ... The fact that the weight of the *shekel* was equal to that of 180 grains of barley seems to indicate that barley preceded silver as the principal monetary unit. From the beginning of the historic period the two currencies functioned side by side both as a standard of value and as medium of exchange ... Nevertheless, over a long period silver was definitely the principal currency and barley an important subsidiary currency employed to facilitate business transactions, especially in rural districts, in face of a shortage of silver ... It is difficult to form an opinion whether the use of silver as a standard of value preceded its use as a medium of exchange.' (Einzig, 1949, p. 211).

13 It is easy to find instances of this approach, including in the classics of anthropology. See, for instance, Firth (1938); Evans-Pritchard (1940); Herskovits (1940); Douglas (1958, 1967); Hart (1986, 2002).

14 Historical writing on ancient Greece sheds some light on this issue. Michell (1957, pp. 314–321), for instance, discusses the use of oxen and of 'talents' of copper and gold as units of value in the Homeric world. Both oxen and the metals were far more frequently used as means of account than as means of exchange. Yet it does not follow that their original monetary use was as abstract units of account. Since both were typical representations of wealth in Homeric society, their monetary role might have been connected with functioning as means of exchange. Moreover, in discussing pre-coinage Greek money, Kim (2001) emphasises the role played by economic factors in inducing monetisation in Archaic Greece, and hence the particular importance of silver in commodity form (bullion). His focus on the economic role of money contrasts with the current interest in the symbolic and broadly non-economic role of money among historians of Ancient Greece. See, for instance, the debate between von Reden (1995, 1997, 2002) and Kurke (1999).

15 This was the thrust of von Mises' (1934) critique of 'acatallactic' doctrines of money's emergence.

16 A suggestion already made by the German Historical School (see Knapp, 1905).

17 Several aspects of this current are discussed in Itoh and Lapavitsas (1999, Ch. 2, p. 10) and Lapavitsas and Saad-Filho, 2000.

18 It also seems to encourage analysis of the social relations that surround money's use, and hence it has attracted the interest of sociologists – for instance, Ingham (1984, 1994, 2000, 2001).

19 The influence of Heihnsohn and Steiger (1983, 1989) on post-Keynesian treatments of this issue is significant (see Wray, 1990). For Heihnsohn and Steiger, money originates in the advance of private property among parties engaging in economic interaction, rather than in the exchange of commodities. For further discussion of this issue, see Itoh and Lapavitsas (1999, Ch. 10).

20 There have also been elaborate neoclassical attempts to build theoretical schemata in which commodities exchange on the basis of credits and debits are settled by money – see, for instance, Hawtrey (1919) and Hicks (1967).

21 The 'endogeneity' of credit-money has for long been recognised by Marxist political economy, though without the same significance attached to it as by post-Keynesianism (Itoh and Lapavitsas, 1999, Ch. 2; see also Lapavitsas, 1991, 2000).

22 A selective list of related literature includes: White (1981, 1992, 2002); DiMaggio and Powell (1983); Pahl (1983, 1999); Stinchcombe (1983); Baker (1987); DiMaggio (1990, 1994); Dodd (1994); Singh (1997); Tilly (1998).

23 Much of this section derives from the debate between Fine and Lapavitsas (2000) and Zelizer (2000). See also Ingham (2001).

24 Essentially 'substantivist' contributions are those of Bohannan (1955, 1959)

and Dalton (1960, 1961, 1969), while 'formalist' ones include Burling (1962), LeClair (1962) and Cook (1966). For later overviews and contributions, see Gudeman (1978), Plattner (1982) and Ortner (1984).

25 Marxist economic anthropology is naturally sympathetic toward the 'substantivists', but rightly stresses the concepts of mode of production and surplus appropriation that are largely absent from the substantivist cannon. Some of the complexities of applying mode of production analysis to non-capitalist societies studied by anthropology can be seen in Godelier (1966, 1973, 1982, 1984); Meillasoux (1973, 1983); Kahn (1978); Kahn and Llobera (1980); Plattner (1989).

26 The issues involved in this debate were not new to anthropology, which has long been concerned with the appropriate methodology for analysis of economic phenomena. Malinowski (1921), for instance, presented some of his early results in economic terms heavily influenced by mainstream theory. Firth (1929, 1938, 1939, 1951, 1959, 1967; Firth and Yamey, 1967), the father of economic anthropology, analysed the economic life of non-capitalist tribal societies by using concepts and methods strongly influenced by neoclassicism. In contrast, Herskovits' (1940) influential tome found neoclassicism inapplicable to 'primitive' societies, a claim that was not to the liking of Knight (1941), who argued in favour of the 'universal principles' of economy.

27 The particularity of local money and its tenacity in the face of competition from more universal money is well-attested in anthropological work. For a relatively recent contribution, see Guyer (1993, 1995).

7 Money as unit of account and means of exchange in a socialist society

1 In Engels' (1892) terms.

2 The reformist outlook inherent to the Second International is most clearly expressed by Bernstein (1899, Ch. 3).

3 Marx's writings on socialism, scanty as they are, could also be used to support the view that a socialist society would operate as a vast factory (Itoh, 1995, Ch. 3). Reconciling socialism as 'aggregate factory' with socialism as 'association of producers' is neither intuitive nor easy.

4 See Itoh (1995, Ch. 4). In the first instalment of the debate on markets and socialism, von Mises (1920) and Hayek (1935) attacked the feasibility of socialism on the grounds that it is impossible to arrive at rational prices for means of production (capital goods) in the absence of the market, and therefore it is impossible to plan aggregate investment rationally. This assertion was rejected by socialists, especially Taylor (1929) and Lange (1936–1937), who argued that capital goods could be rationally priced in a socialist economy through a process of trial and error. The analytical framework used by Taylor and Lange derived from Walrasian general equilibrium.

5 See Auerbach *et al.* (1988).

6 The miraculous powers and insight of the 'entrepreneur' were fundamental to Menger's derivation of money (as shown in Chapter 6).

7 The theoretical treatment of profits as a residual proved to be a major weakness of Ricardian economics, contributing to its eventual decline in Britain (see Meek, 1950).

8 As represented by Gray, Bray and others; see Saad-Filho (1993).

9 In a letter to Annenkov, Marx (1846, p. 105) states: 'Mr Proudhon is, from top to toe, a philosopher, an economist of the petty bourgeoisie . . . He is at one and the same time bourgeois and man of the people. In his heart of hearts he prides himself on his impartiality, on having found the correct balance, allegedly distinct from the happy medium.'

10 For Marx (1867, p. 135), labour of higher skill and greater intensity (complex) contributes more abstract labour per unit time, and hence counts as a multiple of less skilled and intensive labour (simple). This also implies that those who perform skilled or more intensive labour would probably receive higher remuneration than others. Marx (1875, pp. 86–87), for instance, argued that in the early stages of communist society workers who have more skills and work more intensively than average should receive proportionately higher remuneration. Nevertheless, if skills result from education and training rather than from innate capacity and learning-on-the-job, the distinction between complex and simple labour would be attenuated, as long as education was freely and socially provided (see Itoh, 1995, pp. 53–57).

11 Taken together, restrictions on money's ability to buy investment goods and labour power would amount to preventing money from functioning as capital. By the same token, emergence of a capitalist class would be hampered.

12 The idea of labour money has generally made few inroads into existing LETS schemes. Some alternative money schemes, such as 'Ithaca money', have deployed time-based currencies (Lietaert, 2001). Other schemes that deploy 'time-dollars', generated by participants providing services to each other, are even more widespread. Bowring (1998) strongly advocates converting LETS to 'time dollars', presenting this idea as a radical further development of the schemes. Despite mentioning Marx, he does not comment on Marx's rejection of labour money.

Bibliography

Abolafia, M. 1996. *Making Markets*, Cambridge: Harvard University Press.

Adaman, F. and Devine, P. 1996. 'The Economic Calculation Debate: Lessons for Socialists', *Cambridge Journal of Economics*, 20, 523–537.

Akerlof, G. 1970. 'The Market for 'Lemons': Quality Uncertainty and the Market Mechanism', *Quarterly Journal of Economics*, 84, 488–500.

Akerlof, G. 1980. 'A Theory of Social Custom, of Which Unemployment May Be One Consequence', *Quarterly Journal of Economics*, 94, 749–775.

Akerlof, G. 1982. 'Labor Contracts as Partial Gift Exchange', *Quarterly Journal of Economics*, 97, 543–569.

Akerlof, G. 1983. 'Loyalty Filters', *American Economic Review*, 73, 54–63.

Akerlof, G. 1984. 'Introduction', in *An Economic Theorist's Book of Tales*, Cambridge: Cambridge University Press.

Akerlof, G. 1990. 'George Akerlof', in R. Swedberg, (ed.) *Economics and Sociology. Redefining Their Boundaries*, Princeton: Princeton University Press.

Albritton, R. 1991. *A Japanese Approach to the Stages of Capitalist Development*, London: Macmillan.

Albritton, R. 1999. *Dialectics and Deconstruction in Political Economy*, London: Macmillan.

Althusser, L. 1969. *For Marx*, London: Allen Lane, Penguin.

Althusser, L. and Balibar, E. 1970. *Reading 'Capital'*, London: New Left Books.

Aoki, M. 1988. *Information, Incentives, and Bargaining in the Japanese Economy*, Cambridge: Cambridge University Press.

Appadurai, A. 1986. 'Introduction: Commodities and the Politics of Value', in A. Appadurai (ed.) *The Social Life of Things: Commodities in Cultural Perspective*, Cambridge: Cambridge University Press.

Armstrong, W. E. 1924. 'Rossel Island Money: A Unique Monetary System', *Economic Journal*, 34, 422–429.

Arrow, K. 1974a. *The Limits of Organization*, London & New York: W.W. Norton.

Arrow, K. 1974b. *Essays in the Theory of Risk Bearing*, Amsterdam, Oxford/New York: Elsevier.

Arrow, K. 1984. *The Economics of Information*, Collected Papers of Kenneth J. Arrow, Vol. 4, Oxford: Basil Blackwell.

Arrow, K. and Hahn, F. 1971. *General Competitive Analysis*, Amsterdam: North Holland.

Arthur, C. 1993. 'Hegel's "Logic" and Marx's "Capital"', in F. Moseley (ed.) *Marx's Method in 'Capital': A Re-examination*, Atlantic Highlands: Humanities Press.

Auerbach, P., Desai, M. and Shamsavari, A. 1988. 'The Transition from Actually Existing Capitalism', *New Left Review*, 170, 61–78.

Axelrod, R. 1984. *The Evolution of Cooperation*, New York: Basic Books.

Aybar, S. and Lapavitsas, C. 2001. 'Financial System Design and the Post-Washington Consensus', in B Fine, C. Lapavitsas and J. Pincus (eds) *Neither the Washington nor the Post-Washington Consensus: Development Policy at the Crossroads*, London: Routledge.

Baker, B. 1987. 'What is Money? A Social Structural Interpretation', in M. Mizruchi and M. Schwartz (eds) *Intercorporate Relations*, Cambridge: Cambridge University Press.

Baker, W. 1984. 'The Social Structure of a National Securities Market', *American Journal of Sociology*, 89(4), 775–811.

Baker, W. 1990. 'Market Networks and Corporate Behavior', *American Journal of Sociology*, 6, 589–625.

Bardhan, P. 1993. 'On Tackling the Soft Budget Constraint in Market Socialism', in P. Bardhan and J. Roemer (eds) *Market Socialism: The Current Debate*, New York: Oxford University Press.

Bardhan, P. and Roemer, J. 1992. 'Market Socialism: A Case for Rejuvenation', *Journal of Economic Perspectives*, 6, 101–116.

Becker, G. 1965. 'A Theory of the Allocation of Time', *Economic Journal*, 75, 493–517.

Becker, G. 1976. *The Economic Approach to Human Behavior*, Chicago: Chicago University Press.

Becker, G. 1991. *A Treatise on the Family*, Cambridge, Mass.: Harvard University Press.

Becker, G. 1993. *Human Capital*, (3rd edn), Chicago: University of Chicago Press.

Becker, G. 1996. *Accounting for Tastes*, Cambridge: Harvard University Press.

Ben-Porath, Y. 1982. 'Economics and the Family – Match or Mismatch? A Review of Becker's *A Treatise on the Family*', *Journal of Economic Literature*, XX, 52–64.

Bernstein, E. 1899 (1961). *Evolutionary Socialism*, New York: Schocken Books.

Binmore, K. 1998. *Game Theory and the Social Contract: Just Playing*, Cambridge: MIT Press.

Blau, P. 1964. *Exchange and Power in Social Life*, New York: Wiley.

Bloch, M. 1961. *Feudal Society*, Vol. 1, 2, London: Routledge & Kegan Paul.

Brewster Stearns, L. 1986. 'Capital Market Effects on External Control of Corporations', *Theory and Society*, 15, 47–75.

Bohannan, P. 1955. 'Some Principles of Exchange and Investment among the Tiv', *American Anthropologist*, 37(1), 60–70.

Bohannan, P. 1959. 'The Impact of Money on an African Subsistence Economy', *Journal of Economic History*, XIX(4), 491–503.

Bourdieu, P. 1979 (1986). *Distinction: A Social Critique of the Judgement of Taste*, London: Routledge.

Bourdieu, P. 1989 (1996). *The State Nobility: Elite Schools in the Field of Power*, Cambridge: Polity Press.

Bowles, S. 1985. 'The Production Process in a Competitive Economy: Walrasian, Neo-Hobbesian, and Marxian Models', *American Economic Review*, 75(1), 16–36.

Bowles, S. and Gintis, H. 2001. 'The Evolution of Strong Reciprocity', Working Paper, Santa Fe Institute.

Bowring, F. 1998. 'LETS: An Eco-Socialist Alternative?', *New Left Review*, 232, 91–111.

Boyd, J. and Prescott, E. 1986. 'Financiary Intermediary-Coalitions', *Journal of Economic Theory*, 38, 211–232.

Boyd, R. and Richerson, P. 1992. 'Punishment Allows the Evolution of Cooperation (or Anything Else) in Sizeable Groups', *Ethology and Sociobiology*, 113, 171–195.

Braudel, F. 1981. *The Structures of Everyday Life, Vol. I of Civilisation and Capitalism, 15th–18th Century*, London: Collins.

Braudel, F. 1982. *The Wheels of Commerce, Vol. II of Civilisation and Capitalism, 15th–18th Century*, London: Collins.

Braudel, F. 1984. *The Perspective of the World, Vol. III of Civilization and Capitalism, 15th–18th Century*, London: Collins.

Bryant, J. 1980. 'A Model of Reserves, Bank Runs and Deposit Insurance', *Journal of Banking and Finance*, 43, 749–761.

Burling, R. 1962. 'Maximization Theories and the Study of Economic Anthropology', *American Anthropologist*, 64(2), 802–821.

Calhoun, C., LiPuma, E. and Postone, M. (eds) 1993. *Bourdieu: Critical Perspectives*, Cambridge: Polity Press.

Caplow, T. 1982. 'Christmas Gifts and Kin Networks', *American Sociological Review*, 47, 383–392.

Caplow, T. 1984. 'Rule Enforcement without Visible Means: Christmas Gift Giving in Middletown', *American Journal of Sociology*, 89(4), 1306–1323.

Carrier, J. 1991. 'Gifts, Commodities and Social Relations: a Maussian View of Exchange', *Sociological Forum* 6, 119–136.

Carrier, J. 1992a. 'Occidentalism: The World Turned Upside-down', *American Ethnologist*, 19(2), 195–212.

Carrier, J. 1992b. 'Emerging Alienation in Production: A Maussian History', *Man*, 27(3), 539–558.

Carrier, J. 1994a. 'Alienating Objects: The Emergence of Alienation in Retail Trade', *Man*, 29(2), 359–380.

Carrier, J. 1994b. *Gifts and Commodities: Exchange and Western Capitalism since 1700*, London: Routledge.

Carrier, J. (ed.) 1997. *Meanings of the Market*, Oxford: Berg.

Cashdan, E. 1989. 'Hunters and Gatherers: Economic Behavior in Bands', in S. Plattner (ed.) *Economic Anthropology*, Stanford: Stanford University Press.

Chapman, A. 1980. 'Barter as a Universal Mode of Exchange', *L'Homme*, 20(3), 33–83.

Cheal, D. 1987. '"Showing Them You Love Them": Gift Giving and the Dialectic of Intimacy', *Sociological Review*, 35(2), 150–169.

Clower, R. 1967. 'A Reconsideration of the Microfoundations of Monetary Theory', *Western Economic Journal*, 6(4), 1–8.

Coase, R. 1937. 'The Nature of the Firm', *Economica*, 4(16), 331–351.

Coase, R. 1960. 'The Problem of Social Cost', *Journal of Law and Economics*, 3, 1–44.

Codere, H. 1968. 'Money-Exchange Systems and a Theory of Money', *Man*, 3(4), 557–577.

Coleman, J. 1972. 'Systems of Social Exchange', *Journal of Mathematical Sociology*, 2, 145–163.

Coleman, J. 1975. 'Social Structure and a Theory of Action', in P. Blau (ed.) *Approaches to the Study of Social Structure*, New York: Free Press.

Coleman, J. 1988. 'Social Capital in the Creation of Human Capital', *American Journal of Sociology*, 94(Suppl), 95–120.

Colcman, J. 1990. *Foundations of Social Theory*, Cambridge: Harvard University Press.

Coleman, J. 1993. 'The Rational Reconstruction of Society', *American Sociological Review*, 58(6), 898–912.

Coleman, J. 1994. 'A Rational Choice Perspective on Economic Sociology', in N. Smelser and R. Swedberg (eds) *The Handbook of Economic Sociology*, Princeton: Princeton University Press.

Cook, S. 1966. 'The Obsolete "Anti-Market" Mentality: A Critique of the Substantive Approach to Economic Anthropology', *American Anthropologist*, 68(2), 323–345.

Dalton, G. 1960. 'A Note of Clarification on Economic Surplus', *American Anthropologist*, 62(2), 483–490.

Dalton, G. 1961. 'Economic Theory and Primitive Society', *American Anthropologist*, 63(1), 1–25.

Dalton, G. 1965. 'Primitive Money', *American Anthropologist*, 67(1), 44–65.

Dalton, G. 1969. 'Theoretical Issues in Economic Anthropology', *Current Anthropology*, 10(1), 63–102.

Davidson, P. 1972. *Money and the Real World*, London and Basingstoke: Macmillan.

Davidson, P. 1989. 'Keynes and Money', in R. Hill (ed.) *Keynes, Money and Monetarism*, London: Macmillan.

Davidson, P. 1990. 'Why Money Matters: Lessons from a Half-century of Monetary Theory', in *Money and Employment*, collected writings of Paul Davidson, London and Basingstoke: Macmillan.

Davis, J. 1992. *Exchange*, Buckingham: Open University Press.

DeBrunhoff, S. 1973 (1976). *Marx on Money*, New York: Urizen Books.

Deutch, M. 1958. 'Trust and Suspicion', *Journal of Conflict Resolution*, 2(4), 265–279.

Diamond, D. 1984. 'Financial Intermediation and Delegated Monitoring', *Review of Economic Studies*, 51(3), 393–414.

Diamond, D. and Dybvig, P. 1983. 'Bank Runs, Deposit Insurance and Liquidity', *Journal of Political Economy*, 91, 401–419.

DiMaggio, P. J. 1990. 'Cultural Aspects of Economic Action and Organisation', in R. Friedland and A. F. Robertson (eds) *Beyond the Marketplace*, New York: Aldine de Gruyter.

DiMaggio, P. J. 1994. 'Culture and Economy', in N. Smelser and R. Swedberg (eds) *The Handbook of Economic Sociology*, Princeton: Princeton University Press.

DiMaggio, P. J. and Louch, H. 1998. 'Socially Embedded Consumer Transactions: For What Kinds of Transactions Do People Most Often Use Networks?', *American Sociological Review*, 63, 619–637.

DiMaggio, P. J. and Powell, W. 1983. 'The Iron Cage Revisited: Institutional Isomorphism and Collective Rationality in Organizational Fields', *American Sociological Review*, 48, 147–160.

Dodd, N. 1994. *The Sociology of Money*, New York: Continuum.

Douglas, M. 1958. 'Raffia Cloth Distribution in the Lele Economy', *Africa*, 28, 109–122; also published in G. Dalton (ed.) 1967. *Tribal and Peasant Economies*, New York: The Natural History Press.

Douglas, M. 1967. 'Primitive Rationing', in R. Firth (ed.) *Themes in Economic Anthropology*, London: Tavistock Publications.

Dow, S. 1984. 'Methodology and the Analysis of a Monetary Economy', *Economies et Societes*, 18, *Monnaie et Production 1*, reprinted in *Money and the Economic Process*, 1993, Aldershot and Brookfield: Edward Elgar.

Duesenberry, J. 1960. Comment on 'An Economic Analysis of Fertility', in *Demographic and Economic Changes in Developed Countries*, Princeton: Princeton University Press.

Durkheim, E. 1893 (1997). *The Division of Labour in Society*, New York: Free Press.

Einzig, P. 1949. *Primitive Money*, London: Eyre and Spottiswood.

Elster, J. 1982. 'Marxism, Functionalism, and Game Theory', *Theory and Society*, 99(3), 453–482.

Elster, J. 1988. 'Is There (Or Should There Be) A Right to Work?', in A. Guttman (ed.) *Democracy and the Welfare State*, Princeton: Princeton University Press.

Elster, J. 1989. 'Social Norms and Economic Theory', *Journal of Economic Perspectives*, 3(4), 117.

Engels, F. 1892 (1954). *Socialism: Utopian and Scientific*, Moscow: Progress Publishers.

Evans, P. 1996a. 'Introduction: Development Strategies across the Public–Private Divide', *World Development*, 24(6), 1033–1037.

Evans, P. 1996b. 'Government Action, Social Capital and Development: Reviewing the Evidence on Synergy', *World Development*, 24(6), 1119–1132.

Evans-Pritchard, E. E. 1940. *The Nuer*, Oxford: Clarendon Press.

Febrero, R. and Schwartz, P. (eds) 1995. *The Essence of Becker*, Stanford: Hoover Institution Press.

Fine, B. 1975. *Marx's Capital*, London: Macmillan.

Fine, B. 1985–1986. 'Banking Capital and the Theory of Interest', *Science and Society*, XLIX(4), 387–413.

Fine, B. 1997. 'The New Revolution in Economics', *Capital and Class*, 61, 143–148.

Fine, B. 1998a. 'The Triumph of Economics: Or 'Rationality' Can Be Dangerous to Your Reasoning', in J. Carrier and D. Miller (eds) *Virtualism: The New Political Economy*, London: Berg.

Fine, B. 1998b. *Labour Market Theory: A Constructive Reassessment*, London: Routledge.

Fine, B. 1999a. 'From Becker to Bourdieu: Economics Confronts the Social Sciences', *International Papers in Political Economy*, 5(3), 1–43.

Fine, B. 1999b. 'A Question of Economics: Is It Colonising the Other Social Sciences?', *Economy and Society*, 28(3), 403–425.

Fine, B. 2001. *Social Capital versus Social Theory*, London: Routledge.

Fine, B. 2002. *The World of Consumption* (2nd edn), London and New York: Routledge.

Fine, B. and Harris, L. 1979. *Rereading Capital*, New York: Columbia University Press.

Fine, B. and Lapavitsas, C. 2000. 'Markets and Money in Social Theory: What Role for Economics?', *Economy and Society*, 29(3), 357–382.

Fine, B. and Leopold, E. 1993. *The World of Consumption*, London and New York: Routledge.

Fine, B., Lapavitsas, C. and Pincus, J. (eds) 2001. *Development Policy in the Twenty-First Century*, London: Routledge.

Fine, B., Lapavitsas, C. and Saad-Filho, A. 2004. 'Transforming the "Transformation Problem": Why the New Interpretation is a Wrong Turning', *Review of Radical Political Economics*, forthcoming.

Firth, R. 1929. *Primitive Economics of the New Zealand Maori*, London: George Routledge & Sons.
Firth, R. 1938. *Human Types*, London: Thomas Nelson.
Firth, R. 1939. *Primitive Polynesian Economy*, London: George Routledge & Sons.
Firth, R. 1951 (1961). *Elements of Social Organisation*, Westport: Glenwood Press.
Firth, R. 1959. *Social Change in Tikopia*, London: George Allen & Unwin.
Firth, R. (ed.) 1967. *Themes in Economic Anthropology*, London: Tavistock Publications.
Firth, R. and Yamey, B. 1964. *Capital, Saving and Credit in Peasant Societies*, London: George Allen & Unwin.
Foley, D. 1982. 'Realisation and Accumulation in a Marxian Model of the Circuit of Capital', *Journal of Economic Theory*, 28, 300–319.
Foley, D. 1986. *Understanding Capital*, Cambridge: Harvard University Press.
Frazer, J. G. 1900. *The Golden Bough*, Vol. I, II, III, London: Macmillan & Co.
Friedland, R. and Robertson, A. F. (eds) 1990. *Beyond the Marketplace*, New York: Aldine De Gruyter.
Gale, D. and Hellwig, M. 1985. 'Incentive-Compatible Debt Contracts: The One-Period Problem', *Review of Economic Studies*, 52, 647–663.
Godelier, M. 1966 (1972). *Rationality and Irrationality in Economics*, London: NLB.
Godelier, M. 1973 (1977). *Perspectives in Marxist Anthropology*, Cambridge: Cambridge University Press.
Godelier, M. 1982 (1986a). *The Making of Great Men*, Cambridge: Cambridge University Press..
Godelier, M. 1984 (1986b). *The Mental and the Material*, London: Verso.
Godelier, M. 1996 (1999). *The Enigma of the Gift*, Chicago: University of Chicago Press.
Goodhart, C. A. E. 1985. *The Evolution of Central Banks*, Cambridge, Mass.: MIT Press.
Goodhart, C. A. E. 1989. *Money, Information and Uncertainty* (2nd edn), Basingstoke: Macmillan.
Gouldner, A. 1960. 'The Norm of Reciprocity: A Preliminary Statement', *American Sociological Review*, 25(2), 161–176.
Granovetter, M. 1973. 'The Strength of Weak Ties', *American Journal of Sociology*, 78, 1360–1380.
Granovetter, M. 1974. *Getting a Job: A Study of Contacts and Careers*, Cambridge, Mass.: Harvard University Press.
Granovetter, M. 1985. 'Economic Action and Social Structure: The Problem of Embeddedness', *American Journal of Sociology*, 91, 481–510.
Granovetter, M. 1994. 'Business Groups', in N. Smelser and R. Swedberg (eds) *The Handbook of Economic Sociology*, Princeton: Princeton University Press.
Gregory, C. 1980. 'Gifts to Men and Gifts to God: Gift Exchange and Capital Accumulation in Contemporary Papua', *Man*, 15, 626–652.
Gregory, C. 1982. *Gifts and Commodities*, London: Academic Press.
Gregory, C. 1997. *Savage Money*, Amsterdam: Harwood.
Grierson, Hamilton, P. J. 1903. *The Silent Trade: A Contribution to the Early History of Human Intercourse*, Edinburgh: William Green & Sons.
Grierson, P. 1977. *The Origin of Money*, London: Athlone Press and University of London.

Grootaert, C. and van Bastelaer, T. 2002. *The Role of Social Capital in Development: An Empirical Assessment*, Cambridge: Cambridge University Press.

Grossman, S. and Stiglitz, J. 1980. 'On the Impossibility of Informationally Efficient Markets', *American Economic Review*, 70, 393–408.

Gudeman, S. 1978. 'Anthropological Economics; The Question of Distribution', *Annual Review of Anthropology*, 7, 347–177.

Guttman, J. 1996. 'Rational Actors, Tit-for-Tat Types, and the Evolution of Cooperation', *Journal of Economic Behavior and Organization*, 29(1), 27–56.

Guyer, J. 1993. 'Wealth in People and Self-Realization in Equatorial Africa', *Man*, 28(2), 243–265.

Guyer, J. (ed.) 1995. *Money Matters*, Portsmouth, NH: Heinemann; London: James Currey.

Hahn, F. 1965. 'On Some Problems of Proving the Existence of an Equilibrium in a Monetary Economy', in F. Hahn and F. Brechling (eds) *The Theory of Interest Rates*, pp. 126–135, London: Macmillan.

Hahn, F. 1971. 'Equilibrium with Transactions Costs', *Econometrica*, 39, 417–439.

Hahn, F. 1973. 'On Transactions Costs, Inessential Sequence Economies and Money', *Review of Economic Studies*, 40, 449–461.

Hahn, F. 1982. *Money and Inflation*, Oxford: Blackwell.

Harrell-Bond, B. E., Voutira E. and Leopold, D. 1992. 'Counting the Refugees: Gifts, Givers, Patrons, Clients', *Journal of Refugee Studies*, 5(3/4), 205–225.

Hart, K. 1986. 'Heads or Tails? Two Sides of the Coin', *Man*, 21, 637–656.

Hart, K. 2002. *Money in an Unequal World: Keith Hart and his Memory Bank*, London: Texere (originally published as *The Memory Bank*, 2001, London: Profile).

Hart, O and Holmstrom, B. 1987. 'The Theory of Contracts', in T. Bewley (ed.) *Advances in Economic Theory*, New York: Cambridge University Press.

Hawtrey, R. G. 1919 (1950). *Currency and Credit*, Aberdeen: University Press.

Hayek, F. 1935. *Collectivist Economic Planning*, London: Routledge and Kegan Paul.

Heihnsohn, G. and Steiger, O. 1983. 'Private Property, Debts and Interest, Or: The Origin of Money and the Rise and Fall of Monetary Economies', *Studi Economici*, 21, 3–56.

Heihnsohn, G. and Steiger, O. 1989. 'The Veil of Barter: The Solution to the Task of Obtaining Representations of an Economy in which Money is Essential', in J. Kregel (ed.) *Inflation and Income Distribution in Capitalist Crisis*, Basingstoke: Macmillan.

Herskovits, M. 1940 (1952). *Economic Anthropology*, first published as *The Economic Life of Primitive Peoples*, New York: Alfred Knopf.

Hicks, J. 1967. *Critical Essays in Monetary Theory*, Oxford: Clarendon Press.

Hilferding, R. 1910 (1981). *Finance Capital*, London: Routledge & Kegan Paul.

Hirsch, P. 1986. 'From Ambushes to Golden Parachutes: Corporate Takeovers as an Instance of Cultural Framing and Institutional Integration', *American Journal of Sociology*, 91(4), 800–837.

Hirschman, A. 1970. *Exit, Voice and Loyalty*, Cambridge, Mass.: Harvard University Press.

Hirschman, A. 1977. *The Passions and the Interests*, Princeton: Princeton University Press.

Hirschman, A. 1982. *Shifting Involvements*, Oxford: Basil Blackwell

Hirschman, A. 1984. 'Against Parsimony: Three Easy Ways of Complicating Some Categories of Economic Discourse', *American Economic Review*, 74(2), 89–96.

Hirshleifer, J. 1985. 'The Expanding Domain of Economics', *American Economic Review*, 75(3), 53–68.

Hobbes, T. 1651 (1968). *Leviathan*, Harmondsworth: Penguin Books.

Homans, G. 1958. 'Social Behaviour as Exchange', *American Journal of Sociology*, LXII(6), 597–606.

Humphrey, C. 1985. 'Barter and Economic Disintegration', *Man*, 20, 48–72.

Humphrey, C. 1992. 'Fair Dealing, Just Rewards: The Ethics of Barter in North-East Nepal', in C. Humphrey and S. Hugh-Jones (eds) *Barter, Exchange and Value. An Anthropological Approach*, Cambridge: Cambridge University Press.

Humphrey, C. and Hugh-Jones, S. 1992. 'Introduction: Barter, Exchange and Value' in C. Humphrey and S. Hugh-Jones (eds) *Barter, Exchange and Value. An Anthropological Approach*, Cambridge: Cambridge University Press.

Hyde, L. 1983. *The Gift: Imagination and the Erotic Life of Property*, New York: Random House.

Ingham, G. 1984. *Capitalism Divided? The City and Industry in British Social Development*, London: Macmillan.

Ingham, G. 1994. 'States and Markets in the Production of World Money: Sterling and the Dollar', in S. Corbridge, R. Martin and N. Thrift (eds) *Money, Power and Space*, Oxford: Blackwell.

Ingham, G. 1996. 'Some Recent Changes in the Relationship between Economics and Sociology', *Cambridge Journal of Economics*, 20, 243–275.

Ingham, G. 2000. 'Babylonian Madness: Or the Historical and Sociological Origins of Money', in J. Smithin (ed.) *What is Money?*, London: Routledge.

Ingham, G. 2001. 'Fundamentals of a Theory of Money: Untangling Fine, Lapavitsas and Zelizer', *Economy and Society*, 30(3), 304–323.

Innes, R. 1990. 'Limited Liability and Incentive Contracting with Ex-Ante Action Choices', *Journal of Economic Theory*, 52(1), 45–67.

Ioannides, S. 1992. *The Market, Competition and Democracy: A Critique of Neo-Austrian Economics*, Aldershot: Edward Elgar.

Itoh, M. 1976. 'A Study of Marx's Theory of Value', *Science and Society*, 40(3), 307–340.

Itoh, M. 1981. *The Theory of Value and Capital*, (in Japanese), Tokyo: Tokyo University Press.

Itoh, M. 1988. *The Basic Theory of Capitalism*, London: Macmillan.

Itoh, M. 1995. *Political Economy for Socialism*, Basingstoke: Macmillan.

Itoh, M. and Lapavitsas, C. 1999. *Political Economy of Money and Finance*, London: Macmillan.

Iwai, K. 1988. 'The Evolution of Money – A Search for the Theoretic Foundation of Monetary Economics', CARESS Working Paper 88-03, University of Pennsylvania.

James, W. and Allen, N. J. (eds) 1998. *Marcel Mauss: A Centenary Tribute*, New York, Oxford: Berghahn Books.

Jevons, W. S. 1875. *Money and the Mechanism of Exchange*, London: Appleton.

Jones, R. 1976. 'The Origin and Development of Media of Exchange', *Journal of Political Economy*, 84, 757–776.

Kahn, J. K. 1978. 'Perspectives in Marxist Anthropology', *Journal of Peasant Studies*, 5(4), 485–496.

Kahn, J. K. and Llobera, J. R. 1980. 'French Marxist Anthropology: Twenty Years After', *Journal of Peasant Studies*, 8(1), 81–100.

Keynes, J. M. 1921 (1971). *A Treatise on Probability*, Royal Economic Society, London: Macmillan.

Keynes, J. M. 1930 (1973). *A Treatise on Money*, Royal Economic Society, London: Macmillan.

Kim, H. 2001. 'Archaic Coinage as Evidence for the Use of Money, in A. Meadows and K. Shipton (eds) *Money and its Uses in the Ancient Greek World*, Oxford: Oxford University Press.

Kiyotaki, N. and Wright, R. 1989. 'On Money as a Medium of Exchange'. *Journal of Political Economy*, 97, 927–954.

Kiyotaki, N. and Wright, R. 1991. 'A Contribution to the Pure Theory of Money', *Journal of Economic Theory*, 53, 215–235.

Knapp, G. 1905 1924. *The State Theory of Money*, London: MacMillan and Co.

Knight, F. 1921. *Risk, Uncertainty and Profit*, New York: Houghton Mifflin.

Knight, F. 1941. 'Anthropology and Economics', *Journal of Political Economy*, XLIX(2), 247–268.

Kopytoff, I. 1986. 'The Cultural Biography of Things: Commoditization as Process', in A. Appadurai (ed.) *The Social Life of Things: Commodities in Cultural Perspective*, Cambridge: Cambridge University Press.

Kurke, L. 1999. *Coins, Bodies, Games, and Gold: The Politics of Meaning in Archaic Greece*, Princeton: Princeton University Press.

Lange, O. 1936–1937 (1938). 'On the Economic Theory of Socialism', in B. Lippincot (ed.) *On the Economic Theory of Socialism*, Minnesota: Minnesota University Press.

Lapavitsas, C. 1991. 'The Theory of Credit Money: A Structural Analysis', *Science and Society*, 55(3), 291–322.

Lapavitsas, C. 1997. 'The Political Economy of Central Banks: Agents of Stability or Source of Instability?', *International Papers in Political Economy*, 4(3), 1–52. Also published in P. Arestis and M. Sawyer (eds) 2001. *Money, Finance and Capitalist Development*, London: Edward Elgar.

Lapavitsas, C. 2000a. 'On Marx's Analysis of Money Hoarding in the Turnover of Capital', *Review of Political Economy*, 12(2), 219–235.

Lapavitsas, C. 2000b. 'Money and the Analysis of Capitalism: The Significance of Commodity Money', *Review of Radical Political Economics*, 32(4), 631–656.

Lapavitsas, C. 2002. '*The Emergence of Money in Commodity Exchange, Or Money as Monopolist of the Ability to Buy*', SOAS Discussion Paper.

Lapavitsas, C. and Saad-Filho, A. 2000. 'The Supply of Credit Money and Capital Accumulation: A Critical View of Post-Keynesianism', *Research in Political Economy*, 18, 309–333.

Lavoie, D. 1985. *Rivalry and Central Planning*, Cambridge: Cambridge University Press.

LeClair, E. E. 1962. 'Economic Theory and Economic Anthropology', *American Anthropologist*, 64(6), 1179–1203.

Leland, H. and Pyle, D. 1977. 'Informational Asymmetries, Financial Structure and Financial Intermediation', *The Journal of Finance*, 32, 371–381.

Leonardi, R. 1995. *Convergence, Cohesion and Integration in the European Union*, London: Macmillan.

Levi-Strauss, C. 1950 (1987). 'Introduction to the Work of Marcel Mauss', London: Routledge & Kegan Paul.

Levi-Strauss, C. 1958 (1963). 'Structural Anthropology', New York, London: Basic Books.

Levi-Strauss, C. 1962 (1964). 'Totemism', London: Merlin Press.

Levi-Strauss, C. 1949 (1969). 'The Elementary Structures of Kinship', Boston: Beacon Press.

Lietaert, B. 2001. *The Future of Money*, London: Century.

Lindbeck, A. 1995. 'Welfare State Disincentives with Endogenous Habits and Norms', *Scandinavian Journal of Economics*, 97(4), 477–494.

Lindbeck, A. 1997. 'Incentives and Social Norms in Household Behavior', *American Economic Review*, 87(2), 370–377.

Lukacs, G. 1971. *History and Class Consciousness*, London: Merlin Press.

Luce, R. and Raifa, H. 1957. *Games and Decisions*, New York: Wiley.

Malinowski, B. 1920. 'Kula; the Circulating Exchange of Valuables in the Archipelagos of Eastern New Guinea', *Man*, 51, 97–105.

Malinowski, B. 1921. 'The Primitive Economics of the Trobriand Islanders', *Economic Journal*, XXXI(121), 1–16.

Malinowski, B. 1922. *Argonauts of the Western Pacific*, London: George Routledge & Sons.

Malinowski, B. 1926 (1966). *Crime and Custom in Savage Society*, London: Routledge & Kegan Paul.

Malinowski, B. 1929 (1932). *The Sexual Life of Savages*, London: Routledge & Kegan Paul.

Malinowski, B. 1935 (1965). *Coral Gardens and Their Magic. Volume I. Soil Tilling and Agricultural Rites in the Trobriand Islands*, Bloomington: Indiana University Press.

Mandel, E. 1986. 'In Defence of Socialist Planning', *New Left Review*, 159, 5–37.

Mandel, E. 1988. 'The Myth of Market Socialism', *New Left Review*, 169, 108–120.

Marx, K. 1846 (1982). *Letter to Annenkov*, Marx–Engels Collected Works, Vol. 38, London: Lawrence & Wishart.

Marx, K. 1847 (1976). *The Poverty of Philosophy*, Marx–Engels Collected Works, Vol. 6, London: Lawrence & Wishart.

Marx, K. 1859 (1970). *Contribution to a Critique of Political Economy*, Moscow: Progress.

Marx, K. 1867 (1976). *Capital*, Vol. I, London: Penguin/NLR.

Marx, K. 1875 (1989). *Critique of the Gotha Programme*, Marx-Engels Collected Works, Vol. 24, London: Lawrence & Wishart.

Marx, K. 1894 (1981). *Capital*, Vol. III, London: Penguin/NLR.

Marx, K. 1939 (1973). *Grundrisse*, London: Penguin/NLR.

Marx, K. 1975. *Early Writings*, London: Penguin/NLR.

Marx, K. and Engels, F. 1845–1846 (1976). *The German Ideology*, Marx–Engels Collected Works, Vol. 5, London: Lawrence & Wishart.

Marx, K. and Engels, F. 1848 (1976). *Manifesto of the Communist Party*, Marx–Engels Collected Works, Vol. 6, London: Lawrence & Wishart.

Mauss, M. 1925 (1990). *The Gift*, London: Routledge & Kegan Paul.

Meek, R. 1950. 'The Decline of Ricardian Economics in England', *Economica*, 17, 43–62.

Meikle, S. 1995. *Aristotle's Economic Thought*, Oxford: Clarendon Press.

Meillassoux, C. 1973. 'The Social Organisation of the Peasantry: The Economic basis of Kinship', *Journal of Peasant Studies*, 1(1), 81–90, also published in D. Seddon (ed.) *Relations of Production*, London: Frank Cass.

Meillassoux, C. 1983. 'The Economic Bases of Demographic Reproduction: From

the Domestic Mode of Production to Wage-Earning', *Journal of Peasant Studies*, 11(1), 50–61.
Menger, K. 1871 (1981). *Principles of Economics*, New York: New York University Press.
Menger, K. 1892. 'On the Origin of Money', *Economic Journal*, 2, 239–255.
Michell, H. 1957. *The Economics of Ancient Greece*, Cambridge: Heffer & Sons.
Milios, J., Dimoulis, D. and Economakis, G. 2002. *Karl Marx and the Classics*, Burlington: Ashgate.
Mill, J. S. 1848 (1965). *Principles of Political Economy*, Toronto: University of Toronto Press.
Mizruchi, M. and Schwartz, M. (eds) 1987. *Intercorporate Relations*, Cambridge: Cambridge University Press.
Mizruchi, M. and Stearns, L. 1994a. 'A Longitudinal Study of Borrowing by Large American Corporations', *Administrative Science Quarterly*, 39, 118–140.
Mizruchi, M. and Stearns, L. 1994b. 'Money, Banking, and Financial Markets', in N. Smelser and R. Swedberg (eds) *The Handbook of Economic Sociology*, Princeton: Princeton University Press.
Mohun, S. 2003. 'Does All Labour Create Value?', in A. Saad-Filho (ed.) *Anti-Capitalism: A Marxist Introduction*, London/Sterling: Pluto.
Murray, P. 1988. *Marx's Theory of Scientific Knowledge*, Atlantic Highlands: Humanities Press.
Niehans, J. 1969. 'Money in a Static Theory of Optimal Payment Arrangements', *Journal of Money, Credit and Banking*, 1, 706–726.
Niehans, J. 1978. *'The Theory of Money'*, Baltimore: Johns Hopkins University Press.
North, D. C. 1981. *Structure and Change in Economic History*, New York: W.W. Norton.
North, D. C. 1990. *Institutions, Institutional Change and Economic Performance*, Cambridge: Cambridge University Press.
North, D. C. 1999. *Understanding the Process of Economic Change*, London: Institute of Economic Affairs.
Nove, A. 1983. *The Economics of Feasible Socialism*, London: Macmillan.
Oberschall, A. and Leifer, E. 1986. 'Efficiency and Social Institutions: Uses and Misuses of Economic Reasoning in Sociology', *Annual Review of Sociology*, 12, 233–253.
Oh, S. 1989. 'A Theory of a Generally Acceptable Medium of Exchange and Barter', *Journal of Monetary Economics*, 23, 101–119.
Olson, M. 1965. *The Logic of Collective Action*, Cambridge, MA: Harvard University Press.
Orlove, B. 1986. 'Barter and Cash Sale on Lake Titicaca: A Test of Competing Approaches', *Current Anthropology*, 27(2), 85–106.
Ortner, S. 1984. 'Theory in Anthropology since the Sixties', *Comparative Studies in Society and History*, 26(1), 126–166.
Ostrom, E. 1998. 'A Behavioral Approach to the Rational Choice Theory of Collective Action', *American Political Science Review*, 92(1), 1–22.
Ostroy, J. and Starr, R. 1990. 'The Transactions Role of Money', in B. Friedman and F. Hahn (eds) *Handbook of Monetary Economics*, Amsterdam: Elsevier Science Publishers.
Owen, R. 1813–1814 (1976). *A New View of Society*, in *The Life of Robert Owen Written by Himself*, Vol. I, New York: Kelly.

Pahl, J. 1983. 'The Allocation of Money and the Structuring of Inequality within Marriage', *The Sociological Review*, 31(2), 237–262.

Pahl, J. 1999. *Invisible Money: Family Finances in the Electronic Economy*, Bristol: Policy Press.

Paraskevopoulos, C. 2001. *Interpreting Convergence in the European Union*, Basingstoke: Palgrave.

Parry, J. 1986. 'The *Gift*, the Indian Gift and the 'Indian Gift'', *Man*, 21(3), 453–473.

Parry, J. and Bloch, M. (eds) 1989. *Money and the Morality of Exchange*, Cambridge: Cambridge University Press.

Parsons, T. and Smelser, N. 1956. *Economy and Society*, Glencoe: Free Press.

Petersen, M. and Rajan, R. 1994. 'The Benefits of Lending Relationships: Evidence from Small Business Data', *Journal of Finance*, 49, 3–37.

Piore, M. 1996. 'Review of the Handbook of Economic Sociology', *Journal of Economic Literature*, 34, 741–754.

Plattner, S. 1982. 'Economic Decision Making in a Public Marketplace', *American Ethnologist*, 9(2), 399–420.

Plattner, S. (ed.) 1989. *Economic Anthropology*, Stanford: Stanford University Press.

Polanyi, K. 1944. *The Great Transformation*, Boston: Beacon Press.

Polanyi, K., Arensberg, C. and Pearson, H. (eds) 1957. *Trade and Markets in Early Empires*, Glencoe: Free Press.

Posner, R. 1977. *Economic Analysis of the Law*, Little: Brown.

Posner, R. 1981. 'A Theory of Primitive Society, With Special Reference to Law', *Journal of Law and Economics*, 23(1), 1–53.

Poulantzas, N. 1973. *Political Power and Social Class*, London: New Left Books.

Poulantzas, N. 1975. *Classes in Contemporary Capitalism*, London: New Left Books.

Putnam, R. 1993. *Making Democracy Work*, Princeton: Princeton University Press.

Putnam, R. 1995a. 'Bowling Alone: America's Declining Social Capital', *Journal of Democracy*, 6(1), 65–78.

Putnam, R. 1995b. 'Tuning In, Tuning Out: The Strange Disappearance of Social Capital in America', *Political Science and Politics*, 28(4), 664–683.

Radcliffe-Brown, A. R. 1951. *Structure and Function in Primitive Society*, New York: Free Press.

Ramakrishnan, R. and Thakor, A. 1984. 'Information Reliability and a Theory of Financial Intermediation', *Review of Economic Studies*, 51, 415–432.

Roemer, J. 1993. 'Can There Be Socialism After Communism?', in P. Bardhan and J. Roemer (eds) *Market Socialism: The Current Debate*, New York: Oxford University Press.

Rosdolsky, R. 1977. *The Making of Marx's 'Capital'*, London: Pluto Press.

Rothschild, M. and Stiglitz, J. 1976. 'Equilibrium in Competitive Insurance Markets: An Essay on the Economics of Imperfect Information', *Quarterly Journal of Economics*, 87, 355–374.

Saad-Filho, A. 1993. 'Labour, Money and "Labour-Money": A Review of Marx's Critique of John Gray's Monetary Analysis', *History of Political Economy*, 25(1), 65–84.

Saad-Filho, A. 2002. *The Value of Marx*, London: Routledge.

Sahlins, M. 1974. *Stone Age Economics*, London: Tavistock Publications.

Samuelson, P. 1958. 'An Exact Consumption–Loan Model with or without the Social Contrivance of Money', *Journal of Political Economy*, 66, 467–482.

Sayers, R. 1938 (1967). *Modern Banking* (7th edn), Delhi: Oxford University Press.

Schumpeter, J. A. 1954. *History of Economic Analysis*, London: Routledge.

Schwartz, B. 1967. 'The Social Psychology of the Gift', *American Journal of Sociology*, 73(1), 1–11.

Seddon, D. (ed.) 1978. *Relations of Production*, London: Frank Cass.

Sekine, T. 1980. 'An Essay on Uno's Dialectic of Capital' (appended to Uno, 1980).

Sekine, T. 1997. *An Outline of the Dialectic of Capital*, Vol. I, II, London: Macmillan.

Sekine, T. 1998. 'The Dialectic of Capital: An Unoist Interpretation', *Science and Society*, 62(3), 434–445.

Sekine, T. 1999. 'Marxian Theory of Value: An Unoist Approach', *Chiiki Bunseki, Aichi Gakuin*, 37(2), 99–136.

Sen, A. 1976–1977. 'Rational Fools: A Critique of the Behavioural Foundations of Economic Theory', *Philosophy and Public Affairs*, 6, 317–344.

Shapiro, C. and Stiglitz, J. 1984. 'Equilibrium Unemployment as a Worker Disciplining Device', *American Economic Review*, 74, 433–444.

Simmel, G. 1900 (1978). *The Philosophy of Money*, London: Routledge and Kegan Paul.

Simon, H. 1955. 'A Behavioral Model of Rational Choice', *Quarterly Journal of Economics*, 69, 99–118.

Simon, H. 1959. 'Theories of Decision-Making in Economics and Behavioral Science', *American Economic Review*, 49, 253–283.

Simon, H. 1978. 'Rationality as Process and as Product of Thought', *American Economic Review*, 68(2), 1–16.

Singh, S. 1997. *Marriage Money: The Social Shaping of Money in Marriage and Banking*. St Leonards, Australia: Allen & Unwin.

Smelser, N. and Swedberg, R. (eds) 1994. *The Handbook of Economic Sociology*, Princeton: Princeton University Press.

Smith, A. 1776 (1904). *The Wealth of Nations*, Vol. I, II, E. Cannan (ed.), London: Methuen.

Smith, T. 1990. *The Logic of Marx's 'Capital': Reply to Hegelian Criticisms*, Albany: State of New York Press.

Smith, T. 1993. *Dialectical Social Theory and Its Critics*, Albany: State of New York Press.

Smithin, J. (ed.) 2000. *What is Money?*, London: Routledge.

Spence, M. 1973. 'Job Market Signalling', *Quarterly Journal of Economics*, 87, 355–374.

Spence, M. 1974. *Market Signalling*, Cambridge, Mass.: Harvard University Press.

Stearns, L. 1986. 'Capital Market Effects on External Control of Corporations', *Theory and Society*, 15(1–2), 47–75.

Steuart, J. 1767 (1995). *An Inquiry into the Principles of Political Economy*, Vol. I, II, III, IV, in *Works, Political, Metaphysical, and Chronological, of the Late Sir James Steuart*, Vol. I, II, III, IV, V, VI, London: Routledge.

Steuart, J. 1805 (1995). *A Plan for Introducing an Uniformity of Weights and Measures within the Limits of the British Empire*, Vol. V, in *Works Political, Metaphysical, and Chronological, of the Late Sir James Steuart*, Vol. I, II, III, IV, V, VI, London: Routledge.

Stigler, G. and Becker, G. 1977. 'De Gustibus Non Est Disputandum', *American Economic Review*, 67(2), 76–90.

Stiglitz, J. 1974. 'Incentives and Risk Sharing in Sharecropping', *Review of Economic Studies*, 41, 219–255.

Stiglitz, J. 1989. 'Markets, Market Failures and Development', *American Economic Review*, 79(2), 197–220.

Stiglitz, J. 1994. 'The Role of the State in Financial Markets', *Proceedings of the World Bank Annual Conference on Development Economics 1993*, pp. 19–52. World Bank.

Stiglitz, J. 1998a. 'More Instruments and Broader Goals: Moving Toward the Post Washington Consensus', The 1998 WIDER Annual Lecture, 7 January, Helsinki.

Stiglitz, J. 1998b. 'Towards a New Paradigm for Development: Strategies, Policies and Processes', Prebisch Lecture, UNCTAD, Geneva.

Stiglitz, J and Weiss, A. 1981. 'Credit Rationing in Markets with Imperfect Information', *American Economic Review*, 71, 393–410.

Stinchcombe, A. 1983. *Economic Sociology*, New York: Academic Press.

Strathern, M. 1985. 'Kinship and Economy: Constitutive Orders of a Provisional Kind', *American Ethnologist*, 12(2), 191–209.

Strathern, M. 1988. *The Gender of the Gift*, Berkeley and Los Angeles: University of California Press.

Swedberg, R. (ed.) 1990. *Economics and Sociology, Redefining Their Boundaries*, Princeton: Princeton University Press.

Swedberg, R. (ed.) 1996. *Economic Sociology*, Cheltenham: Edward Elgar.

Swedberg, R., Himmelstrand, U. and Brulin, G. 1987. 'The Paradigm of Economic Sociology: Premises and Promises', *Theory and Society*, 16, 69–213.

Tarrow, S. 1996. 'Making Social Science Work Across Time and Space: A Critical Reflection on Robert Putnam's "Making Democracy Work"', *American Political Science Review*, 90(2), 389–397.

Taylor, F. 1929 (1938). 'The Guidance of Production in a Socialist State', in B. Lippincot (ed.) *On the Economic Theory of Socialism*, Minnesota: Minnesota University Press.

Thomas, N. 1991. *Entangled Objects: Exchange, Material Culture, and Colonialism in the Pacific*, Cambridge, Mass.: Harvard University Press.

Tilly, C. 1998. *Durable Inequality*, Berkeley: University of California Press.

Timberlake, R. 1984. 'The Central Banking Role of Clearinghouse Associations', *Journal of Money Credit and Banking*, 16(1), 1–15.

Titmuss, R. 1970. *The Gift Relationship: From Human Blood to Social Policy*, London: Allen and Unwin.

Tonnies, F. 1887 (1955). *Community and Association*, London: Routledge & Kegan Paul.

Townsend, R. 1979. 'Optimal Contracts and Competitive Markets with Costly State Verification', *Journal of Economic Theory*, 21, 265–293.

Uno, K. 1950–1952 (1980). *Principles of Political Economy* (trans. T. Sekine, from a 1964 edn), Brighton: Harvesten.

Uzzi, B. 1999. 'Embeddedness in the Making of Financial Capital: How Social Relations and Networks Benefit Firms Seeking Financing', *American Sociological Review*, 64(4), 481–505.

Valeri, V. 1994. 'Buying Women but not Selling Them: Gift and Commodity Exchange in Huaulu Alliance', *Man*, 29(1), 1–26.

von Mises, L. 1920 (1935). 'Economic Calculation in the Socialist Commonwealth', in F. Hayek (ed.) *Collectivist Economic Planning*, London: Routledge and Kegan Paul.

von Mises, L. 1934 (1953). *The Theory of Money and Credit*, Appendix A: 'On the Classification of Monetary Theories', London: Cape.
von Reden, S. 1995. *Exchange in Ancient Greece*, London: Duckworth.
von Reden, S. 1997. 'Money, Law and Exchange: Coinage in the Greek Polis', *Journal of Historical Studies*, 117, 154–176.
von Reden, S. 2002. 'Demos' *Phiale* and the Rhetoric of Money in Fourth-Century Athens', in P. Cartledge, E. Cohen and L. Foxhall (eds) *Money, Labour and Land*, London and New York: Routledge.
Voutira, E. and Harrell-Bond, B. E. 1995. 'In Search of the Locus of Trust: The Social World of the Refugee Camp', in E. V. Daniel and J. C. Knudsen (eds) *Mistrusting Refugees*, Berkeley: University of California Press.
Wallace, N. 1980. 'The Overlapping Generations Model of Fiat Money', in J. Kareken and N. Wallace (eds) *Models of Monetary Policy*, Minneapolis: Federal Reserve Bank of Minneapolis.
Walras, L. 1926 (1984). *Elements of Pure Economics* (trans. W. Jaffe from the 'edition definitive'), Philadelphia: Orion.
Weber, M. 1930. *The Protestant Ethic and the Spirit of Capitalism*, Unwin: London.
Weber, M. 1968. *Economy and Society: An Outline of Interpretive Sociology*, in two vols, G. Roth and C. Wittich (eds), New York: Bedminster Press.
Weeks, J. 1981. *Capital and Exploitation*, London: Edward Arnold.
Weiner, A. 1976. *Women of Value, Men of Renown*, Austin and London: University of Texas Press.
Weiner, A. 1985. 'Inalienable Wealth', *American Ethnologist*, 12, 52–65.
Weiner, A. 1988. *The Trobrianders of Papua New Guinea*, New York: Holt, Rinehart & Winston.
Weiner, A. 1992. *Inalienable Possessions*, Berkeley and Los Angeles: University of California Press.
White, H. 1981. 'Where Do Markets Come From?', *American Journal of Sociology*, 87(3), 517–547.
White, L. 1984. 'Competitive Payment Systems and the Unit of Account', *American Economic Review*, 74(4), 699–712.
White, H. 1992. *Identity and Control*, Princeton: Princeton University Press.
White, H. 2002. *Markets from Networks*, Princeton: Princeton University Press.
Williamson, O. 1975. *Markets and Hierarchies*, New York: Free Press.
Williamson, O. 1979. 'Transaction-Cost Economics: The Governance of Contractual Relations', *Journal of Law and Economics*, XXII(2), 233–261.
Williamson, O. 1985. *The Economic Institutions of Capitalism*, New York: Free Press.
Williamson, O. 1996. *The Mechanisms of Governance*, New York: Oxford University Press.
Williamson, O. 2000. 'The New Institutional Economics: Taking Stock, Looking Ahead', *Journal of Economic Literature*, Vol. XXXVIII, 595–613.
Woolcock, M. 1998. 'Social Capital and Economic Development: Toward a Theoretical Synthesis and Policy Framework', *Theory and Society*, 27(2), 151–208.
Wray, R. 1990. *Money and Credit in Capitalist Economies*, Aldershot: Edward Elgar.
Zelizer, V. 1983. *Morals and the Market: The Development of Life Insurance in the United States*, New Brunswick: Transaction.
Zelizer, V. 1987. *Pricing the Priceless Child: The Changing Social Value of Children*, New York: Basic Books.

Zelizer, V. 1988. 'Beyond the Polemics on the Market: Establishing a Theoretical and Empirical Agenda', *Sociological Forum*, 3(4) (reprinted in Swedberg, 1996).
Zelizer, V. 1994. *The Social Meaning of Money*, New York: Basic Books.
Zelizer, V. 1996. 'Payments and Social Ties', *Sociological Forum*, 11(3), 481–495.
Zelizer, V. 1998. 'The Proliferation of Social Currencies', in M. Callon (ed.) *The Laws of the Market*, Oxford: Blackwell.
Zelizer, V. 2000. 'Fine Tuning the Zelizer View', *Economy and Society*, 29(3), 383–389.

Index

abstract labour 24–5
Akerlof 143 n22, 94, 95, 101–2
Althusser (Althusserianism) 14, 141 n11
Arrow 92, 94–5
Austrian School 114–17, 133

bank 77, 83, 84, 101; assets and liabilities 79–84; capital 79, 80; monitoring 80–1, 146 n15, 86, 133; profit 79–80; reserves 80, 82–4, 85
Bardhan 133
barter 62, 64–6, 115, 120–4; 'difficulties' of 56, 113–14, 116, 117
Becker 94
Bourdieu 147 n21
Bowring 151 n12

capital as set of social relations 21, 109–11; circuit of 21–2, 41, 42
capitalism and markets 3, 18–19, 29, 127, 133–4; and non-market relations 33, 37; as mode of production 14–17, 61
capitalist production 17–18, 42
central bank 71, 84–6
chartalism 119–20
class relations 17–21, 74–5, 92, 100, 104, 106–7, 127, 132–4, 136
Clower 117–18
Coase 99
Codere 122
Coleman 31, 107
collective action 18, 44, 137, 139
commercial (trade) bill 76, 145 n11; discounting of 77–82
commercial capitalist 78
commitment 39, 40, 43, 91
commodity and capitalist social relations 9, 12–14, 22–5, 36–7, 129–30; and non-market relations 33; as fundamental component of markets 9, 22; 'fetishism' 19–21; form of, 27; relative to products 3, 9, 10–12; sale relative to purchase 51–2
commodity exchange 11–12, 64–6
concrete labour 24, 142 n15
credit, 3; banking (monetary) 69–70, 71, 76–82; commercial (trade) 39–40, 69–70, 71, 72–82; power and trust in relations of 68–9, 74–82, 76–81, 106
credit money 65, 77, 79, 123
credit system 142 n7, 69, 70–2, 86, 87

Dalton 129
Davidson 122
default 77, 78, 79
Diamond 146 n15
direct exchange 37, 55–8, 65–6, 118, 120, 122, 124
division of labour 69–70, 73, 113
Dow 122
Duesenberry 104
Durkheim 4

economics 15; game-theoretic 95–7, 101, 102, 114, 118; of information 91, 101–4; of institutions 15, 91, 98–100; of transactions costs 15, 98–9, 133
economic 'base' 15–17, 100
egoism 10, 142 n2, 92–3
Einzig 148 n12, 121
Elster 93
'embeddedness' 104–7, 128
Engels 16, 131–2
exchange value 25, 29, 34, 37; development of 22–4, 56, 57

financial assets 11, 27, 29, 54, 145 n1, 127
financial intermediation 76, 82, 83–4
Fine 12, 14, 20, 97, 109, 110, 141 n9, 142 n15, n18, n3, 143 n18, n20, 146 n13, 147 n20, n21, 149 n23
Firth 35, 150 n26
'foreign-ness' of commodity owners 54, 57, 61, 62, 65–7, 68–9, 73, 86, 127, 131, 134, 138
Formalists 128–30

general equilibrium theory 92–3, 94, 101–3, 114, 115, 117–18, 150 n4
Granovetter 105–7
Gregory 33–4
gift 2; and usefulness, 40–1; exchangeability 33–7; 'pure' 35; relative to commodity 31–2
Godelier 36, 150 n25
gold 64, 85
Grierson 122
Grierson H. 62

Hahn 148 n8
Harris 12, 14, 141 n9
Hayek 150 n4
Heihnsohn 149 n19
Herskovits 144 n9, 150 n26
hierarchy 32, 36, 38, 44, 73, 75, 99; and capitalist production 15, 17–18
Hirschleifer 146 n6
Hirschman 146 n3
Historical School 115, 149 n16
Hyde 142 n4

International Monetary Fund (IMF) 1, 110
information 93, 96, 97, 105, 107; asymmetry of 75, 83, 101–4, 110–11
Ingham 147 n17, 149 n18
Itoh 141 n7, 144 n4, 145 n1, 146 n12, 149 n17, n19, n21, 150 n3, n4, 151 n10

Jevons 56, 114

Keynes 120
Kim 149 n14
Kiyotaki 118
Knapp 120, 148 n5, 149 n16
kula 41

labour market 18–19, 25, 105, 107, 136, 138
Labour money 135–9
labour power 42–4, 136
Lange 150 n4
Lapavitsas 142 n15, 142 n18, 144 n2, n6, n10, 145 n1, n4, n6, 146 n12, n17, n20, 148 n6, n10, 149 n17, n19, n21, n23
Lavoie 133
Levi-Strauss 31
Local Exchange Trading Systems (LETS) 131, 138–9

Malinowski 34–5, 40–1, 150 n26
Mandel 133
market 3; and socialism 131–4; as theoretical category 9, 124, 127; in produced commodities 13; in non-produced objects 14, 26–30; 'pretend' 10, 14, 27
'marketability' ('saleability') 144 n8, 115–17, 118
Marx: on banks 78; on commodity 'fetishism' 19–21; on communism 132; on contradictions between use value and value 54–5; on human consciousness 16–17; on labour money 136; on methodology 13, 140 n6; on skilled labour 151 n10; on the 'riddle' of money 53
Mauss 31, 34–5, 41
Meikle 140 n6
Menger 144 n8, 114–17, 118, 119, 150 n6
merchant capitalist 78
Methodenstreit 115
Michell 149 n14
Milios 141 n11, 141 n14
Mises von 148 n1, 149 n15, 150 n4
Mohun, 142 n19
money 101; and form of value 53–4, 57–64, 112, 122, 130; and power 49, 52, 61, 66–7; and social custom 49, 52, 59–64, 65, 116, 118, 123–4; and social norms 49, 51, 53, 59, 63–6, 118; as foundation of trust in credit relations 69–70, 73–5; and value substance 53–6; as means of exchange 113–18, 135–9; as monopolist of ability to buy 3, 49, 52–3, 58, 59, 60, 62–3, 112, 124, 128, 130; as representative of value 55, 56; as resolution of contradictions between use value and value 54–6; as unit of account 112, 114, 119–24, 135–9; as 'universal equivalent' 56, 57, 60, 61, 124; functions of 123–4;

money *continued*
peculiar character of 49, 52–3, 117; idle (hoards) 71–2, 77–8, 82–4; 'riddle' of 53, 55, 56, 112; use value (usefulness) of 50, 62–4, 65
money-dealing capitalist 78
money market 71, 82–4, 85
'moral hazard' 75–6, 86
moral obligation 57, 132, 139; and gifts 31–2, 37; and use value 38–9

Nash 95–6
network theory 2, 91, 104–7
Niehans 117
non-market relations and gift exchangeability 36; and labour power 42–4; in gifts compared to commodities 32–3.
North 15, 98–100
Nove 133

Owen 131, 136

Parsons 104
Polanyi 31, 128–30
Post-Keynesianism 122–3, 145 n6
Post-Washington consensus 109–11
potlatch 41
power 32, 37, 40, 44, 92, 99, 105–7, 132; and bank operations 76–87; and capitalist production 17–18, 136; and money 49, 52, 61, 66–7; as foundation of credit 74–82
product relative to commodity 3, 9, 10–12
property rights 15, 17, 99, 132–3, 137
Proudhon 136
Putnam 108

rationality as individual choice, 10, 31, 50, 91–111, 115–16, 129; social (aggregate), 71, 134
real estate (land) 27, 29, 54, 127
reciprocity 31, 35–7, 108
Ricardianism 135–6
Roemer 133

Saad-Filho 140 n6, 141 n14, 142 n15, 145 n6, 149 n17, 150 n8
Sahlins 31, 140 n4
Sekine 141 n7, 144 n6
'silent trade' 62
Simon 146 n2
Simmel 126–7, 144 n1
Smith 11–12, 56, 113
social capital 2, 4, 31, 91, 107–11
social custom 43, 49, 52, 57, 73, 94, 128, 134; and exchange value 28–9; and money 59–64, 65, 116–17, 118, 123–4
social norms 2, 86, 91–111, 128; and length of the working day 43–4; and money 49, 51, 53, 59, 63–6, 118; and wages 43.
social 'superstructure', 15–17, 100
socialism and labour money, 135–9; and markets, 131–4; and non-economic relations, 132, 134
solidarity 44, 91, 95, 97; and capitalist production 18
Steiger 149 n19
Spence 101
Steuart 119, 145 n5
Stiglitz 101, 110, 148 n27
Substantivists 128–30

Taylor 150 n4
Tonnies 4
Townsend, 145 n10
trust 1, 3, 32, 36, 37, 43, 91, 95, 97, 100, 107–8, 110, 132, 139; and capitalist commercial relations 38–9; and bank operations 76–87; as foundation of credit 68–9, 106

Uno 13
use value 32–3, 74; and non-market relations 37–9, 41
Uzzi 106

value and capitalist social relations 10, 14, 53–4; as social norm 25, 28; relation of form to substance 24–9, 53–4, 124, 127; 'relative versus equivalent' 57–64

Walras 114
Washington Consensus 109–11
Weber 4, 148 n5
Weeks 12
Weiner 33, 36
wergeld 122
White 116
Williamson 15–16, 98–100
World Bank 1, 110
Wray 123, 149 n19
Wright 118

Zelizer 148 n2, 124–8